ARBITRATION AND
BUSINESS ETHICS

ARBITRATION AND BUSINESS ETHICS

A STUDY OF THE HISTORY AND PHILOSOPHY OF THE
VARIOUS TYPES OF ARBITRATION AND THEIR
RELATIONS TO BUSINESS ETHICS

BY

CLARENCE F. BIRDSEYE

AUTHOR OF "ENCYCLOPÆDIA OF GENERAL BUSINESS AND
LEGAL FORMS," "REVISED STATUTES, CODES AND
GENERAL LAWS OF NEW YORK," "INDIVIDUAL
TRAINING IN OUR COLLEGES," ETC.

WITH A FOREWORD BY

CHARLES L. BERNHEIMER

CHAIRMAN OF THE COMMITTEE ON ARBITRATION OF THE
CHAMBER OF COMMERCE OF THE STATE
OF NEW YORK

D. APPLETON AND COMPANY
NEW YORK   LONDON
1926

331.155
B532c

COPYRIGHT, 1926, BY
CLARENCE F. BIRDSEYE

OCT 22 1931
293126
Gift.

PRINTED IN THE UNITED STATES OF AMERICA

FOREWORD

THESE pages give the clearest account which I have read of the true meaning of arbitration as a whole, and of its various types. Mr. Birdseye bases his arguments upon the broad needs of the merchant. Thereby he furnishes the correct viewpoint for courts, lawyers and laymen. He has rendered a real service to the cause of organized business by his demonstration that the primary value of commercial arbitration is an important factor in the field of business ethics. By his historical references and his statements of the facts, he has simplified and illumined the ethical features which were in danger of being lost sight of in the fight for the statutory reform of common law arbitration.

I hope that every one interested in arbitration and better commercial methods will read this book, and that thus we may all find it easier and more rewarding to work for the higher business ends which are here so clearly set forth.

CHARLES L. BERNHEIMER.

PREFACE

THE word *arbitration* is applied to at least four radically different methods of settling disputes, exclusive of political international arbitrament; and this must be kept constantly in mind if we are to get a clear understanding of the philosophy, history, objectives and application of the differing forms of arbitration.

First: Arbitration is, strictly speaking, an inherent and important part of the trade and ethical machinery provided by an organized trade association to control the dealings of its members with each other. This machinery is chiefly concerned with the technical and ethical conduct of a highly specialized business, and to that end seeks to make it almost impossible that disputes shall arise in the future.

Ordinarily, under these rules, such differences are amicably settled by the members themselves. In a few instances, the dispute may be referred to a fellow member for informal adjustment (conciliation). In rare cases, formal arbitration under the rules may be necessary.

Thus commercial arbitration is an essential, but little used, function, in administering the affairs of self-governing bodies of men doing a homogeneous business with each other, such as guilds, exchanges, boards of trade or trade associations. Its awards are enforced through the powers of a self-governing body whose constitution, by-laws, rules and regulations are drawn, enforced, and, if necessary, amended in order to make the whole trade machinery run smoothly, and so as to carry out the larger purposes of the institution, preserve the sacredness of members' contracts, and settle the infrequent disputes that are certain to arise in trading under its very technical rules.

The aggregate bulk and value of the transactions of such trade organizations, whose disputes as they may arise in the future are to be thus settled by commercial arbitration, are thousands of times as great as those involved under all the other forms of arbitration.

As time progresses, the trade machinery works more smoothly, and the need for arbitration becomes almost negligible because the trade ethics and the guild or club spirit have developed and become dominant. Indeed, in the case of the institution whose annual transactions are the largest in the country, and equal to the country's total wealth, there has not been an arbitration for years, and the chief executive could not recollect when the last arbitration took place.

The history, functions and scope of commercial arbitration and its relation to business ethics are discussed in Part I.

Second: Common law arbitration, as we know it, was evolved under the earlier English or American court decisions, unaffected by statute. It never had much value because the courts soon held: (*a*) that an agreement to arbitrate a future dispute was against public policy and not enforceable; and (*b*) that either party to an arbitration might withdraw at any time before the actual award. Common law arbitration has become so discredited that its volume is hardly more than infinitesimal when compared with the other types, and it is being displaced by statutory arbitration. Yet unfortunately the ordinary man knows and thinks only of this futile and unfair common law type, and naturally is prejudiced against the three other predominant and useful forms, because he judges and measuers them by it, and not it by them. Part II treats of common law arbitration.

Third: The evils of common law or court-made arbitration were and are curable only by statute. This came about easily in England in the latter half of the last century, but in this country the first adequate statutory reforms were inaugurated only a few years ago through the Chamber of Commerce of the State of New York, under the leadership of its committee on arbitration.

The history of this wonderful reform and its effects upon business organization and ethics will be found in Part III.

Fourth: Negotiations between employers and employees, so far as they relate to making a new bargain as to services to be rendered in the future, are not arbitration, industrial or otherwise, but are and should be considered merely as collective bargaining. Industrial arbitration, in the proper sense, is confined to the orderly adjustment of future disputes—usually as to working conditions rather than wages—which may arise during the life of the formal agreement between employer and employees to govern their future relations; such adjustments to be made by certain agreed tribunals of various types and powers set up by the underlying collective bargain contract.

This form of arbitration will be discussed in Part IV.

Part V considers some further examples of applied arbitration, some reforms which should be adopted in this country, and the conclusions as to the future of arbitration and the growth of business ethics.

Heretofore common law arbitration has been adopted and used as the standard by which to appraise the scope, usefulness, application and ethical and business value of the other kinds, but since the common law type lacks most of the better attributes and qualities of the other types, it has proved entirely useless as a standard. This has been like using a scow to admeasure the advantages, parts and performances of all other seagoing vessels, even up to a modern ocean liner.

I shall follow exactly the opposite course and adopt commercial arbitration as the standard. The other types will be measured by it to show how far they fall short of the perfection of its theory, working parts and performances. The ocean liner perfection of strict commercial arbitration will serve to bring out and emphasize the imperfections and lacking parts of the other and lower types—especially of the scowlike common law arbitration.

Many persons, and especially many lawyers, associate arbitration chiefly with the common law variety. They do not understand that its greatest field is in commercial arbitration, in which form it is in ordinary use in connection with exchanges, boards of trade and trade associations dealing in homogeneous products or commodities; and that common law arbitration in this sense has few if any of the features of the commercial type.

CONTENTS

	PAGE
Foreword, by Charles L. Bernheimer	v
Preface	vii

PART I
COMMERCIAL ARBITRATION

CHAPTER
I. The natural habitat of strict commercial arbitration and its relation to business ethics.	3
II. The present tendency to organize and suborganize in all phases of life along altruistic and ethical lines	9
III. Commercial arbitration and business ethics under the English craft guilds	16
IV. Commercial arbitration and business ethics among the international merchants of medieval Europe	23
V. The necessity of speedy and expert decisions of commercial disputes	30
VI. The ethical objects of organized business.	34
VII. The minimizing of disputes under proper business organization	41

PART II
COMMON LAW ARBITRATION

VIII. The nature, origin and scope of the common law.	55
IX. The frailties and failures of common law arbitration	62
X. How the rules governing common law arbitration have been changed throughout the British Empire by act of Parliament and by the spread of commercial arbitration and business ethics.	69

CONTENTS

PART III

STATUTORY ARBITRATION

CHAPTER		PAGE
XI.	The difficulties in changing the statutes and court decisions governing common law arbitration in the the United States	81
XII.	The history of arbitration in the Chamber of Commerce of the State of New York, A.D. 1768-1910.	87
XIII.	The history of arbitration in the Chamber of Commerce of the State of New York—continued: A.D. 1910-1926.	94

PART IV

INDUSTRIAL ARBITRATION

XIV.	The English Industrial Revolution of 1760; the growth and meaning of trade unions.	119
XV.	Collective bargaining and industrial arbitration . .	128

PART V

OTHER EXAMPLES OF ARBITRATION; MISCELLANEOUS; CONCLUSIONS

XVI.	Other examples of arbitration.	143
XVII.	Official administrative arbitration by nonjudicial functionaries	151
XVIII.	Conciliation	154
XIX.	Compulsory and voluntary arbitration.	159
XX.	Commercial courts and small claims court . . .	162
XXI.	Conclusions	165

APPENDICES

I.	Ordinaunces of the Arte or Mystery of Clothworkers of the City of London.	181
II.	Objects of organized business	187

CONTENTS

		PAGE
III.	Arbitration clause from Standard Exhibition Contract used by members of Motion Picture Producers and Distributors of America, Inc.	189
IV.	Arbitration law and court rules of Illinois	192
V.	Arbitration law and court rules of New York	199
VI.	Arbitration law of New Jersey	211
VII.	Arbitration law of Oregon	216
VIII.	Chapter 251 of the General Laws of Massachusetts as amended by Chapter 294, Acts of 1925	219
IX.	United States Arbitration Act	223
X.	The Hart Schaffner and Marx Labor Agreement	229
XI.	Anthracite Agreement of February 17, 1926.	246
XII.	Suggestions to chambers of commerce, trade associations and other bodies for plan for offering arbitration facilities to members and non-members.	248
XIII.	National Wholesale Lumber Dealers Association.	255
XIV.	The Rubber Association of America, Incorporated; rules and regulations governing arbitrations	265
XV.	Agreements to submit future disputes to arbitration.	273
XVI.	Forms of submission	277
XVII.	Practice and procedure before arbitrators	281
XVIII.	Awards	284

PART I
COMMERCIAL ARBITRATION

ARBITRATION AND BUSINESS ETHICS

CHAPTER I

THE NATURAL HABITAT OF STRICT COMMERCIAL ARBITRATION AND ITS RELATION TO BUSINESS ETHICS

ALMOST invariably, strict or pure commercial arbitration is found only in connection with a combination of the following elements, *viz.*:

First, a self-governing business organization, incorporated or voluntary, having full power, by expulsion, suspension or otherwise, to enforce directly upon its members its proper mandates of any kind, including the awards of its arbitration tribunal.

Second, the members must be engaged in trading with each other in homogeneous products, commodities or securities.

Third, this trading must be under self-imposed rules and regulations or standardized or uniform contracts which relate usually to the condition, grades and grading, deliveries, terms and other trade details—often highly technical—worked out to cover the peculiar conditions prevailing in that particular market. These rules will also govern the conduct of members in other particulars, provide for the care and use of the common property, and in many other ways resemble the by-laws and management of a well-run club.

These by-laws, rules and regulations are designed, primarily, so to standardize and simplify transactions between members and to build up business ethics and mutual confidence that disputes will become almost impossible. If occasionally they do arise, they are so simplified and so much matters of routine that usually they are amicably settled on the spot between the parties themselves. Very infrequently informal or formal conciliation may be resorted to before friendly fellow members or the official agencies maintained by the organization for such unusual contingencies. In very rare instances it may be necessary to invoke the services of the regular committee on arbitration, but usually only where there is doubt as to the meaning and application of an underlying rule, or where new conditions show that existing rules are inadequate and may require amendment.

In the case of the institution having the largest annual transactions in the country, this process has been carried on another step to its logical conclusion, and arbitration has been practically superseded by official interpretation of the rules. That is, in any case of doubt the executive official of the institution is asked, probably by telephone, for his interpretation of the rule governing a particular transaction, and that interpretation is implicitly followed.

Fourth, the by-laws or rules of the organization provide that the compulsory arbitration of future disputes not disposed of amicably or by conciliation, shall be carried on before a recognized and official tribunal composed of impartial experienced and honored fellow members, who are experts in everything connected with the articles dealt in and in regard to the technical rules of the organization covering such dealings.

Fifth, in every instance, this expert tribunal keeps in mind, if necessary, the larger ethical and business interests of the organization and its members as affected by the particular dispute. Whenever necessary or desirable, amendments to the rules are suggested to and made by the proper officials of the organization rather than through the enactments of a non-expert and politically minded legislature or the decisions of a non-expert and not commercially minded court of justice. In some instances, trading conditions require that these changes shall be frequent and drastic.

Sixth, underlying and enveloping and giving life and vision to the foregoing elements is the ethical and guild spirit which was responsible for the original birth of the organization. That spirit grows and is strengthened as the decades pass by, and as new generations gain control who were reared under the better conditions of the new collectivism, and who have not personally experienced the evils of the older individualism which finally forced an unwilling combination of discordant trade rivals. That spirit works increasingly for better business ethics and methods, for the sacredness of contracts, for mutual confidence in fellow members' integrity and good faith, for loyalty to the organization and its ideals, for a realization that the whole is greater and better than any of its parts, for a united effort to make the future better than the past, and to lend a hand.

All of these are important features in the strict commercial arbitration which is inherent and necessary in the conduct of exchanges, boards of trade, trade associations and similar bodies whose members deal with each other in homogeneous products, commodities or securities. In administering the affairs of such an association, strict commercial arbitration is incidental and not accidental. It is an essential part of the organization's machinery of operation without which unethical practices and constant litigation might lead to hard feeling and ultimate disruption, and prevent the larger and better growth of the particular business in which the members have a common interest.

This becomes more and more evident as the institution becomes older, and more experienced, self-conscious and successful. Usually the formation of such organizations is forced by adverse business conditions and the existence of too many unethical practices. Only gradually do the evils of individualism give way to the advantages of collective trade organization. The earlier jealousies between members must be changed into jealousy for the good of the whole and for the good name of the craft. The club spirit and the solidarity of the guild may be of slow growth. It may take time for the better men to shape the craft policies. The new trade and operating machinery may be intricate and experimental and its users inexperienced. But in the end the machinery will work so smoothly and the ethical spirit be so strong that disputes between members will be almost absolutely avoided and most differences will be amicably settled as mere routine matters. The statistics given in Chapter VII show that eventually in such organizations official arbitration becomes a negligible item in a year's operations.

The larger activating forces in connection with such strict commercial arbitration are business ethics, the best good of the whole membership, the just enforcement of contracts and the carrying out of a general craft policy which will improve business conditions and make possible a larger volume of transactions.

It must be clearly held in mind that the mere avoidance of litigation or the relief of the courts do not have much or any weight in connection with strict commercial arbitration. The activating motives are of a much higher nature. On the contrary, in this form of business association, arbitration, in its strictly commercial form, has an important but increasingly inconspicuous and infrequent part in a great ethical and highly organized and specialized trade machinery.

Strict commercial arbitration refers exclusively to future disputes. A gyroscope does not perform any of the functions of the engines or propeller which furnish the power, nor of the hull in which the cargo is carried. Rather it is intended to steady the craft and make it more comfortable and safe when conditions are bad. When the going is smooth the gyroscope may be cut off for long periods, but it is always ready for use in case of need. Its steadying effect is felt throughout the entire craft, and without performing the functions of any other part it tends to make every other do better work. In the same sense, its arbitration tribunal is a sort of gyroscopic attachment in an exchange or trade association. It tends to make the workings of all parts of the institution more safe and comfortable, especially when conditions are bad, and it is less and less used as the navigation of the institution is better understood. Its gyroscopic and ethical functions are far more important than its actual use in settling disputes.

It will become more and more evident as we proceed that no other kind of arbitration has all of these surroundings and characteristics, or such a habitat; and that, therefore, neither common law, statutory, nor industrial arbitration has the enormous potential field or all the advantages of strict commercial arbitration; and, hence, that no one of these forms has all the qualities necessary to fit it for use as the general standard of measurement of arbitration as a whole.

CHAPTER II

THE PRESENT TENDENCY TO ORGANIZE AND SUBORGANIZE IN ALL PHASES OF LIFE ALONG ALTRUISTIC AND ETHICAL LINES

FOR a long time a new method of doing business has been increasingly adopted throughout our land almost as surely, swiftly and extensively as the telephone, the typewriter or the automobile. Yet few persons realize its growing prevalence and power. Even fewer realize that it is not a newly discovered agency like the telephone, the typewriter and the automobile; but that it is a revival, in modern form and efficiency, of a quickening power which worked overtime in the Renaissance and sudden expansion of manufacturing and merchandising six or seven centuries ago.

Our extraordinary commercial growth in the old as well as in new lines of business, and the disorders and disturbances which inevitably accompany such sudden growth strongly resemble those of post-Crusade Europe. Therefore our business world, following the laws of business which apparently govern it as surely as the natural laws govern the physical world, has been forced to revamp and modernize the powerful agency so highly developed by the English guilds and the international merchants of the Middle Ages, in order to solve the same kind of difficulties and problems that beset these earlier business organizations.

Above all, hardly any one has paused to study out the true meaning and far-reaching potential power of this business instrumentality, and what are to be its moral, ethical and economic effects upon the future conduct of business or in counteracting some present unethical practices and forces.

This force, which is constantly gaining headway, is the increasing organization and coördination of capital as well as of labor into self-governing units to which members can be admitted, and from which they may be expelled, or within which they may be otherwise disciplined, solely under the rules of the body itself. These rules are made and enforced by the members, without outside interference, and extend to the personal conduct of members so far as that is detrimental to the well-being of the organization itself or of fellow-members or of the branch of business which they represent.

These privileges were difficult to obtain in the early days. Now they are considered to be an inherent right in any self-governing church, club or social organization, or stock, produce or other exchange, trade association or chamber of commerce, or similar business body.

Of recent years modern business has tended more and more to organize itself into stock, produce, cotton, real estate and other exchanges and boards of trade, and into banking and trade associations, chambers, associations or boards of commerce, Rotary and Kiwanis Clubs, and other similar bodies—all more or less modeled on the club or the church.

This tendency is not peculiar to business, but is a part of a great national movement to organize and suborganize, which characterizes the age and is plainly discernible in the religious and club life of the country. We have about 240,000 churches of hundreds of different sects and denominations, with a nominal membership of almost fifty millions. The clubs and fraternal or secret organizations run into the tens of thousands and their membership into tens of millions. The underlying objects of these religious, social and business bodies are service, coöperation, uplift and mutual improvement, and an altruistic and ethical attempt thereby to meet the evils inherent in the daily conditions which surround their members. If they take on a corporate form, they are usually membership or non-profit-sharing corporations as distinguished from stock or profit-sharing companies; but some of the largest, like the New York Stock Exchange and the New York Clearing House Association, are purely voluntary associations.

Even labor, to meet the terrible oppressions and social and economic catastrophes which followed the English Industrial Revolution of 1760 and the introduction of factories and city tenement house life, was compelled to band together for self-protection and uplift. As a result, labor in the United States is thoroughly organized, chiefly under the American Federation of Labor, with its 107 national and international unions, 4 departments, 49 state branches, 901 city centrals, 523 local trade and federal labor unions, embracing and representing over 36,000 local unions, and 2,900,000 paid-up members with a total membership of about 3,500,000. In addition there are the railway brotherhoods, with about 450,000 members, the Amalgamated Clothing Workers with 140,000 and the Industrial Workers of the World claiming 30,000 members.

This great modern movement toward organization for mutual protection and improvement and general uplift is also very evident in business, commerce and finance. A pamphlet on "Commercial and Industrial Organizations of the United States," issued by the United States Department of Commerce, March 1, 1923,[1] gives the names and ad-

---
[1] Miscellaneous Series, No. 99.

dresses of over 11,000 such organizations, made up, approximately, of 1,500 international, interstate and national bodies, and 2,000 state and 7,700 local organizations; and this includes only those which replied to the department's request for information.

This list is slightly misleading because in some instances it duplicates international, national and state and many local associations which are in fact branches of a central organization covering the same line of trade. It has been estimated that there are 3,000 local chambers of commerce or similar commercial bodies under other names in the United States. The Chamber of Commerce of the State of New York publishes a list of 1,800 of such local commercial organizations in cities having a population of 5,000 or more. Not all of these chambers of commerce, exchanges, trade associations, etc., have compulsory or voluntary arbitration provisions in their constitutions or by-laws, but many have, and more and more they are offering arbitration facilities.

These figures are given to show the constantly increasing tendency of modern business to organize for better business methods and more ethical aims, and to eliminate abuses as far as possible in the fields so organized. Arbitration, commercial or statutory, is only one of their methods of accomplishing this result.

Whether these bodies exist for religious, social, labor or business ends, it is evident, first, that they were formed primarily to uplift and benefit the cause in which they are enlisted as well as their members as individuals, or, vice versa, to help their members and thereby the cause.

Their second common characteristic is that internal dissensions and disputes between their members are not taken around the corner to the nearest justice of the peace or other civil magistrate to be adjudicated. In other words, be it church or club, trade union or trade association, chamber of commerce or stock or other exchange, it would never think of airing its ordinary affairs before the civil courts. The rules of the organization provide that such internal troubles or disputes shall be settled by the church dignitaries, or by the officials or appropriate committees of the club, labor union, exchange, trade association or chamber of commerce. Our court calendars are not clogged by this class of differences.

Evidently it could not be otherwise. Such appeals to the civil courts would destroy the usefulness and sanctity of the churches and the benefits of the clubs and labor and business organizations.

It is the chief end and function of stock, produce, cotton, coffee and sugar and other exchanges or boards of trade or trade associations to regulate dealings between their members in the homogeneous articles or commodities in which they traffic. These dealings are usually on the floor or in the pit of the exchange, under very carefully drawn and stringent regulations. In trade associations the dealings are chiefly through contracts in prescribed and standardized forms which seek to cut out all possible chances for dispute. In these instances the transactions are highly technical in their nature—simple and everyday details to the members, but almost unintelligible to outsiders. For example, the many grades and gradings of cotton, wheat, coffee, silks and other staples, seem almost childish to the uninitiated, and yet they have been carefully evolved to promote and safeguard wholesale dealings. It is to transactions of such a nature that commercial arbitration and the arbitration rules of commercial bodies primarily apply.

This has been so in the past, as we shall see, and always must be so, if there is to continue to be specialized wholesale trading in stocks, bonds, cotton, grain, lumber and other commodities and staples.

In 1916, the committee on arbitration of the Chamber of Commerce of the State of New York and the committee on prevention of unnecessary litigation of the New York State Bar Association, acted jointly in preparing rules for the prevention of unnecessary litigation. Their report was approved by the Chamber of Commerce on November 2, 1916, and by the New York State Bar Association on January 13, 1917. In referring to the desirability and value of standardized contracts the joint committee said:

> This necessity of business has led to the employment of counsel in the preparation of important contracts, and, finally, to the standardization of many kinds of contracts, such as deeds, mortgages, insurance policies, promissory notes, bills of lading and the like.
>
> These standard contracts are necessary to the transaction of ordinary business and represent the wisdom and experience of ages. Many contracts, however, are not capable of standardization, and these are the contracts that cause the most disputes and litigation.
>
> On the basis of space devoted to each subject, in a standard digest of all reported cases, it seems that of all the litigation in the State of New York concerning non-standardized contracts, about 28 per cent concerns the meaning of the instrument. In contrast with this the percentage of litigation concerning the meaning of standardized contracts, it may be well to note, ranges only from 3 to 7 per cent.
>
> These figures are to be taken as nothing more than approximate; but they are, nevertheless, useful as showing the value of the standardization, or careful preparation, of contracts. They clearly show that uncertainty of meaning is the great breeder of disputes and litigation.

ORGANIZING FOR ALTRUISM AND ETHICS

Commercial arbitration, as defined in Chapter I is not new or even recent. Six or seven centuries ago, it existed in a very complete and advanced form in the ordinances of the English craft guilds, as shown in Chapter III. During the Middle Ages, it was highly developed in the consular courts and consular service of the international merchants of Europe, as described in Chapter IV. Through these courts was evolved the *lex mercatoria* or law merchant which lies at the very foundation of all our commercial, shipping and international terms, customs and rules.

Therefore we shall digress, in the next two chapters, to consider the nature and history of organized business in the Middle Ages in Europe, and the improvement in business ethics and the forms of strict commercial arbitration which developed under the conditions of trade which then prevailed.

CHAPTER III

COMMERCIAL ARBITRATION AND BUSINESS ETHICS UNDER THE ENGLISH CRAFT GUILDS

The English guilds were of three kinds; the municipal guilds, guilds merchant, and craft guilds. It is not necessary in this connection to go at length into the arbitration rights of the early English municipal guilds or guilds merchant. At first all kinds of guilds were closely affiliated with the Church, which was all powerful at that time. The guild merchant was intimately connected with its local municipal guild, and was more of a religious fraternity than a craft guild. By the fifteenth century the guild merchant had largely disappeared except in a few instances where it had become a religious fraternity or had been completely merged in the municipal organization. These guilds merchant were formed under special charters or licenses, and were associations for the purpose, among others, of mutual arbitration. Their members were compelled to arbitrate within the guild before litigating elsewhere, and there were many cases of English guilds merchant which had the power to try actions between their members or between their members and outsiders who voluntarily submitted to their jurisdiction.

A pure form of commercial arbitration was developed under the English craft guilds, which originated in the twelfth century, and were homogeneous in that they covered all transactions between the members belonging to a particular craft. They, too, had a distinctly religious and fraternal and mystical side, and usually had two names: "The Company of the Grocers," which was also "The Fraternity of St. Francis." Each guild was considered as an art, trade or mystery.

The earliest and most important charter was that granted to the weavers by Henry I, which gave them control of that trade. Thereby they claimed the right to arbitrate between their members, and also to hold a hallmoot, which was a petty court with jurisdiction over their members, and their households and employees, "in a plea of debt, contract or small transgression," thus combining a limited criminal jurisdiction with their full civil authority over their members.

In 1155, the bakers of London were recorded in the Pipe Roll, or tax list of the Exchequer, as paying six pounds sterling yearly for the privilege of having a guild, and they were subsequently found holding their hallmoots. The later English craft guilds asserted and if possible assumed the right to hold hallmoots in addition to their arbitration rights.

There were few if any factories in England prior to the English Industrial Revolution of 1760. The various crafts were carried on from generation to generation in the homes of the masters, in which the apprentices and often the journeymen resided. A common law indenture of apprenticeship was practically a legal adoption of the boy until he became twenty-one years of age, as is shown by the following form,[1] of comparatively recent date.

THIS INDENTURE witnesseth that E. H., an infant under the age of twenty-one years, the son of J. H., of Providence, in the

[1] Birdseye's Abbott's *Encyclopædia of General Business and Legal Forms*, p. 195.

state of Rhode Island and Providence Plantations, an yeoman, hath put himself, and by these presents doth voluntarily and of his own free will and accord, and with the consent of his aforesaid father, J. H., put and bind himself apprentice to J. O., of Smithfield, in the state aforenamed, to learn the art, trade or mystery of a wheelwright, after the manner of an apprentice, to serve from the day of the date of these presents ten years nine months and twenty-four days, to be complete and ended. During all which said term the said apprentice his master faithfully shall serve, his secrets keep, his lawful commands gladly obey. He shall do no damage to his said master, nor see it done by other, without letting or giving notice thereof to his said master. He shall not waste his said master's goods, nor lend them unlawfully to any. He shall not commit fornication nor contract matrimony within said term.

At cards, dice, or any other unlawful game, he shall not play, whereby his said master may have damage from his own goods, or the goods of others. He shall not absent himself by day or by night without his said master's leave, or haunt alehouses, taverns or playhouses, but in all things behave himself as a good and faithful apprentice ought to do towards his said master.

And he, the said master, for himself, his executors and administrators, does hereby promise to teach and instruct, or cause the said apprentice to be taught and instructed, in the art, trade or calling of a wheelwright by the best ways and means he can, and to provide for said apprentice good and sufficient meat, drink and apparel, both in sickness and in health, and lodging and washing and other necessary fitting for such an apprentice.

And at the expiration of said time abovesaid, the said master to dismiss said apprentice with one new suit of apparel for all parts of his body, both woolen and linen, fitting for such an apprentice, besides his wearing apparel, and likewise to learn said apprentice to read, write, and cipher as far as the rule of three. And that at the expiration of such apprenticeship he will give to such apprentice a certificate in writing that such apprentice has served at such trade or craft a full term of apprenticeship as specified in this indenture.

IN WITNESS WHEREOF, we, the parties, do hereunto interchangeably set our hands and seals, the eighteenth day of June, A.D. 1777.

Signed, sealed and delivered in presence of   J. O. (L. S.)
A. Y.   J. H. (L. S.)
F. O.   E. H. (L. S.)

After his apprenticeship the young man, now become a journeyman, frequently married into the master's family or lived on or near the premises. There was great personal and trade loyalty to the establishment and home in which the journeyman had learned his trade, and with which he was likely to be connected for life unless he migrated to another place or set up business for himself.

Hence and of necessity, the ordinances of the craft guilds covered not only the matters which related to the craft itself, but to the government of the daily lives of and relations between the master members and their families, servants, journeymen and apprentices, to an extent which would not be possible to-day. A list of the titles of the hundred ordinances of the Clothworkers is given in Appendix I. Of these only one related to arbitration, and that is given below. Apparently small misdemeanors or ordinary disputes concerning debts or contracts were tried in the hall-moot, while the wardens and assistant wardens had special jurisdiction over any discord, strife or debate which at any time thereafter might fortune to happen for any cause or matter whatsoever it be, between members or their journeymen, serving men or apprentices, or between any of the aforesaid persons or any others of the said art or mystery of Clothworkers.

The following is an exact copy of the provisions for Arbitration in the ordinances of the Clothworkers' Guild.

An Ordynaunce for controversies to be decyded by the Master Wardenes and Assistauntes.

Item It is ordayned ordered and establyshed that frome henceforthe yf any dyscorde stryfe or debate at any tyme hereafter shall fortune to happen for any cause or matter whatsoever it be betwyxte one houshoulder and an other or howshoulders and others of the sayde Company or Fellowshippe of Clotheworkers or betweene them or any of theyr jorneymen servingmen or apprentices or betweene any of the aforesayde persones or any others of the sayde Arte or Mystery of Clotheworkers which without prejudice of the lawes of the Realme may be appeased and reformed by good and wyse meanes That then the sayde parties before they move or attempte by course of lawe any suite betweene them or one agaynste the other in that behalfe shall firste shewe theyr matter and cause of theyr greefe with the circumstaunces of the same to the Master and Wardenes of the saide Arte or Mystery of Clotheworkers for the tyme beinge or some of them to thintente y^t by theyr good dyscretions some quiet order and good ende may be taken therin to the satisfaction of such parties and by their assent accordinge to righte and equitie in eschewinge of further trouble and suite of lawe And yf it shall seeme to ye saide Master and Wardenes or the more parte of them that the matter is difficulte and beyonde their reache to ende and determyne the same for lacke of better understandinge of the lawes of the Realme or the customes of ye saide Citie of London That then any of the said partyes soe greeved as aforesayde maye take theyr remedy one agaynste the other by order of lawe without any further licence to be obtayned and had at the handes of ye saide Master and Wardens or any of them in that behalfe But yf the said Master and Wardens or the more parte of them for the tyme beinge shall ende and determyne any cause matter or thinge betweene any of the sayde parties in forme aforesaide by assent of the parties and yet neverthelesse the saide person or persones havinge any matter or cause ended before them will afterwards prosecute and followe suite in lawe the one agaynst the other without lycence had and obtayned in that behalfe soe to doe of the sayde Master and Wardens for the tyme beinge or the more parte of them Then the person so offending shall forfett and pay the some of Forty Shillings of lawfull Englishe money at the least or a greter some suche as shalbe thoughte meete and reasonable by ye saide Master Wardens and Assistaunts or the more parte of them accordinge to the greatnes of the matter or cause in controversie betweene them so it exceede not the some of Twenty Poundes.

Thus it is evident that this early arbitration by the craft guilds reached every phase of life in which there might be a discord, strife or dispute which affected the guild in general or the members or their families or employees in particular, but that it did not apply to outsiders.

We shall find this same thought running through all commercial arbitration, as through the affairs of a club or a church. Disputes may involve the larger interests of the organization as well as the matters immediately at issue between the contestants. The ordinances or rules made by the whole body for the common welfare must be held in mind in deciding the dispute. This corresponds to the questions of public policy or of the common good which may arise in an ordinary litigation, and upon which the final decision may rest.

Another point to be observed here is that, at least in the beginning, arbitration under the craft guilds involved many questions which could not then have been intelligently or adequately tried in an ordinary lawsuit. Courts of equity had not then been established, but many questions of an equitable nature must have come before these arbitrators, who were a regular and permanent court of trade experts which functioned for centuries, and which must have worked out, in each guild, the body of precedents under which they conducted their company, fellowship, fraternity, craft, art, trade, guild or mystery—for it was called by all these names.

Their decisions were intended to build up and be a part of a code of business conduct and ethics, and even in the craft guilds the close connection between commercial arbitration and business ethics was very evident. To-day, also, commercial arbitration is to be regarded largely as a means for the formulation and construction of a code of business practice and ethics for any particular body by a tribunal of its own experts, rather than as a substitute for ordinary legal procedure or as a means of relieving the courts. As the organization's original purpose was to improve ethical and trading conditions, it follows that arbitration, as an important part of its machinery, must have been instituted for the same object.

The jealousy with which the guilds guarded their powers to enforce their own decrees and awards is shown by an ordinance of The Worshipful Company of Grocers, organized in A.D. 1345, and second in importance only to the Livery Companies of London. After providing for arbitration before the wardens, the ordinance proceeds:

> And if by chance one party be unwilling to abide by their directions and complain to other officers, all who shall be warned of the Fraternity shall go with the wardens in order to oppose him, except in cases of felony or other actions amenable to the law.

CHAPTER IV

COMMERCIAL ARBITRATION AND BUSINESS ETHICS AMONG THE INTERNATIONAL MERCHANTS OF MEDIEVAL EUROPE

PRIOR to the Crusades—A.D. 1096 to 1276—the Arabs were the great merchants of eastern Europe and the East. Many of their business forms, names, customs and laws and much of their sea law and terms were adopted bodily by commercial Europe and still form the basis of our commercial law and practice. It was the Saracens who, about A.D. 941, introduced arithmetic into Europe.

After the Crusades a large trade sprang up between the Far East on the one side and England and western Europe on the other. Speaking generally, goods were landed in Venice on the east or Genoa on the west of Italy, and from there they were distributed throughout Europe on the backs of horses or mules or by vessels. Venice usually sent her goods overland into Europe, but Genoa was the chief shipping port to western Europe and England. Florence was the banking and financial center, while Pisa, in a smaller way, covered both commerce and business.

At that time, the word *merchant* strictly meant a person who dedicated himself to commerce, and the international merchants became organized as a great profession, second only to the Church and possibly to knighthood. It ranked far above manufacturing, which was regarded as merely a set of local trades in the hands of the various craft guilds. These international merchants did business chiefly through the many great fairs of France, Spain, Germany and England, which were held annually or oftener in various cities. To these the merchants, traveling together for protection, carried their goods from the East or the products of their own country, and sold them for cash for local consumption or exchanged them for native products offered at the fair. These and other goods were then taken on to the next fair and the process repeated there; but, as we shall see, the transactions of each fair were closed then and there between the merchants before they journeyed on together to the next fair.

The chief English fair was that of Stourbridge,[1] which was annually proclaimed on September 4th, opened on the 8th and continued for three weeks. The erection of temporary buildings for the fair commenced on August 24th; the builders being allowed to destroy the grain on the spot if it were not cleared by that date, and the owners being authorized to destroy the booths on Michaelmas Day, if they were not removed by that time. The fair occupied about half a mile square which was divided into streets, in each of which they dealt in some special article, such as ironmongery, cloth, wool, leather, and ultimately every conceivable commodity; and the streets bore the name of the article dealt in. The Italian merchants brought eastern wares, Italian silks, velvets and delicate glass; and the Flemish, the linens of Liége and Ghent. Spain sent iron; and Norway, tar and pitch. There were wines from Gascony, Spain and even Greece. The Hanse towns contributed furs and amber, and possibly the precious stones of the East—supplied through Moscow and Novgorod. England sent her great wool packs which were the envy of other nations. Wales offered tin. Salt came from the springs of

---

[1] Bewes, *Romance of the Law Merchant*, pp. 93 *et seq.*

Worcestershire, lead from Derbyshire, and iron from the Sussex forges. Also there was much agricultural produce, which was then grown in greater abundance in England than anywhere else except Flanders.

The general plan of these fairs, the transactions thereat and the pilgrims and others who attended them are well illustrated by this extract from Bunyan's *Pilgrim's Progress*, describing the Vanity Fair:

> Almost five thousand years agone there were pilgrims walking to the Celestial City . . . and Beelzebub, Apollyon and Legion, with their companions, perceiving by the path that the pilgrims made, that their way to the city lay through this town of Vanity, they contrived here to set up a fair; a fair wherein should be sold all sorts of vanity, and that it should last all the year long: therefore at this fair are all such merchandises sold, as houses, lands, trades, places, honours, preferments, titles, countries, kingdoms, lusts, pleasures, and delights of all sorts, as whores, bawds, wives, husbands, children, masters, servants, lives, blood, bodies, souls, silver, gold, pearls, precious stones, and what not.
>
> And, moreover, at this fair there is at all times to be seen juggling, cheats, games, plays, fools, apes, knaves, and rogues, and that of every kind.
>
> Here are to be seen, too, and that for nothing, thefts, murders, adulteries, false swearers, and that of a blood-red colour.
>
> And as in other fairs of less moment, there are several rows and streets, under their proper names, where such and such wares are vended; so here, likewise, you have the proper places, rows, streets (*viz.* countries and kingdoms), where the wares of this fair are soonest to be found. . . . This fair, therefore, is an ancient thing, of long standing, and a very great fair.

Usually the wholesale international trading was carried on at these fairs, while the local retail interchange of native products took place at the local markets which met frequently throughout the year.

For our present purpose, it is chiefly necessary to notice but a few features of these great fairs. These were the Peace of God, or of the Church; freedom of the international merchants from local law; the merchants' consular courts; and the great celerity with which the fair courts and the consular courts disposed of their cases—with no appeal.

Just as our American Indians had an eternal peace at the salt springs to which they all must flock, so at first by the feudal lord, subsequently by the Church, and sometimes by treaty, it was provided that there should be peace and comity at the fairs (the Peace of God) even if some of the nations might be at war. Nor did the laws of the state or of the locality prevail as between the international merchants themselves, but only their law merchant. Disputes between outsiders or between the merchants and outsiders were governed by the law of the fair or "fair law." There was strict extraterritoriality at each fair, and the merchants settled their disputes before their own consular courts before they journeyed on to the next fair.

For example, a Middle Age Spanish law decreed that:

If the merchants of oversea ports have any action among themselves, no judge of our land ought to judge it; but they must answer according to their own laws and their own judges.

Magna Charta provided that:

All Merchants shall have safety and security in coming into England, and going out of England, and in staying and in traveling through England, as well by land as by water, to buy and sell, without any unjust exactions, according to ancient and right customs, excepting in the time of war, and if they be of a country at war against us; and if such are found in our land at the beginning of a war, they shall be apprehended without injury of their bodies and goods until it shall be known to us, or to our Chief Justiciary, how the Merchants of our country are treated who are found in the country at war against us; and if ours be in safety there, the others shall be in safety in our land.

Under the law merchant, the arbitration of disputes between these international merchants was before their own consular courts, which were of four classes:

First, the itinerant consul or consuls—who traveled with their compatriot traders, watching over their interests and judging their differences.

Second, the permanent consulado, or consuls having similar but greater powers in the cities of their own country, where they and their prior formed the local commercial court.

Third, the consulate which was organized as a fixed institution in foreign trading cities, with administrative and judicial jurisdiction of their nationals, who were predominantly merchants. This last class survives in our commercial consular service and in extraterritorial courts, such as those in China at present and formerly in Egypt and Turkey.

Fourth, there were even more permanent courts in the towns visited by the itinerant merchants, in which the word *consuls* was usually applied to the judges of the merchants; which courts, or the municipal court of the prior and the consuls, later developed throughout Europe into standing commercial courts.

In medieval Europe these international merchants took their law with them, and there was little or no opposition, except in England, to having their disputes judged by their own consuls. Certain countries refused admission beyond the ports, and then it was a practice to carry consuls on board visiting ships, although in important towns there might be a resident consul.

The promptness with which suits between strangers and natives were to be tried in these early days is shown by the customs of Newcastle-on-Tyne during the reign of Henry I when such cases were to be disposed of before the third turn of the tide. In the time of Edward I it was provided that ordinary suits with strangers should be completed from day to day. In case of fire they should be completed from hour to hour, and in case of stranger mariners, from tide to tide. At Stourbridge, the mayor held his "court of the dusty feet," at which disputes arising at the fair, so long as they were not between the merchants, were determined from morn till night with no appeal.

The important points here are that as soon as commerce began to take on an organized form, even 600 or 700 years ago, it had to provide its own rules and its own machinery, one item of which was arbitration, both local and itinerant, which decided cases on the spot, so that the disputes arising at a certain fair could be settled before the body of merchants moved on to the next fair; that out of the decisions thus made in regard to such commercial transactions emerged the law merchant or *lex mercatoria,* as distinguished from the civil or church or local laws in Europe or the common law in England; that the consular courts were the progenitors of the commercial courts which are very usual throughout Europe and deal wholly with commercial or business disputes; and that the law merchant, which was the direct product of these consular court experts, is the foundation of our present international commerce and of very many of our domestic commercial and transportation terms and customs. It is proving itself a remarkably broad and solid foundation, capable of bearing any strains put upon it in these modern times, and shows the great advantage of having court decisions based upon a personal knowledge by the judge of the trade rules and conditions involved.

This also evidences the high standards of commercial honor and good faith which prevailed among these organized itinerant merchants of many nationalities. In those disturbed times they had little to stand upon except their own code of honor and a general agreement to ostracize in future dealings every merchant who did not perform all his agreements with the greatest punctiliousness.

CHAPTER V

THE NECESSITY OF SPEEDY AND EXPERT DECISIONS OF COMMERCIAL DISPUTES

ORGANIZED business prefers and even requires prompt decisions of its disputes by experts acquainted with the technical points involved, rather than a formal trial at some uncertain future time before a court of justice of nonexperts. If trial of any kind is delayed, witnesses may forget, or die, or be lost, and other evidence may vanish. Legal expenses run on day by day. Business needs prompt certainty as to where it stands and as to its liabilities and available assets. The direct and indirect losses and expenses of a delayed court trial often exceed the whole amount involved; but if the rules of his organization or a clause in his contract provide for arbitration before a recognized arbitration tribunal, the merchant knows that he will have a speedy decision upon the merits of his particular dispute.

Further, he knows that probably there will be no need of expert evidence and that the issues will be narrowed to a few questions of fact, because the trial will be had before a committee of experts who understand all the technical points involved, who probably know all the parties, and who, in deciding the issues, will have in view the larger interests of the organization or business itself.

In courts of law, technical questions and trade customs and rules are usually decided after hearing the conflicting evidence of expert witnesses; and in this connection it is

NEED OF SPEEDY AND EXPERT DECISIONS

well to remember the classification of liars made by a learned and well-known jurist—"plain liars, damned liars and expert witnesses." At least this quotation contrasts the courts' regard for the conflicting testimony of high-priced expert witnesses and the merchants' desire that their disputes shall be settled before experts chosen from their own ranks.

Even arbitration is likely to be avoided by prior voluntary amicable adjustment or by conciliation, but more especially by the fact that any dispute will be tried before trusted fellow member experts who probably have had many years of experience upon the arbitration committee, and who are acting under standardized contracts or ancient rules and regulations which have been carefully devised, revised and improved to cover every exigency.

Every exchange and board of trade has its standing arbitration committee made up of highly honored members who give their time for a nominal sum. Trials can be brought on before such a committee in the course of a few days, while the facts are fresh and evidence available. Thus a merchant's rights are definitely and fairly fixed without any delay or any unnecessary trouble or expense, and he can turn his mind to other more important matters.

These questions of time and certainty become more and more important to the merchant as his business expands and becomes more and more intricate, and he gladly welcomes every rule or regulation, or any standardized contract or other agency of his exchange or board of trade or trade association which hastens a decision of any dispute arising in his business.

The importance of these elements to the merchant was forcibly brought out in 1874 by the argument of Elliott C. Cowdin, long the chairman of the executive committee of the

Chamber of Commerce of the State of New York, before the judiciary committee of the New York Senate, in advocacy of the bill to establish a court of arbitration for the port of New York, as detailed in Chapter XII.

It must be generally admitted that hitherto our legal tribunals have been altogether inadequate to speedily investigate and promptly decide upon purely commercial and business disputes.

I but express the general feeling of business men when I say that, in the controversies which arise among them, they desire, above all things, that these controversies be rapidly as well as equitably decided. In the vast majority of cases, promptness of decision, by a competent and disinterested arbitrator, is their ideal of justice. Procrastination is the thief, not only of their time, but of their energies. Prolonged lawsuits are the tumors and cancers of business men, eating into the very substance of their life. What feeling of security, financially, can any man have, if, among transactions amounting often to hundreds of thousands of dollars a month, distributed among scores of individuals, a portion of these are held in doubt for many weary months and even years.

To the business man, tardy justice is practically injustice. A speedy verdict against his own judgment of the merits of his case would often be better for him than a slow verdict confirming it; because, independent of the inevitable expenses incurred, the fret and worriment of the controversy distract his mind, and subtly impair his capacity to manage the ever-recurring emergencies of his daily affairs.

Moreover, prolonged lawsuits lock up or cut off the merchant's resources, as well as undermine his energies. Indeed, gentlemen, have we not sometimes seen business men so harassed, so completely unstrung, by cases postponed or appealed, that they have at last lost confidence in the equity of legal proceedings?

There always has been a tendency in business communities to settle business disputes by some form of reference or arbitration. Even in ancient times there were particular magistrates for deciding upon commercial controversies. In Athens, for example, the magistrates boarded the ships to decide maritime disputes, in order that the interests of merchants might not suffer from delay, and they were required to give their decisions with the utmost promptitude.

The system of arbitration which has gradually found its way into the practice of European nations, has its source in the jurisprudence of Justinian. Tribunals for the settlement of commercial disputes now exist in France, Germany, Russia, Austria, Spain, Italy, Belgium, Denmark, and, indeed, for the most part throughout Europe. France took the lead in establishing these courts of arbitration. The French Tribunal of Commerce, virtually instituted in 1563, during the reign of Francis II, though it has, especially in the present century, been subjected to important alterations and modifications, has practically existed, with little interruption, for more than three hundred years. In the language of the original decree of 1563, its object was "the shortening of lawsuits and adjusting the differences between merchants trading in good faith, without being restrained within the subtleties of the law."

CHAPTER VI

THE ETHICAL OBJECTS OF ORGANIZED BUSINESS

IN the growth of ordinary unorganized business, disputes increase in number and variety much faster than the volume of the business itself; in a geometrical rather than an arithmetical ratio. These disputes may be honest ones in regard to the grading, condition, classification or transportation of the merchandise itself, or they may arise from unethical acts and practices by a few individuals. Because such practices are frequently successful they are likely to spread and taint the whole course of unorganized business and affect men who otherwise would not think of resorting to them. This rule as to the increase of disputes and unethical acts is an important reason why business must organize more and more scientifically as its volume increases. Otherwise it tends to seek a lower and not a higher level, to engender a greater expense and confusion, and the better merchants are likely to be tarred with the stick of the least ethical.

More and more the guiding mottoes and characteristics of big business and organized business are service and business honor. Some of our largest banks and trust companies boast that they offer over fifty kinds of service to their customers. Never before has the average customer gotten more for his money, all things considered. Our present volume of business transactions could not have been reached

ETHICAL OBJECTS OF ORGANIZED BUSINESS

unless these new and better notions of service and business honor had first grown correspondingly. The-customer-be-pleased theory extends every day; partly because business is best based upon a reputation for honorable dealing, and partly because of carefully supervised advertising—whether of the "money-back" variety or not. The day of Yankee wooden nutmegs has passed.

The sacredness of contracts grows daily among business men. More and more it is becoming axiomatic among them that neither party to an agreement should have the privilege of changing any of its provisions without the consent of the other. This is most clearly understood where the contract is in standardized printed form, such as those carefully prepared and prescribed by an exchange, board of trade, trade association or governmental agency, for the very purpose of preventing misunderstandings and disputes between members or by ordinary men of business.

Such a contract becomes the most ordinary thing in an office, so that even an office boy can fill in its blanks. A dispute under such a contract becomes the most out-of-the-ordinary thing in the office; and certainly not a reason why litigation should ensue and lifelong business relations and friendships should be severed for a mere trifle which two business men can adjust in a few moments without the thought of calling in a lawyer. At most, they think only of referring the matter to some fellow member or to their trusted friends on the arbitration committee. If necessary or desirable because of changed conditions, they readily unite to get the rules or the standardized contracts amended so that such a dispute shall not arise between others in the future.

Under the spirit of modern organized business, the sacredness of the contract, the value of the business connection and friendship, and the best traditions of the guild are the things of real moment, and a dispute is merely an incident in the larger matters, and arbitration is merely a means to prevent bad blood.

In other words, in an exchange, or board of trade or other business organization, as in a club, the members have 999 points in common for every difference that is important enough for an arbitration. In most instances this proportion is far too small. Therefore arbitration in such an organization becomes merely one of many details for the better conduct of business and the improvement of trade relations, rather than a method of preventing litigation or relieving the courts.

The careful organization of business through exchanges, boards of trade, trade associations, standardized contracts or other methods, only partly of modern origin, is not primarily to eliminate disputes. Rather it is to eliminate the abuses and wastes of all kinds which lead to such disputes; to fix standards; formulate uniform business rules; cultivate the get-together spirit; and foster business friendships and confidence in place of unscrupulous and unethical competition. This organization of business, by producing uniformity and understanding, cuts out all thought of litigation at the same time that it provides a friendly means of conciliating any dispute, and expert tribunals of its own through which differences may or must be arbitrated. The only way in which the natural law of the geometrical increase of disputes in unorganized business can be thwarted is by the higher organization of business by itself, so that it can detect and remedy in an expert way its own ethical and administrative weaknesses.

And right here we may see clearly the very close connection between strict commercial arbitration and better business ethics which is not inherent in any other form of arbitration.

True business ethics are not a matter of forms or methods any more than music is a matter of keys or strings or instruments, or true oratory a question of the language or color of the orator. On the contrary such ethics are an atmosphere and enfolding power which consciously and unconsciously bend and sway every one within their field of action and make him do better work for the common good. Improved methods are not manacles, nor do required forms become fetters. Rather, these are the best instruments so far devised for accomplishing a common and desirable end at that particular time and stage of the business.

As an engineer constantly goes over his locomotive to be sure that every part is functioning correctly, so the experts of a business organization are constantly going over its parts to make sure of their proper functioning; and at the same time they are watching all its working parts to ascertain how improvements may be made in the future. Over all is the United States Department of Commerce making a broad national and international survey, gathering and disseminating essential and enlightening statistics, and working for and with the business of the country for higher and better ends and results.

Because the use of improved business methods may elevate the ideals and ideas of those who are interested therein, these very methods may thereby become obsolete and unfitted to accomplish the higher ends to which they have shown the way. Hence, as the experienced members of organized business watch its workings they must constantly seek for and install new methods and instruments better fitted for new and higher ends.

This tendency to improve the education of new members and then to improve by organization the atmosphere in which coworkers shall labor is not new. It was first seen in the crafts, for as early as A.D. 1565 a law was passed in England providing that no one should practice any trade who had not served a seven years' apprenticeship therein; and that usually meant that the apprenticeship must be served with a master who was a member of a craft guild.

The practice of medicine and surgery in the city of New York was first regulated June 10, 1760, and afterwards by an act of March 27, 1792. On March 23, 1797, the first general regulation throughout the state was adopted, authorizing the chancellor, a judge of the supreme court or common pleas or a master in chancery, to license physicians and surgeons on receiving evidence of their having studied two years.[1] Now however, the statutes of New York also recognize as professions dentistry, veterinary medicine, pharmacy, optometry, chiropody, nursing, public accountancy, certified shorthand reporting, and architecture, and provide for the licensing of those who are to practice many lines of business. In addition, mining, civil, electrical, metallurgical, mechanical, industrial and aeronautical engineering and many other professions are recruited from college and university graduates holding diplomas in these respective subjects.

Simultaneously, as already shown, business has organized in exchanges, boards of trade, trade associations, chambers of commerce, and other similar bodies, intended to advance the common good of those engaged in that line of business. Their affairs are controlled by the stronger and better class

---
[1] 2 R. L. 1813, p. 219.

ETHICAL OBJECTS OF ORGANIZED BUSINESS

of their members and they have many of the characteristics of a well-organized church or club. The ethical phase is most prominent, and the rules, regulations and customs are designed to improve constantly the ethical side of the organization, for it is realized that thereby the common good is fostered. This is shown by reference to the objects of these associations as stated in their several charters or constitutions.[2]

All these exchanges, trade associations and other similar organizations have more or less complete and comprehensive rules and regulations, which, in the main, refer to the conduct of their particular business, and govern the grades, grading, condition, terms, times and other intricate details of trading between members. The actual dealings may take place upon the floor or pit of the exchange with the simplest memorandum of the transaction, to be subsequently mutually confirmed and executed by the office forces of the members. In other organizations the contracts are made through elaborate uniform printed agreements which cover every detail; as in the standard arrival and spot contracts of the American Spice Trade Association. The front of these contracts contains a few items as to the quantity, article, quality, approval, price, shipment, terms, weight, tares and insurance of a particular transaction, with the further provision that "all questions arising out of this contract shall be subject to the rules of the American Spice Trade Association, printed on the reverse side of this contract." The main contract, printed in small type upon the back, contains about 950 words under fifteen subdivisions.[3]

---

[2] See Appendix No. II.
[3] Birdseye's Abbott's *Encyclopædia of General Business and Legal Forms*, p. 832-836, Forms 1102, 1103.

It should constantly be borne in mind that all strict commercial arbitration presupposes a permanent and time-honored tribunal of conscientious and experienced experts, able and anxious to decide each dispute upon its merits and with a view to the future good of their own organization as a whole.

CHAPTER VII

THE MINIMIZING OF DISPUTES UNDER PROPER BUSINESS ORGANIZATION

HAVING shown the true habitat, meaning and history of commercial arbitration, it remains only to prove by concrete and irrefutable examples that the rules, regulations, uniform or standardized contracts, and ethical conduct and atmosphere of exchanges, boards of trade and trade associations do : (*a*) make it almost impossible for disputes and especially for unethical disputes to occur; and (*b*) render it likely that such disputes, which are usually in the form of natural mistakes and errors arising in the whirl of business, will ordinarily be amicably settled between the parties; or occasionally may require conciliation through the informal or official action of fellow members or of the organization; or in very unusual and infrequent instances may make it necessary that otherwise unsolvable disputes be brought before the arbitration authorities of the organization. (*c*) In some instances, the process will go so far that official interpretations of the rules will supplant the resort to arbitration.

The important and basic thing is that disputes are prevented, that good faith is not impugned, and that friendships are not broken. In a sense there is no thought of the prevention of litigation or the relief of the courts. Organized business, more and more, is seeking to make its contracts and methods so perfect and complete that disputes cannot arise; and in its constitutions, by-laws and written regulations, the provisions as to arbitration are a negligibly small part of the whole.

In order to make the parts of the organization work together satisfactorily, either individually or as a whole, there is a constant endeavor to promote a general atmosphere of friendliness and cordiality, and this is nothing more than the constant and scientific lubricating which any great piece of machinery requires to make all its parts work together satisfactorily.

It is not difficult to prove the foregoing statements. If we except accident and criminal cases, there is not, relatively and considering the volume and intricacy of the business transactions involved, one thousandth as much litigation to-day as there was in the beginning of the nineteenth century. This is because the organization of business has taken at least ninety-five per cent of the total business transactions out of the field of potential litigation by regulating them most wisely and minutely, and by making them subject to commercial adjustment, conciliation and arbitration. The remainder of the dealings is done under such improved methods and influences that the need and the will to litigate is very much minimized. Transactions involving hundreds of millions, and even billions of dollars are daily carried through without the thought of litigation, although, as already shown, ordinarily litigation tends, in unorganized business, to increase much faster than the volume of business, unless that natural law is checked by better and newer ideals and methods. A few examples will clearly prove the truth of the above statements.

The New York Stock Exchange is not incorporated, and

MINIMIZING BUSINESS DISPUTES

has always resisted any efforts to force it to incorporate. In 1925 the official transactions of the Exchange amounted to over $50,000,000,000 (market value) of stocks and bonds, an average of almost $200,000,000 for every working day. There are listed upon the Exchange about 1012 different issues of stocks and 1330 issues of bonds, of many differing kinds and descriptions. The total transactions of the Exchange represented a turnover of several times the total par value of these listed stocks and bonds.

These dealings were very intricate and required at least two days to complete. From the standpoint of the sellers they involved over $50,000,000,000; and from the standpoint of the buyers, an equal amount.

There were many different operations in carrying through these complicated transactions in any one of which disputes or errors might arise. (1) There were the rapid-fire purchases and sales of the $50,000,000,000 between the members on the floor, which appear to the onlooker in the gallery to be confusion worse confounded; (2) these must be followed by telephonic reports of every item by both parties to their respective offices; and (3) advices thereof by the offices to their various principals; (4) the confirming of each and every purchase and sale, on the same afternoon, by and between the respective selling and purchasing houses; and (5) their reports to the Stock Exchange Clearing House; (6) the clearing thereat; (7) the drawing and certifying of checks in payment; and (8) the delivery of the checks and certificates of stock by two o'clock the next afternoon. Also this frequently involved (9) the actual transferring, and (10) registering of the stock certificates by differing banks or trust companies. (11) In addition, every transaction in stocks on the floor must be transmitted, by wire and thousands of stock tickers, to every considerable community in the land.

Necessarily such huge and intricate transactions must have been attended with tens of thousands of mistakes, errors and differences. Yet the records of the Exchange show that in the whole year of 1925 there were only twenty-four official arbitrations and not a single litigation necessary to take care of all the mistakes, errors and differences which arose out of highly technical and complicated transactions involving $50,000,000,000, carried on in the apparent bedlam of an active market upon the floor of the New York Stock Exchange, by or on behalf of its 1100 members. This is the more striking because arbitration is not compulsory under the rules of the Exchange; but in speaking of this a leading official said, "I cannot conceive of a case where a member would not accept arbitration if offered, whether by a fellow member or an outsider."

One thing is evident in this instance. As the years have passed, the self-adopted constitution, rules, customs and dealings of the Exchange have created a new atmosphere which has eliminated substantially all disputes. Personal hostility and suspicion between the members have been replaced by a spirit of honorable dealing and the assumption of the good faith of all fellow members.

This is quite different from the atmosphere of sixty years ago when some members of the Exchange were proved to have resorted to the most unethical and illegal practices, protecting themselves by buying up judges of the New York Supreme Court, who were afterwards threatened with impeachment for their actions in this connection. In those times, a famous member of the Exchange used to say in a crisis, "Well, boys, we'll have to injine 'em."

MINIMIZING BUSINESS DISPUTES

Transactions in the New York Stock Exchange are conducted strictly under its constitution, and

> no person elected to membership shall be admitted to the privileges thereof until he shall have signed the Constitution of the Exchange. By such signature he pledges himself to abide by the same, as the same has been or shall be from time to time amended, and by all rules and regulations adopted pursuant to the Constitution.[1]

The constitution of the New York Stock Exchange, and the rules of its governing committee pursuant to the constitution embrace about 500 paragraphs, which provide for fifteen standing committees, including that for arbitration, and for four special committees. It requires only four of these paragraphs to cover the provisions as to the appointment of the arbitration committee, its composition, powers, procedure and the appeals from its decisions. Relatively these paragraphs are little used in the daily transactions of the Exchange, compared with those which provide, in the greatest detail, how business shall be conducted.

Surely this example of pure commercial arbitration in a voluntary business organization doing a homogeneous business demonstrates clearly that the Exchange does not consider that the chief function of its arbitration committee is to prevent litigation or relieve the crowded calendars of the courts of New York City. In this respect all commercial bodies using compulsory arbitration follow the rule of the craft guilds where, as shown in Appendix No. 1, only one ordinance out of a hundred related to arbitration.

There are voluntary associations formed in various cities throughout the country to clear the daily transactions between member and other banks. The transactions, clearings

---
[1] Article XII, Sec. 5.

and balances, of the New York Clearing House Association for the year ending September 30, 1925, amounted to $306,595,037,911.57 in all, or an average of $1,011,864,811.58 per business day. For the week ending March 6, 1926, they aggregated $7,797,141,202.20 or an average of about $1,300,000,000 per business day. Yet this was not the largest week on record. The present total transactions are at a rate of over $320,000,000,000 per annum.

In this Association the member banks, in case of doubt, call up the manager and inquire what is the rule governing the point in question, and then follow his ruling. On very rare occasions the manager refers the matter to the clearing house committee for decision.

The constitution of the Association contains eight lines in regard to the arbitration committee, but the manager could not remember when that committee had been called upon to act. Nor did he know of any litigations between the members as such in regard to the hundreds of billions of dollars of clearing house transactions. Of course this did not apply to the underlying transactions of the customers and depositors of the various banks as covered by notes or checks deposited in such banks.

Possibly this is the most striking example of the ability of modern self-governing business organizations to iron out disputes between their members without any resort to the nonexpert courts and juries, and even without conciliation or arbitration under their own rules.

In this instance even the need of arbitration has become a sort of vermiform appendix, its functions being replaced by an occasional official interpretation of the rules which in itself is sufficient to prevent disputes.

The total wealth of the whole country has been officially

MINIMIZING BUSINESS DISPUTES

estimated as $320,000,000,000, as of 1922. The turnover or transactions of the New York Clearing House now exceed this amount, without requiring a single arbitration or lawsuit, but merely official interpretations of rules, which are invariably followed.

The New York Produce Exchange may also be mentioned to show how infrequently it is necessary to invoke commercial arbitration in this and other similar exchanges and boards of trade throughout the country, whose members deal in grain, sugar, coffee, and other food products, and cotton and similar homogeneous articles. All such bodies come within the definitions of Chapter I and furnish examples of strict commercial arbitration as carried on by self-governing business bodies, trading in homogeneous products.

Originally incorporated in 1862 as "The New York Commercial Association," the objects of the New York Produce Exchange were stated as follows in its charter:

> The purpose of said corporation shall be to provide and regulate a suitable room or rooms for a produce exchange in the city of New York, to inculcate just and equitable principles in trade, to establish and maintain uniformity in commercial usages, to acquire, preserve and disseminate valuable business information and to adjust controversies and misunderstandings between persons engaged in business.

Subsequently the Exchange was given power to make provision for the widows and families of deceased members.

The charter, by-laws and the several trade rules of the New York Produce Exchange governing transactions in different kinds of products cover over 300 octavo pages, and about 1500 paragraphs, and, besides the control of the property and affairs of the Exchange, provide regulations for transactions among members in the following products:

provisions, meats, lard, flour, petroleum, cotton seed, vegetable oils, waxes and fats, animal oils and fats, hay and straw, butter and cheese, naval stores, and the grading, inspecting, weighing, sampling, warehousing and dealing in futures in some or all of these various articles, with provisions as to canal boats, lighterage, sail and steam vessels, and charter parties and bills of lading for the same, margin depositories, etc., etc.

Of the thirty-five standing and trade committees, the provisions as to the arbitration committee cover about a page and a half out of 300, while those as to the complaint committee take in five pages. With all these complicated affairs, transactions and interests, subject to so many errors, omissions, mistakes and human failures, there were only eighteen sittings of the arbitration committee upon sixteen regular arbitrations during the last fiscal year, and about the same number of arbitrations in which special questions as to technical dealings, such as charter parties, lighterage, etc., were submitted to mutually selected specialists in those lines. Their awards had the same force and effect as those of the regular arbitration committee. So far as was known to officials there was not a single litigation between members of the Exchange.

The same conditions hold true in all other exchanges dealing in homogeneous articles. Their constitutions, by-laws, rules and regulations are chiefly devoted to regulating transactions between members so as to prevent disputes and to simplify and minimize those which arise, and so as to create an atmosphere of good fellowship between members in which a settlement of any dispute becomes a friendly act or a matter to be covered by conciliation or arbitration.

Furthermore constant changes in the articles to be dealt

MINIMIZING BUSINESS DISPUTES 49

in and new methods of doing business require corresponding amendments in the by-laws, rules and regulations. These are not made by application to a nonexpert and politically minded legislature or nonexpert judge and jury, but, with the advice of experienced counsel, are worked out by experts acquainted with all the new and old facts and conditions, and then promulgated as an approved law to govern members in future dealings.

The same rule holds true in connection with trade associations. In these, transactions between members are usually conducted under uniform and standardized contracts which have been prepared by learned counsel under the instructions of astute clients, and which have been tested out in daily transactions involving millions of dollars.

In such agreements every contingency and technical detail in future transactions is intended to be provided for. As a very minor feature of such contracts, and merely to assure the settlement of the few disputes arising under them which have not been amicably disposed of by the parties or by conciliation, there is generally a provision for compulsory arbitration; usually under the rules of a prescribed business organization, and frequently under the laws of a particular state where the procedure and effect of arbitrations are fully covered by statute. In most instances the actual cases of arbitration bear but a very insignificant ratio to the volume of the whole transaction.

The motion picture industry is the most recent and striking example of how the wise and careful organization of a business tends to eliminate disputes and the causes for disputes, to improve business policies and ethics, and to work out successful conciliation and arbitration.

The Motion Picture Producers and Distributors of

America, Inc., was organized under the board of trade article of the Business Corporations Law of New York, with Will H. Hays as president.

This industry has three principal branches: (a) the producers, who purchase the stories, hire the cast, make the pictures, cut, edit and title them, and complete a finished negative from which the positive prints shown in the theaters are made; (b) the distributors, who advertise, sell and deliver the positive prints to the exhibitors on the dates agreed upon; and (c) the exhibitors or motion picture theater owners or lessees, who display the pictures to the public in their 20,000 theaters. A century ago, if we could imagine its existence at that time, such a new and complicated industry would have been the source of untold litigation to be settled by nonexpert judges and juries.

Over ninety-five per cent of the contracts between distributors and exhibitors are made under the association's uniform exhibition contract, which covers the minutest technical and business details and contains stringent provisions for compulsory arbitration of future disputes.[2] The association has organized, in thirty-three key distributing centers of the United States, film boards of trade, composed of the branch managers of each distributing company doing business in that district. These arrange for preliminary conciliation, if possible, but select a representative from three distributing companies, alternating frequently, who, with three other members selected by the exhibitors or theater owners, constitute the arbitration board for that district. A seventh arbitrator is chosen only in case of a tie vote.

During the year 1923, the first year of conciliation and

---

[2] See Appendix No. III.

MINIMIZING BUSINESS DISPUTES

arbitration, these boards heard and disposed of more than 5,000 cases, over ninety per cent unanimously, and about ten per cent by five to one or four to two votes. Twenty-two cases in the United States required a seventh arbitrator, and only two were taken to court. In addition over 25,000 disputes were settled by conciliation between the parties themselves, because, before arbitration, they were brought into touch with each other and encouraged to sit down calmly and discuss their differences.

In 1924 the record was as follows: There were 11,197 disputes involving $2,119,622.26, fifteen of which required a seventh arbitrator. One dispute was litigated before and four after arbitration. Five thousand six hundred and ninety-seven differences, involving $871,035.74, were settled and disposed of by conciliation—that is before the board met and without submission. Four thousand eight hundred and seventy-five awards, involving $1,077,968.99, were made. Three hundred and thirty-two disputes, involving $132,115.48, were withdrawn by complainants, and 293, involving $38,502.35, were dismissed for want of jurisdiction, etc. Five hundred and twenty disputes, involving $140,234, were pending in January, 1925, and only one litigation on September 10, 1925. Twenty-one complaints were made to the New York office by distributors protesting against decisions of boards of arbitrators and seventeen by exhibitors. Thirty-four of these complaints were adjusted by the New York office, and four were pending on January 1, 1925.

During the year 1925, 11,887 disputes, involving $2,542,544.40, were disposed of by awards, conciliation, dismissal, etc. Of these, 4,269, involving $802,747.60, were settled before submission; 554 were withdrawn by complainants;

292 were dismissed; 539, involving $205,216.71, were pending on December 31, 1925; 5,450 awards, involving $1,351,206.72 were made. Twenty-two disputes required a seventh arbitrator, one dispute was litigated before arbitration and seventeen after. About March 1, 1926, the parent body adopted a new uniform contract based upon a three years' experience, which is expected to avoid many differences.

Many hundreds of examples could be added to the foregoing to illustrate and illumine the outstanding and predominant objects of modern business organization and the relatively rare need to use therein commercial arbitration, whether voluntary or involuntary.

Formal commercial arbitration is less and less frequently called into use as business men learn how to conduct their organizations. The volume of disputes conciliated under the various types of arbitration is referred to in Chapter XVIII.

General Grant once said that he knew only two tunes. One was "Yankee Doodle," and the other wasn't. So, in a way, there are but two kinds of arbitration One is commercial arbitration and the other isn't. The transactions involved in all the other kinds represent but a small fraction of the financial values subject to the rules and regulations and strict commercial arbitration of organized business.

Having thus explained strict commercial arbitration, let us turn to the common law, statutory and industrial types and any modifications or admixtures thereof, and respectively measure them by the standards already set up.

PART II
COMMON LAW ARBITRATION

CHAPTER VIII

THE NATURE, ORIGIN AND SCOPE OF THE COMMON LAW

As already shown, rules of law governing commerce were developed largely on the continent of Europe in connection with the *lex mercatoria* or law merchant. Undoubtedly this was partially a survival of commercial law as it had been worked out among the eastern nations and the Romans before and after the beginning of the Christian Era, and as it was introduced into Europe by the Arabs, chiefly after the Crusades. Thereafter the wholesale commerce of Europe and of England was carried on almost exclusively at the great fairs, and its retail transactions through the local markets. The trading between merchants, whether at the fairs or not, was governed by the law merchant. Dealings at the fairs, if not strictly between merchants, were governed by the law of each fair, or the "fair law."

Out of the consular courts of the types mentioned in Chapter IV there have survived all over continental Europe the commercial courts of to-day. These specialize in transactions which relate to business and commerce in all forms, including many phases of transportation. At first these courts were the spontaneous product of the merchants themselves, as set forth in Chapter IV. In recent times, as the various countries have systemized and codified their laws, these courts have been incorporated in the regular judicial system, with jurisdiction over commercial cases and presided over by judges who are experts in this branch of the law.

Throughout continental Europe the importance of trading and commerce was generously recognized and business was freely accorded the right to be governed by the law merchant. In England this right was begrudgingly conceded, and it is not difficult to see why this was so.

England was insular and provincial in many particulars. She had no great codes of statute law such as the continental nations had inherited from the Roman Institutes. Her common law related almost entirely to feudal estates and to rights in real and personal property. At the very period that continental Europe felt a revival of trade in connection with the end of the Crusades, the few Norman nobles in England were striving to establish a strict feudal power over the earlier Saxon nobles whom they largely supplanted, and over the Saxon lower classes who vastly outnumbered them, and who were to absorb them racially in a few generations. The great social and legal struggles of England during the twelfth to the sixteenth centuries were in connection, at first, with the consolidating of the Normans' feudal system and later with the assimilation of the Saxon and Norman races and their racial customs and laws. While on the Continent commerce and trade were more and more asserting their power, there was going on in England a political and social struggle, which was to last at least 500 years, between the few conquering and dominant Normans and their descendants and the far greater number of virile and oppressed Saxons. During this period the chief vital forces of both races were concentrated upon constructing and reconstructing a new social and political body of law which related almost entirely to feudal rights and customs and real property. The dominant classes of that time were militarily and politically and not commercially minded.

Within five centuries after the Norman Conquest, England had twenty-seven different sovereigns, good, bad and indifferent, of five houses or families. The many reforms under the better kings were overturned, if possible, by the bad ones. As we look back we can see that England's history since the Norman Conquest, A.D. 1066, has been a great kaleidoscopic struggle for personal freedom and constitutional government—even since her Industrial Revolution of 1760.

All this accounts for the backwardness of the development of the common law in regard to commercial questions. As a matter of fact commercial law in England and America is almost entirely an adoption and adaptation of the law merchant, rather than a self-development, as in the case of the real property law.

The English law of contracts was of the most rudimentary form. Hardly any one could read or write except the clergy. In Pollock and Maitland's *History of the English Law*,[1] it is stated that the law of contracts held "but an inconspicuous place among the institutions of English law." Its fundamental and ordinary rules, thoroughly familiar to-day, had "perished in the general breaking up of the Roman system, and had to be painfully reconstructed in the Middle Ages." "Even in the schemes of Hale (1609-1676) and Blackstone (1723-1780) it appears as a mere supplement to the law of property."

Because hardly any, even of the landed nobility, could read and write, the written document,

---
[1] Vol. II, p. 182.

which few have the art to manufacture, is regarded with mystical awe; it takes its place beside the *festuca* (the notched stick which was the emblem of a contract in early days); ... setting one's hand to it is a *stipulatio:* it is delivered over as a symbol along with twig and turf and glove. ... It is chiefly used as a means of creating or transferring rights in land by way of gift, sale, lease or gage; it is rarely used for the purpose of creating or attesting the creation of purely personal rights.[2]

Writing was but little used except in deeds or wills, and these were usually executed by the seal or signet, rather than by the signature.

On the contrary, the merchants of Europe were accustomed to carefully drawn contracts which they could read and understand. Cohen says that:[3]

Without reviewing further this development, no student of the common law under which we live can fail to realize that for very simple and ordinary rules of contract, accepted as commonplaces to-day, and finding firm base in the customs of merchants and general acceptance under the Roman law, it nevertheless took centuries of English judicature and parliamentary action before they became part of the great English common law.

Page on History of the Law of Contract,[4] says that:

No general theory of contract was developed or attempted during the early period of the common law;

and

We must acknowledge that our present principles cannot be applied to the early common law; and on the other hand we must also acknowledge that many of the peculiar principles of the early common law either are obsolete or are arrested in development, and that modern contract law owes part of its ideas to

---

[2] *Ibid.*, pp. 190, 191.
[3] Cohen, *Commercial Arbitration and the Law*, p. 65.
[4] Page, *History of the Law of Contract*, Vol. I, p. 21; Cohen, *op. cit.*, pp. 65, 66.

COMMON LAW; NATURE, ORIGIN AND SCOPE 59

the gradual infusion of Roman law and part to the original stock of the common law.

The common law was not a written code like those of the Continent, derived from the Roman law. It was made up chiefly of decisions of the courts. When these became unusable and impracticable in any particular case, a statute of Parliament was passed; but, strictly, that was statutory and not common law. The literature upon estates and rights in real and personal property was voluminous from the beginning, but that upon commercial questions came very late. In the first edition of Blackstone's *Commentaries upon the Laws of England,* written about 1755, and first published about 1765, there were 110 chapters and many appendices. Of these only a part of one chapter was devoted to the acquiring of personal property by contract, and this was solely in connection with eleven other ways in which title might be acquired.

Blackstone says that the early legislators [5]

took all imaginable care in ascertaining the rights, and directing the disposition, of such property as they considered lasting (real property), and which would answer to posterity the trouble and pains which their ancestors employed about them; but at the same time entertained a very low and contemptuous opinion of all personal estates which they regarded only as a transient commodity. . . . Our ancient law books, which are founded upon the feodal provisions, do not therefore often condescend to regulate this species of (personal) property. There is not a chapter in Britton or the mirrior, that can fairly be referred to this head; and the little that is to be found in Glanvil, Bracton and Fleta, seems principally borrowed from the civilians.

Undoubtedly the underlying thought of those who resorted to English common law arbitration was to enable

---
[5] Bk. II, Ch. 24.

the parties to avoid litigation with its expenses and delays. Ordinary English justice moved slowly and cumbrously. It did not sit from day to day, or hour to hour, or tide to tide, as has been shown to be the case in certain fair and other courts. The ordinary sessions were few and far between, and split many hairs over the law and local customs. Still later, and in very recent years, when the calendars of the courts became greatly clogged, the thought was carried even further, and arbitration came to be regarded as a means to relieve the overburdened courts rather than the parties. Nowhere do we find in common law arbitration any suggestion of the higher business ethics and ideals which lie at the very foundation of strict commercial arbitration of any time or clime, nor any provision for the orderly settlement of future disputes.

On the contrary, too often the course of a true-to-legal-type common law arbitration is as follows: A has a just claim for $1,000 against B, who unjustly and unethically claims that the work was not properly done, or that the goods were not as agreed, and offers to compromise at $200. The duly appointed compromisers, whose appointments may be revoked at any time, hear the case and divide by two the sums of $1,000 and $200, and bring in a compromise award of $600. A is outraged because he knows that B would have compromised at more than $600, and B is delighted at the success of his unethical scheme, and feels justified in working it on others—for he is strictly within the letter of common law arbitration; the essence of which is, too often, not business ethics or the fulfillment of a contract, but compromise.

Therefore we must not expect to find, under the common law, any development of the principles and practice of commercial arbitration, and we shall not be disappointed in that regard. Admittedly, the arbitration provisions in the ordinances of the English craft guilds were entirely distinct from the common law, and were worked out by the guilds themselves upon ethical principles and without regard to the courts.

Undoubtedly the reference of disputes to settlement by friends, rather than by physical combat, must have antedated the courts; but it is evident that the common law could furnish no congenial soil for the fair and just settlement of commercial disputes by arbitration, as that was understood elsewhere in Europe, and that no commercial courts could grow up in early England as they had developed upon the continent.

CHAPTER IX

THE FRAILTIES AND FAILURES OF COMMON LAW ARBITRATION

STRICTLY speaking, common law arbitration developed under the earlier English or American court decisions unaffected by legislative provisions. It was court-made law as distinguished from statutory enactments or commercial regulation. It never had much value because the courts soon held: (1) that either party to an arbitration might withdraw at any time before an actual award; and (2) that an agreement to arbitrate a future dispute was against public policy and not enforceable.

The rules governing common law arbitration were evolved through the infrequent decisions of the early English courts, upon unrelated differences, between persons who had no common interest except in regard to an existing dispute, and who wished merely to avoid the delay and expense of ordinary litigation. It was not before a recognized permanent expert or nonexpert tribunal entitled to respect. It was merely a temporary and really worthless makeshift, and might well earn the contempt of the judiciary.

Under this court-made law an arbitrator was regarded, not as a person exercising judicial functions of any kind, but merely as an agent or an attorney-in-fact, appointed to confer with an opposing agent or attorney-in-fact, to effect a compromise of an existing dispute upon the best terms

FAILURES OF COMMON LAW ARBITRATION

possible. Such an appointment was revocable at any time before the award was actually made, because at common law such an agent's power, when not coupled with an interest, is revocable by his principal at any time. Hence the courts ruled that a party might revoke his submission at any time before the actual rendering of the award; and further that there was no way of enforcing the award except by another action to be brought upon the award itself.

The arbitrator was not regarded as a member of a tribunal to judge of the merits of the controversy, because this would have been usurping the rights of the courts. Too frequently common law arbitration has been carried out by having each party appoint a prejudiced partisan—or near lawyer—who is almost obligated to vote on the side of his appointer under any circumstances. There is likely to be the same spirit of jockeying in naming the third arbitrator or umpire.

This method of settling disputes resembles that of many labor controversies where, by collective bargaining, and probably with much publicity in the newspapers, prejudiced committees of employers and employees try to work out a compromise as to future working conditions and scale of wages. It is utterly different from a meeting of a tribunal of impartial experts to get at the real merits of the dispute, to interpret and enforce an existing contract, to cut out all chicanery, bad faith and sharp practices, to administer even-handed justice, and at the same time safeguard the interests and dignity of the parent body, as in commercial arbitration. Strict common law arbitration is not, in any sense, before a recognized, expert and permanent tribunal, but only before one appointed for the occasion.

Unless the common law rule has been changed by statute,

64   ARBITRATION AND BUSINESS ETHICS

an agreement to arbitrate may be revoked by either party before the award. Thus a long delay may be caused, and the party who honorably holds to his submission to arbitrate may suffer great disadvantage through the disclosure of his evidence, the tampering with witnesses and in other ways.

Common law arbitration received another black eye when the early English courts further decided that an agreement to arbitrate a future dispute, whether standing alone or constituting merely some part of a larger contract, was against public policy and unenforceable—although this is probably the only instance where those courts have so held in regard to any form of duly executed contract, between competent parties, which was not in its nature illegal. Therefore common law arbitration is confined only to existing disputes. We have already seen that substantially all commercial arbitration relates to future disputes, and that in this field lies its chief value. We shall find that the same is true of industrial arbitration and frequently in regard to the statutory type. It is most important to a merchant to have his contracts exactly fix all his rights, including the expert forum in which disputes must be adjudicated. He has no fear in regard to contracting away his right to go into an inexpert court of justice, years behind in its calendar, and he has no desire to trust his intricate and technical trade problems to an ordinary petit jury.

The early English courts gave five reasons why they should not enforce an agreement to arbitrate a future dispute: (a) the contract is in its nature revocable; (b) such contracts are against public policy; (c) the covenant to refer is but collateral to the main contract, and may be disregarded, leaving the contract keeper to his action for dam-

FAILURES OF COMMON LAW ARBITRATION 65

ages for breach of such collateral covenant; (*d*) any contract tending to wholly oust the courts of jurisdiction violates the spirit of the laws creating the courts, in that it is not competent for private persons either to increase or diminish the statutory juridical power; (*e*) arbitration may be a condition precedent to suit, and as such valid, if it does not prevent legal action, or seek to determine out of court the general question of liability.

Even where the transaction was in the form of a bond to arbitrate, it was held that the agreement to arbitrate could not be recovered upon, but that the bond, being under seal, might be enforced as a sealed instrument if the obligor refused to perform.

This continued to be the law in England until 1855 when the rule was reversed in the House of Lords in the case of Scott *vs.* Avery, in which it was distinctly stated that the original reason for the rule was the desire of the early judges, who were paid by fees and not by salaries, to prevent any litigation from getting away from them. It would not have done for any layman or member of the bar to have thus aspersed the motives of the judges, but this was baldly stated by Lord Campbell in his opinion in Scott *vs.* Avery, as reported in 25 Law Journal (Exchequer), 313.[1]

Lord Campbell explained this position of the early courts toward arbitration in the following words:

The doctrine had its origin in the interests of the Judges. There was no disguising the fact that, as formerly, the emoluments of the Judges depended mainly, or almost entirely, upon fees, and as they had no fixed salary, there was great competition to get as much as possible of litigation into Westminster Hall, and a great scramble in Westminster Hall for the division

---

[1] This clause was carefully omitted from the official report of the case as given in 5 House of Lords Cases, 811, 851.

of the spoil. And hence the dispute between the different Courts about a *latitat,* a *capias,* and a *quo minus,* the *latitat* bringing business into the Court of Queen's Bench, the *capias* into the Court of Common Pleas, and the *quo minus* into the Court of Exchequer. And they had great jealousy of arbitrations whereby Westminster Hall was robbed of those cases which came not into the King's Bench, nor the Common Pleas, nor the Exchequer. Therefore they said that the Courts ought not to be ousted of their jurisdiction, and that it was contrary to the policy of the law to do so.

Evidently some judges also felt that the submission of disputes to laymen, no matter how well qualified, was derogatory to the dignity of the courts, because it implied that they could not decide the cases as well as the arbitrators. In one case it was also suggested [2] that some of the earliest authoritative English cases were decided upon a misunderstanding of the earlier Norman law, and thereafter slavishly followed.

All these things tended to dampen the inclination of parties to arbitrate under the common law, and to discourage the habit of using this simple, inexpensive and expeditious method of settling disputes. In these instances the parties undoubtedly did desire to avoid the expense and delay of early English litigation, and it was this which the courts resented.

The early American colonies were under the English law until July 4, 1776, and thereafter the states took over the English common law as it stood on that date, and thus inherited this common law attitude as to arbitration, which could be changed only by a statutory provision, or by a reversal of the policy of the courts, as was done in the case

---

[2] Hough, J., in U. S. Asphalt R. Co. against Trinidad Lake P. Co., 222 Federal Reporter, 1006.

of Scott *vs.* Avery. The latter decision, reversing the earlier English doctrine, was followed by the English courts and supplemented by wise statutes under which commercial arbitration has made great headway throughout the British Empire.

But the harm had been done in America, for our courts slavishly followed the earlier English doctrines which still prevail in many states, and are sufficient to justify the prejudices of many lawyers and others against arbitration as they understand it; for they know little or nothing of the commercial or statutory types. Usually these vicious common law conditions can be changed only by legislation, which specifically validates and enforces agreements to arbitrate future or existing disputes, and makes them irrevocable, and provides how arbitration shall be conducted, preferably before regularly constituted tribunals, and how the awards of the arbitrators shall be enforced.

It is evident, however, that the common law arbitration lacks substantially all the requisites for commercial arbitration set forth in Chapter I. It applies only to isolated existing disputes, and not to those arising in the dealings of a self-governing organization, whose members deal in homogeneous commodities or securities under self-imposed regulations relating to future disputes, to be adjusted before tribunals of experts who consider the ethical as well as contractual interests, and are concerned with the higher interests of the parent body. In view of the history and conduct of common law arbitration, as above set forth, it is not surprising that fair-minded business men and lawyers, unacquainted with the theory or practice of commercial arbitration, should oppose common law arbitration as understood in the past. Moreover many lawyers feel, like the

68 ARBITRATION AND BUSINESS ETHICS

earlier English judges, that arbitration would reduce their own fees by taking cases out of the courts, and therefore should be avoided.

The gyroscopic advantages of strict commercial arbitration constantly appeal to those who use it, but are not considered by those who approach the subject from the standpoint of common law arbitration, because the latter type possesses none of these larger advantages.

CHAPTER X

HOW THE RULES GOVERNING COMMON LAW ARBITRATION HAVE BEEN CHANGED THROUGHOUT THE BRITISH EMPIRE BY ACT OF PARLIAMENT AND BY THE SPREAD OF COMMERCIAL ARBITRATION AND BUSINESS ETHICS

It is curious how careful we have been in this country to maintain, in so many states, the supposed sacredness of the old common law doctrines in regard to arbitration, while in England they have fully realized what a clog they are, and have changed and abolished them by statutes of the British Parliament and by adopting and applying commercial arbitration in the broadest way.

About 1915 the Chicago Association of Credit Men sought to encourage commercial arbitration by establishing a permanent bureau. In order to ascertain conditions in England, Mr. Samuel Rosenbaum, of the Philadelphia bar, was sent to London to study the subject. After spending seven months in England Mr. Rosenbaum made an exhaustive report, in 1916, upon commercial arbitration in England.

He showed how, after the American Civil War, there had arisen

an enoromus number of disputes between cotton shippers and traders in the South, on one side, and the factors in the Liverpool cotton market on the other, ranging from differences over liability for war risks to the condition in which shipments of cotton were arriving in the Mersey.[1]

Thereupon the members of the Liverpool Cotton Association inserted in all their contracts a clause requiring disputes to be submitted to the arbitration committee of their association. The success of this movement was so great that similar committees and arbitration clauses were adopted by the Liverpool Corn Trade Association and the General Brokers' Association. London then copied the Liverpool plan and the London associations existing in the corn, oil seed, cotton, coffee and other trades set up their own arbitration committees, and were followed by the stock, coal, produce and other exchanges, and by the architects, engineers, estate agents, auctioneers and other similar groups.

In 1889, after a dozen years of agitation, an Act was passed consolidating and revising the law of arbitration and providing in a schedule a simple set of rules to govern the procedure in all arbitrations where no agreement to the contrary was made by the parties. The need for such a simplification in the law is eloquent of the extent to which the principle of arbitration had spread through the English business world. A letter in the *London Times* in 1883 (probably from Lord Bramwell) said: "It is strange that those who call for changes in the procedure of our courts rarely allude to arbitration. Yet what would be their condition but for the fact that the whole trades and professions have virtually turned their backs upon them and uniformly settle their disputes by arbitration."

To-day there is not a trade or professional organization in England that does not provide some means for the arbitration of disputes that arise among members or between members and

---

[1] *A Report on Commercial Arbitration*, by Samuel Rosenbaum of the Philadelphia Bar. Bulletin XII, American Judicature Society, October, 1916.

others, and frequently between non-members engaged in similar work. It is not surprising, therefore, that by this means a great volume of litigation is avoided and commercial disputes kept out of court.[2]

Mr. Rosenbaum shows that there is an almost complete absence of commercial cases from the trial lists of England's High Court of Justice, and continues:

> But the reason for the comparative rarity of English commercial trials goes deeper than that. Efficient though the English courts are in disposing of all but 3 per cent of their great volume of business without letting it come to trial, there is a large mass of disputes in mercantile and other matters that is never brought into the duly constituted courts of law at all. These disputes, instead of forming the basis of lawsuits, are, for a variety of causes, and in a variety of modes, submitted to arbitration, and there has grown up in England a law, practice and custom of arbitration, which is daily growing in bulk and authority and may almost be said to amount to a system of jurisprudence in itself. Just as the characteristic legislative impulse to-day in America is to create administrative tribunals, composed largely of non-lawyers, for the decision of questions arising out of our new industrial legislation, so the characteristic tendency in English legal procedure is likewise away from the courts, but towards "domestic" tribunals whose awards in arbitration are sought after more than the judgments of the courts.[3]

The practice of arbitration among members of an exchange such as the Stock Exchange rests so completely upon the power of the Exchange to discipline its members that it offers no points of special interest in a study of arbitration generally. A member of such a close corporation is bound to conform to the rules or he is cut off completely, and the arbitrations there take place because the rules make them compulsory rather than because they are expressly provided for in individual contracts.

In the trade associations the position is different, and they cover by far the largest part of this field, as may be gathered

---

[2] *Ibid.*, p. 15.   [3] *Ibid.*, p. 11.

from the following answer given by the Council of the London Chamber of Commerce in 1885 to the Royal Commission on Depression of Trade and Industry, in response to an inquiry as to what trades or industries were of special importance in London: "The wholesale distributing trade, comprising merchants, brokers and dealers of all sorts, probably covers the largest area, and employs the largest capital and the most labor of any in the City. It imports, stores and re-distributes the natural produce and manufactures of all nationalities, and it is probably to it, together with its assistants, the carrying trade on land and water, that London owes its position as the commercial emporium of the world." Every branch of trade in these lines is well organized, and few trades are not included among the members of the associations. The primary object of a trade association is, in general, coöperation for the benefit of the trade, and this takes several concrete forms. The most important is the publication of drafts of contracts for use in trade dealings, in the preparation of which the collective experience of the members is available. Contract forms are provided by each association for all the most frequent transactions engaged in by its members so that there may be uniformity in the separate undertakings. The contracts are worded in great detail to cover every contingency that may arise, and are naturally so worded as to give the association members every possible protection without placing obstacles in the way of business. By reason of the fact that every influential merchant or broker in any particular line is a member of the association in his trade, it is practically impossible to buy or sell goods of any kind in any bulk in the London market without using one of the contract forms insisted on by the trade associations.

Varied though these forms are, because they cover every conceivable subject, from the purchase of a parcel of Argentine oil seed to the erection of an electric power house in Russia, there is one clause common to them all and that is the clause by which the parties agree to submit to arbitration any disputes arising out of the contract. The clause itself varies considerably in text and content, although its import is always the same. In its simplest form it is a bare agreement to arbitrate differences in the manner usual in the trade; the following clause from a form of sale note in use on the Corn Exchange in Mark Lane is an illustration:

"Goods sold ex ship to arrive to be taken without refusal, but any dispute arising out of this contract to be settled by arbitration in the usual manner, as per rules of the London Corn Trade Association."

The association named in this clause has a complete and efficient code of arbitration rules which are thereby incorporated in the contract.

Another form of clause is the following, from a contract form of the London Oil & Tallow Trades' Association (Form No. 6, 1915, for Linseed Oil in barrels, clause 11):

"Any dispute on this contract to be settled by arbitration in London as soon as it may arise, in accordance with the rules endorsed on this contract."

On the back of the contract form is printed a set of rules for arbitration, outlining the procedure which has been found most satisfactory to the oil and tallow trades.

Still another brief form is the following, quoted from the Refiners' Beet Contract of the Sugar Association of London:

"This contract is subject to the rules of the Sugar Association of London, as fully as if the same had been expressly inserted herein, notwithstanding either or both of the parties to it be not a member or members (as the case may be) of the Association."

The rules of the Association require all disputes to be submitted to arbitration and provide for the procedure to be followed. In some associations the arbitration clause is longer and more detailed, containing in itself directions for the procedure instead of incorporating a separate set of rules by reference. The most frequent form is one which names the arbitrators or the manner of their appointment or provides for a certain number (one, two or three) and, as to the rest, leaves the procedure to be regulated by the Act of 1889. A carefully drawn one is the following, from the Standard Clauses of Contract published jointly by the Institution of Gas Engineers and the Society of British Gas Industries:

"All or any differences or disputes or doubt or disagreements or questions that may arise out of or in connection with the contract, at whatever time they may arise whether during the progress of the work or after its completion or before the final payment shall be made, whether before, concerning or after the giving of any certificate by the engineer in relation to the contract and whether relating to the interpretation of the contract or the meaning of the specification or drawings or other documents forming the contract, and whether relating to the methods or manner of carrying out the work or the quality or suitability or sufficiency of workmanship or materials, and whether concerning extras or costs or payments or rights or liabilities of any kind whatsoever, and whether relating to any of the preceding or any other question of a like or different nature shall be referred to the arbitration of both the President of the Institution of Gas Engineers and the President of the Society of British Gas Industries for the time being respectively either for determination by them or by such person or persons as they may appoint and in such manner as both the Presidents may think best or direct. Provided always that any arbitration shall be deemed to be a submission to arbitration within the meaning of the Arbitration Act of 1889 or any amending statute thereof."

More frequently the chief specification in the clause is as to the number of arbitrators, as the following quotation will illustrate, from the arbitration clause (16) of the F. O. B. contract supplied by the Timber Trade Federation of the United Kingdom:

"Should any dispute arise under this contract which it may be found impossible to settle by amicable arrangement, the same shall forthwith be referred to the decision of a third party to be mutually agreed upon, or in default of agreement to two arbitrators, one to be appointed by the sellers and one by the buyers. Such arbitrators shall, previously to entering upon the arbitration, appoint an umpire, and the arbitration shall be subject to the English Arbitration Act of 1889 or any subsisting statutory modification thereof or substitution therefor. . . . In the event of either side failing to appoint their arbitrator within seven days after being requested through the agents under this contract so to do, the arbitrator thus required shall be appointed by the President or failing him by the Vice-President of the Timber Trade Federation of the United Kingdom on the application of either party.

"In the case of a claim not exceeding £25, or on less than 25 standards the dispute shall, if not amicably settled, be referred to one arbitrator, and in default of the parties agreeing to his appointment, he shall be appointed by the President or failing him by the Vice-President. . . .

"Every arbitrator or umpire shall be selected from members of the timber trade or from the arbitrators approved by the Timber Trade Federation of the United Kingdom or by the Scandinavian Sawmillers' Association."

The last clause refers to the official list of arbitrators published by the Association in which opposite each name is stated the grades of wood in which the man named is most proficient.[4]

As to the enforceability in England of contracts to arbitrate future disputes, Mr. Rosenbaum said:

In England the inherited antipathy of courts to arbitration has been cured by a course of legislation which though extending over a period of nearly two centuries, is now gathered and codified in the Arbitration Act, 1889. The two outstanding features of the law are that a submission to arbitration cannot be revoked, and that an award of the arbitrators may be enforced like a judgment of the courts.[5]

After a careful review of Mr. Rosenbaum's report it appears:

(a) That in England substantially all the trades and businesses have been formed into self-governing associations doing a homogeneous business, and that, therefore, the organization of business, upon an elaborate and scientific basis, has been carried very much further than in the United States.

---

[4] *Ibid.*, pp. 15-18.   [5] *Ibid.*, p. 19.

(*b*) That in England substantially all commercial business is done under the rules of associations which provide for arbitrating future disputes between their members, or under carefully drawn trade association contracts containing an arbitration clause covering future disputes.

(*c*) That few commercial cases do or can get into the courts, although the present English court procedure is uniform and very simple and provides for conciliation and arbitration to prevent the necessity of trying cases before juries.

(*d*) That so far as possible in England official arbitration is provided for in many fields relating to condemnation, assessing lands, opening roads, levying taxes, public improvements, and many other governmental administrative functions, in a manner and to an extent not followed in this country.

(*e*) That there are provisions in the English statutes by which specific questions of law arising in arbitration proceedings may be referred to the courts for decision, but that this procedure is resorted to in very few cases.

(*f*) That the will to arbitrate, rather than to litigate, is constantly growing in England. The advantages of arbitration are clearly recognized and are constantly being extended to new fields. Arbitration provisions are inserted, as often as possible, in new statutes requiring quasi judicial proceedings, so that there are very many classes of statutory arbitrators of whose existence we have not dreamed in this country.

(*g*) That these statutory provisions are often applicable to transactions arising or being carried out in any subdivision of the British Empire or any other parts of the world, as in the case of Lloyds, who provide for arbitration in

London under salvage contracts with contractors in many foreign ports.

Thus, we see that the use of arbitration provisions or clauses as to future disputes is bound to grow in this country as business is more carefully organized, and that we may expect great advances in this field in future years; also that the sooner we grasp this great lesson in modern business organization and apply it in a large way wherever possible, the sooner we will reap its great advantages, and, to the same extent, relieve the overcrowded calendars of our courts.

The facts so far stated make it apparent why common law arbitration cannot furnish an adequate standard by which to test the value of other types of arbitration. This will become even more evident as we proceed to consider the history and principles of statutory and industrial arbitration.

In Part III we shall discuss the evolution and present status in the United States of statutory arbitration which have been brought about by the unselfish and high-minded efforts of merchants to cure, by legislation, some of the frailties and failures of common law arbitration and to extend to ordinary business disputes some of the inherent advantages of strict commercial arbitration, very much along the lines which have been followed in England.

PART III
STATUTORY ARBITRATION

CHAPTER XI

THE DIFFICULTIES IN CHANGING THE STATUTES AND COURT DECISIONS GOVERNING COMMON LAW ARBITRATION IN THE UNITED STATES

By his ruling in Scott *vs.* Avery, in 1855,[1] Lord Campbell solved many of England's difficulties in regard to common law arbitration, so far as this could be done by a complete reversal by the courts themselves of their former decisions. Yet only a part of these difficulties could be overcome by any unaided action of the courts; and few, if any, of the inherent advantages of strict commercial arbitration could be gained through mere court decisions or rules. It required positive action by Parliament to broaden the scope of common law arbitration, provide for adequate court procedure, make arbitration awards as effective as court decrees, and render it possible to set up in England commercial arbitration on the broad scale and scientific basis set out in Mr. Rosenbaum's report referred to in Chapter X.

Such statutory changes were made from time to time, culminating in the Act of 1889. This was a comparatively simple legal task in England, where all such questions are under the control of the Parliament which exercises for England, Scotland, part of Ireland and many portions of the British Empire, most of the legislative powers which in this country are the joint and several functions of our federal

---
[1] See pp. 65, 66.

and state governments and sometimes of the legislative bodies of our counties, cities or towns.

All this is quite different in the United States. The rights, powers and decisions of our federal, state and local courts overlap and differ greatly in the various jurisdictions, and are annually changed and amended by hundreds of statutes. No other part of our government exhibits more clearly the complicated, illogical and contradictory structure of our federal, state, territorial, dependency and federal district governments and courts, with the underlying and constant conflict of the limitations of the United States Constitution and the aggressive claims of state rights.

It is necessary to explain more fully the nature and extent of this conflict of laws in order to see how herculean is the task of changing the ancient rules in regard to common law arbitration.

First, there is the federal government to which certain limited powers were given by the states under the United States Constitution. The federal government has, among its powers, jurisdiction through the Congress and executive and the federal courts over: (*a*) international; (*b*) interstate; (*c*) maritime; and (*d*) certain constitutional questions; (*e*) over the affairs of the federal District of Columbia which is governed by the laws of Congress administered by one of its committees; and (*f*) certain powers over the federal territories and dependencies.

Second, there are forty-eight independent states of the Union which have almost exclusive control of their intrastate affairs, including arbitration, but joint jurisdiction with the United States over many matters.

Third, the large federal dependencies and territories, like Alaska, Hawaii, Porto Rico and the Philippines, have a

DIFFICULTIES IN CHANGING COMMON LAW 83

major control over many of their own affairs like arbitration.

Fourth, the jurisdiction of the United States courts is usually exclusive within the powers given to them by the United States Constitution, but does not extend to very large fields wherein the state courts are supreme within their own jurisdiction. These United States courts (April 5, 1926) function as follows: There are (*a*) the chief justice and eight associate justices of the United States Supreme Court, with final appellate and some original jurisdiction; (*b*) United States Court of Claims, with one chief justice and four associate justices; (*c*) United States Court of Customs Appeals, with a presiding judge and four associate judges; (*d*) thirty-seven United States circuit judges, appointed in nine circuits, which together embrace the forty-eight states and Alaska, Hawaii, Porto Rico and the Canal Zone; (*e*) one hundred and twenty-five United States District Court judges, scattered through eighty-one districts in the forty-eight states; (*f*) in Alaska, four district judges in four districts; (*g*) in the Canal Zone, a district judge; (*h*) in Hawaii, a Supreme Court with a chief justice and two associate justices, a Circuit Court, with eight justices in five circuits, and two United States District Court justices; (*i*) in Porto Rico, a Supreme Court with a chief justice and four associate justices, and a United States District Court judge; (*j*) in the District of Columbia, a Court of Appeals with a chief justice and two associate justices, a Supreme Court, with a chief justice and five associate justices, four police court judges, a Juvenile Court judge, and four municipal judges.

In many things the practice of these courts is uniform under rules of the United States Supreme Court, but in other respects each court of original and appellate jurisdiction has its own rules. Moreover, the lower courts are like chameleons whose color changes more or less with the color of the objects about them. So these United States courts of original jurisdiction, so far as possible, conform to the practice and procedure of the several states in which they are located. The procedure and practice of the United States courts of original jurisdiction vary with those of the various states in which they act, and no two states have exactly the same practice and procedure. It is evident, therefore, that an act of Congress and probably some rules of court would be necessary to bring about changes in regard to common law arbitration within the jurisdiction of the United States courts.

Fifth, the procedure, practice and rules of the courts of the forty-eight independent states differ materially between themselves, and are being constantly amended by legislative enactments. Even if two states started with the same procedure and practice, their historical development would be different within a few years, because their legislatures would not be likely to make identical changes therein. In the various states there is a very great diversity in the structure, names and powers of the courts, which include the principal appellate tribunal, minor appellate courts of limited local jurisdiction, many courts of higher original jurisdiction in the various counties or other parts of the state, many city, county and probate courts, and those of the nature of justices of the peace, having exclusive or coördinate jurisdiction over petty debts and crimes. At the same time there are other distinctively criminal courts dealing with the major and minor offenses.

Sixth, in the federal dependencies, the courts are a sort

DIFFICULTIES IN CHANGING COMMON LAW

of cross between the federal and state courts, with local idiosyncrasies of their own, and also many differences inherited from the Spanish or other races from which they were acquired.

This is sufficient to indicate how difficult it must be and has been to obtain uniformity in regard to arbitration in these fifty-five or more jurisdictions. In only one instance is there anything like similarity and uniformity. The Uniform Negotiable Instruments Law has been adopted in all these jurisdictions except the state of Georgia, but with a few trivial changes in some of the other states. In no other case is there anything like uniformity in the court rules or statutes of the various federal, state, territorial, dependency and local jurisdictions.

In many and probably most of the state jurisdictions, where not directly changed by statute, the courts still maintain the earlier common law rules that an agreement to arbitrate a future dispute is nonenforceable and that either party to an arbitration may withdraw therefrom at any time before an actual award has been rendered; and these rules are sustained by the reasonings of the earlier English decisions which were so emphatically reversed in the case of Scott *vs.* Avery.

But the legislative process must go further if statutory arbitration is to have much value. The statutes must provide for the making of rules for the orderly conduct of such arbitrations, and that awards shall have the force of court decrees, so that judgment may be entered thereupon as of course and enforced like the corresponding processes of a court.

Admittedly the working and results of any statutory arbitration, taken as a whole, are and must be quite different from those of strict commercial arbitration which is only a cog in the workings of an organization whose primary object is to improve ethical and other conditions in a particular industry or business, dealing in homogeneous products, and which has inherent power to enforce its rulings upon its members, as set forth in Part I.

With this picture in our minds of the intricate, involved and overlapping court jurisdictions of the United States and her states and dependencies, we pass now to the history of statutory arbitration as developed up to the present time, largely under and through the efforts of our oldest commercial organization, the Chamber of Commerce of the State of New York.

CHAPTER XII

THE HISTORY OF ARBITRATION IN THE CHAMBER OF COMMERCE OF THE STATE OF NEW YORK, A.D. 1768-1910

STATUTORY arbitration in the United States has been chiefly evolved through the unremitting efforts and example of an old, powerful and respected commercial institution, which has persistently, wisely and in an unselfish and public-spirited manner attempted by itself or through the agencies which it inspired or fanned into life to establish a country-wide system of statutory arbitration in face of the difficulties set forth in the last chapter.

The Chamber of Commerce of the State of New York, commonly known and usually referred to herein and elsewhere as the New York Chamber of Commerce, organized on April 5, 1768, had as one of its objects the "adjusting of disputes relating to trade and navigation." At its first meeting, on May 3, 1768, it appointed

a committee until the first Tuesday in June next for adjusting any differences between the parties agreeing to leave such disputes to this Chamber, and that they do attend every Tuesday or oftener as business requires at such places as they may agree upon, giving notice thereof to the president.

The records of the Chamber show that such arbitration committees were appointed at every succeeding monthly meeting for over 100 years, and until the formation of a permanent court in 1874.

The royal charter to "The Corporation of the Chamber

of Commerce in the City of New York, in America" bears date March 13, 1770. Its rights and privileges were confirmed by an act of the New York State legislature passed April 13, 1784, the first session after the Revolutionary War; but under the name of "The Corporation of the Chamber of Commerce of the State of New York."

The Chamber functioned in New York City during the Revolutionary War, the city being under martial law after the entrance of the British troops in 1776. The original minutes of those monthly arbitration committees from July 6, 1779, to November 1, 1792, now in the New York Public Library, cover 230 cases of arbitration in about thirteen years. These were of three distinct classes:

(1) by agreement between the parties;
(2) during the Revolutionary War, causes sent by the police authorities, as in the following:

Gentlemen We beg leave to refer to your consideration a commercial dispute between Messrs. Donaldson & White and Mr. Henry White and we request you would be pleased to give us your opinion on the matter in controversy.
We are Gent. your most obt. Humbe Servants
    Andrew Elliott Sup. Gen'l
    D. Matthews Mayor
    Peter Dubois Magt. of Police

The committee's answers seem to have been addressed to "The Gentlemen of the Police," or "To the Superintendent General and Officers of Police."

(3) some cases were referred by the British commandant of the city, who is addressed as

Your Excellency,
Major General James Patterson, Esq.
Commandant of New York, Etc., Etc., Etc.

There never have been many arbitrations between the members of the Chamber, but the heading of an early meeting after the state charter reads:

New York, 12th August, 1784.
We the subscribers being a Committee for the present month appointed by the Chamber of Commerce of this City to settle disputes that may arise between any members of said Chamber or any other partys of men that chuse to leave their disputes to be settled by us——.

From the beginning these committees on arbitration might do their work in vain, for under the common law, which was then in force in New York State, the parties might withdraw at any time after submission and before the award, and there was then no statute under which an award could be enforced. For generations the Chamber sought without avail to have these conditions changed by the legislature. Yet few if any of those who submitted their disputes sought to take advantage of these legal loopholes, and almost invariably the awards have been carried through by the parties.

The 230 cases referred to above cover distinctly commercial disputes relating largely to shipping, partnership and other issues which would have come before a European commercial court. On October 2, 1781 (seventeen days before the surrender of Cornwallis at Yorktown, Virginia), Andrew Elliott, the British Superintendent General, wrote to the Chamber of Commerce:

As I was and still am of the opinion that mercantile disputes cannot be adjusted in a more appropriate and more equitable way than by a reference to respectable merchants, it gave me great satisfaction when the method was so generally agreed to, and I flatter myself that notwithstanding the trouble it gave individuals that it would at least be continued as long as I had any concern in the Superintendency. I shall be much concerned if these, my expectations, should be disappointed.

The present juncture of affairs (evidently referring to the siege at Yorktown) does not seem favorable for any new plans to be adopted. It has long been proposed (I hope events are not distant that may admit of a trial) to revive such part of the civil authority by which justice may be administered to the community. Individuals will then be free from the burthen of adjusting mercantile disputes, and I shall be relieved from a most fatiguing and anxious situation, but I beg you will assure the Chamber of Commerce that in all situations I shall ever retain the highest sense of assistance and support they have afforded me.

In 1855 the Chamber amended its by-laws so as to provide for "The Committee on Arbitration" of five members, and "The Committee on Appeals," to consist of the president, first and second vice-presidents, treasurer, and chairman of the committee on arbitration of the Chamber. No case could be appealed which did not involve more than one hundred dollars, nor, if the decision of the committee on arbitration had been unanimous, where the amount did not exceed five hundred dollars.

In 1839 the Chamber began a movement to establish a tribunal or court of commerce with powers to determine all litigation between merchants, the trials to be by juries taken solely from the classes of merchants and tradesmen, the jurors to determine by bare majority and to be judges of the law and facts. The agitation continued for about twelve years, but was finally dropped, largely because such a proposed court would be unconstitutional without an amendment to the state constitution.

Nevertheless much interest in the subject was stirred up

in the Chamber. The subject of a commercial court became one of such great interest that it was renewed at the meeting of 1860. On April 15, 1861, an act was passed by the New York legislature "conferring legal powers upon 'the Arbitration Committee of the Chamber of Commerce of the State of New York.'"[1] The act was accepted by the Chamber at a meeting held on April 25, 1861, and the procedure of the Chamber was somewhat modified, and, as so amended, was followed from 1861 to 1874.

At a meeting held October 2, 1873, it was determined to inquire into the expediency of establishing a tribunal of commerce for the speedy, judicial and economical settlement of disputes between merchants and others, and if desirable to apply to the legislature. It was shown that the New York Stock Exchange, the Produce Exchange, the Grocers' Board of Trade, the Chamber itself and other incorporated bodies had arbitration provisions, but that many of these arbitrations had no direct sanction of law, and were dependent only upon the mutual good faith of the parties for their operation and success. Also, that the number of these arbitrations would, probably, aggregate as many as the causes determined during the year in either of the superior local courts.

The tendency to arbitrate private differences has been accelerated by the example set by our own nation and England, in submitting their differences to the Geneva Tribunal of Arbitration; and like happy results seem to have been accomplished. Shall this feature in our business and commercial life continue to exist, and fitfully display itself in irregular methods, or shall it be recognized, sanctioned by law, and provided with an established forum and home?

---

[1] Laws of 1861, Ch. 251.

In 1874 the New York legislature authorized the establishment of the Court of Arbitration for the Port of New York, and the Honorable Enoch L. Fancher was appointed as arbitrator or judge under the provisions of the act. The opening of the court on October 15, 1874, was attended with much ceremony. Many bankers, merchants, shipowners and lawyers were present. Wm. E. Dodge, Sr., President of the Chamber, occupied the chair, and David Dudley Field, Elliott F. Shepard, Erastus Brooks, David M. Stone and others spoke.

During the succeeding years, the court heard and decided important questions relating to the Statute of Frauds, the performance of contracts, general average, rights of owners as against consignees, of landlord and tenant, of owner and builder, of buyer and seller, of responsibility under charter parties, of shipowners and consignees as to the removal of goods, the distinction existing between a partnership and a joint interest in a venture, the duty of seller and purchaser as to custom house liquidations, rights of brokers on sale of goods to arrive, what is a reasonable time for delivery of goods sold on contracts, the distribution of damages in cases of collisions between two negligent vessels, of liability of builders and subcontractors where changes are made from plans and specifications, the rescission of contracts and the burden of proof after delivery of merchandise, the right to salvage on recovery of derelict goods lost at sea, the rights of architects to commissions and many other difficult questions.

It is evident that Judge Fancher acted rather as a court of law in deciding many new and intricate points which arose in connection with commercial disputes. His reputation was so well known that, by consent of parties, cases

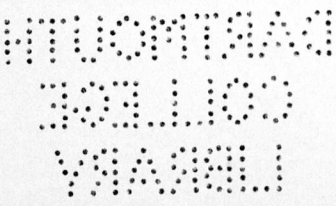

were referred to him as a referee. Unfortunately there was some dispute as to how the expenses of the court should be paid, and from 1875 to 1878 the state did not provide these expenses. In 1878 it appropriated two years' salary of Judge Fancher and the clerk, but repealed the provisions of the act that these salaries should be paid by the state of New York. Nevertheless the court continued and Judge Fancher, at his own expense, considered difficult cases submitted to the court and made important decisions. The court practically ceased with the death of Judge Fancher on February 9, 1900. The act has never been repealed, and no provisions have been made to continue the court, except that on March 15, 1922, Governor Nathan L. Miller, of the State of New York, appointed Mr. Charles L. Bernheimer, as judge of the Court. Mr. Bernheimer, who still holds the position, has never exercised any of its functions.

CHAPTER XIII

THE HISTORY OF ARBITRATION IN THE CHAMBER OF COMMERCE OF THE STATE OF NEW YORK—CONTINUED: A.D. 1910-1926

THE panic of 1907, as every one knows, brought about many peculiar conditions. One which had a very lasting effect was an experience of Mr. Charles L. Bernheimer, the president of a New York concern, which was the successor of the first cotton goods converting house in the country. This company was the subject of sharp practices by a customer in Chicago who insisted that certain cases of goods shipped were not according to order. When directed to return the goods, all but one of the original cases were sent back intact, but that case had been emptied and filled with odds and ends of shopworn and out-of-date merchandise of a previous season, purchased from the seller, which had accumulated on the customer's hands. The market price had declined sharply. Litigation was the only remedy available.

Outraged at this unethical act, Mr. Bernheimer determined to see what could be done to stop such practices. He found that since the death of Judge Fancher the arbitration machinery of the Chamber of Commerce of the State of New York was not functioning to the extent of its possibilities. Sending to England for all possible literature upon the subject, Mr. Bernheimer studied arbitration and the commercial court as they had developed in the country after Lord

Campbell's decision in Scott *vs.* Avery, in 1855. He also had the New York Chamber of Commerce send out for any information that could be obtained on the subject in this country and Canada, and informed himself as to commercial courts upon the continent of Europe. After several years of careful study of the whole subject he moved that the Chamber appoint a special committee to consider and report upon the need of reëstablishing in the Chamber a court or committee of arbitration, and if desirable to suggest a feasible plan for such arbitration.

On March 3, 1910, the special committee was appointed, and included among its members Alexander E. Orr, a former president of the Chamber and of the New York Produce Exchange, which had always had stringent and successful arbitration rules, and Frank A. Ferris, a prominent provision merchant long identified with arbitration in the same exchange. Two other members were James Talcott, the well-known head of a leading dry goods house, and Henry Hentz, the dean of the New York Cotton Exchange, which also had compulsory arbitration. These men have long since passed away. Mr. Bernheimer was made chairman of this special committee, and has ever since remained the chairman of the Chamber's committee on arbitration and its guiding spirit, and the recognized leader in and authority upon arbitration in this country.

The special committee's report was a modest but very definite one. It recited the history of arbitration in the Chamber, the formation of a Court of Arbitration for the Port of New York at the Chamber's suggestion, and the passing of that court after about twenty years of precarious existence. The committee then recommended the return to the former simple system of an arbitration committee, to be supplemented by a panel, to be from time to time revised by the arbitration committee, of not less than fifty members of the Chamber willing to act as official arbitrators under the rules. The published list has since grown to about 650 names, who are classified as doing business in 175 different lines of business.

Any commercial matter in dispute might be submitted under the official form of submission to: (*a*) an official arbitrator as sole arbitrator; or (*b*) to two outside parties not necessarily members of the Chamber, who must select from the list a third arbitrator; or (*c*) in certain important cases to the committee on arbitration or a quorum thereof. This is the system which still prevails with some slight modifications.

The following résumé is made from the printed annual reports of the committee on arbitration, to show what has been accomplished by it directly or through its efforts or inspiration during the past sixteen years.

A. *The educational work of the committee on arbitration and its results.* From the beginning of Mr. Bernheimer's chairmanship the committee on arbitration has laid down and steadfastly pursued a large and definite campaign of education, whose results, direct and indirect, are becoming more and more evident every year, both here and abroad.

The committee's pamphlet, issued in 1911, containing an explanation of its system, and rules and regulations, a handbook for arbitrators, the New York law on arbitration, etc., was distributed to the members of the Chamber (then fifteen hundred), to two thousand members of New York bar associations, to important organizations throughout the world, and to some of the state and foreign governments that applied for copies. Many leading newspapers and magazines became interested, and hundreds of commendatory editorials and articles were published. An extensive correspondence was carried on in ever-increasing volume with organizations and individuals throughout the United States and abroad.

Thus from the beginning the committee recognized and carried forward the Chamber's general policy of service and public duty, and of the sanctity of contracts.

In its report of 1913, the committee said:

> The committee's work of education has taken a wide range, and we are confident has created widespread interest in the subject of commercial arbitration. . . . It has conceived its function to be larger than that merely of administering arbitration for the benefit of such of our members as care to avail themselves of its facilities. It has conceived its duty to be to inspire throughout this country, as well as other countries, a spirit of arbitration and conciliation—believing that by so doing it was contributing the Chamber's share towards eliminating some of the obstacles in the way of commercial and industrial peace

In carrying out this policy, the committee has sought to get other chambers of commerce throughout the country to follow the example of the New York Chamber in their own localities, and this policy has been generally adopted.

A few exchanges formerly provided for arbitration of disputes arising on the floor, but this has now become practically universal. Trade associations of all kinds have enthusiastically adopted forms of uniform trade contracts providing that any dispute arising thereunder shall be arbitrated and that the decision of the arbitrators shall be final.

By addresses, matter furnished to newspapers and magazines, by correspondence and personal interviews, and by its own example, the Chamber of Commerce of the State of New York has sought to set forward the general cause of arbitration and conciliation.

The committee had twenty-two disputes before it in 1911, including one between a nonmember and an English firm, which was decided within a month at a cost of sixty dollars.

In 1912 the new plan showed more clearly its many and many-sided advantages. The committee reported that:

The very existence of the Chamber's system, the very presence of a committee elected to administer it, and the mere offer of arbitration were sufficient in many cases to bring the disputants together, and an otherwise expensive and irritating litigation turned into a friendly settlement. . . .

Business men of high standing and large affairs served as arbitrators and gave their time and experience to the settling of disputes . . . and frequently even the defeated party voiced his satisfaction with the promptness, inexpensiveness, fairness and courtesy of the proceedings.

The committee continued and broadened its efforts at conciliation.

Through its good offices the disputants were enabled to continue amicable personal relations leading to an adjustment. . . . It involved countless interviews and a vast amount of correspondence. The results, however, justified the labor expended.

The annual reports of the arbitration committee since 1911 show the spirit by which the committee has been governed, and in which it has constantly done its work. In 1912 it fully outlined the work which it thought it ought to do, and it has kept very closely to this line ever since. In 1914 it said that:

The spirit of the committee has brought out clearly that there is a universal sense of honor among business men, and that as a practical working matter this sense of honor may be made the basis for the avoidance of litigation. It has made clear, also, that the collective conscience of a group, organized into a chamber of commerce or merchants' association of any locality, is a power for the maintenance of standards of honor of greater influence in certain directions than the force of law and much less expensive of time, money and energy in its operation. The establishment of tribunals of commercial arbitration by trade bodies, it is seen, brings out those standards of commercial honor in the community which are the very best, and brings to bear in the enforcement of such standards the collective conscience of the commercial community.

In 1915 it reported that it received daily new proofs of the adaptability, flexibility and fairness of its system.

The arbitrators chosen from the Chamber's list invariably exhibit not only the intelligence and fairness that was reasonably to be expected from the high character of the men chosen, but a fidelity in the performance of their duty rising to a degree of enthusiasm.

In 1916 it distinctly sensed the "big brother" nature of its work and said:

The Chamber is instrumental in establishing and developing throughout the country, in mercantile and civic associations, systems of arbitration, mediation and conciliation based upon our experience. Our Chamber stands for principles of mediation, conciliation and arbitration in business disputes. This is known wherever the name of the Chamber is known. In consequence, appeals for advice and information are received from all over this country, as well as abroad. The Committee's efforts tend to prompt other commercial and civic and professional bodies of men to institute systems of their own, adapted, of course, to their specific needs and in harmony with their own laws, customs and opinions. Many systems have been thus established, and your committee is in frequent conference and has voluminous correspondence in this field of its activities.

These organizations are now spreading the gospel which the committee preaches in the name of this Chamber—good-will between men—business honor—the elimination at the source of unnecessary business friction—the saving to the merchant of time, trouble and expense—the application of common sense and equity to business misunderstandings. And throughout, the committee urges that the best guaranty of the enforcibility of arbitration agreements is the sense of commercial honor in the business community. We do not believe business men generally will avail themselves of the technicalities of the law to escape the morally binding effect of an agreement to arbitrate.

In 1917, the committee called attention to George Washington's will, which required that all possible controversies relating to his estate, worth a million dollars and devised to nearly two hundred beneficiaries, should be submitted

"to three impartial and intelligent men, known for their probity and good understanding," who "shall unfettered by law or legal construction declare their sense of the Testator's intention."

By far the largest field of the committee's activity during the last year, as in the past, has been informal arbitration, wherein complete satisfaction can be recorded. Most of the cases are so complex that if they were put through the ordinary processes of litigation, the parties would have had imposed upon them such expenditure of time and money as would make it almost impossible to secure real justice. . . .

Of course, in the cases of informal arbitration there is nothing binding but a gentleman's word of honor to abide by the settlement; but we have yet to hear of a settlement thus obtained which has not been scrupulously observed. Your committee is convinced that the friendly intervention of our Chamber acts as an almost irresistible moral force.

The business man needed equally to learn how to prevent controversy from arising and how to take care of it when it did arise, with good sense, straightforwardness and efficiency.

In 1918 the committee said:

That the old merchant, Malynes, who wrote in 1622, said that it was not so much what the law regarded as binding as what merchants would say concerning a breach by one of them, for "the honour of merchants is so delicate and tender that it must be cared for as the apple of a man's eie."

In speaking of transactions with foreigners, the committee said:

All applicants know in advance that the guiding thought of the committee is to safeguard the good name of the American business man, and, by guarding against false impressions and using preventive measures, to forestall the feeling that the American business man resorts to trickery or evasion in the performance of his obligations. . . .

Many questions are put to the committee during the course of the year which do not involve actual arbitration. These questions it answers broadly, covering some times a more comprehensive field than would be required for a mere answer confined to the question propounded. This policy it pursues because, after all, the work of the committee, like that of the teacher, is to widen the mental horizon and to develop correct habits.

Nor must it be assumed that the cases or problems presented to the committee can be disposed of at once. They very often require patient and persistent attention. One foreign case took two and a half years before results were obtained, and there are now pending foreign cases in which the committee has been active for periods of not less than twelve months. The process of mediation by correspondence is slow, but more effective and much quicker than litigation. . . .

This work could not be done without the voluntary and painstaking services of the arbitrators, who include not only members of the Chamber selected from the Official List of Arbitrators, but also those non-members who have served with great seriousness of purpose and earnestness of work. Your committee is glad to record that in every instance these men have risen to the importance of the occasion, have set aside their own business engagements, have divested themselves of all personal and business bias, and have performed their work bearing in mind only the rendition of such public service, as, through this Chamber, they could freely give to their fellow merchants, no matter where those fellow merchants might be doing business. The committee takes this opportunity to express its great obligation to all of these gentlemen.

In 1919 the committee reported:

Such transactions and others, involving large sums, frequently reaching as much as one hundred thousand dollars and, in one instance, several million dollars (whether handled by means of formal arbitration, mediation and conciliation) or activities in legislatures, or furtherance of co-operation with sister institutions, or inducing them to establish arbitration systems of their own, or efforts to bring into existence the legal validation of arbitration agreements—these all indicate in a faint way to the Chamber the radius within which your committee has been operating, insistently and persistently. Always bearing in mind that our work is not merely to furnish arbitration facilities in such cases as we have designated, but to serve worthily and constructively in bringing out, wherever we may, the value of the principle of commercial arbitration; which principle briefly stated embraces "the maintenance of commercial honor, the prevention of unnecessary litigation, the elimination of the law's delays and the preservation of friendly business relations."

In 1920 and 1921 the committee showed the success of its efforts to promote wise statutory changes in connection with arbitration and its intervention in court to sustain the constitutionality of such statutes; and reported that the New York Court of Appeals had held that the obligation of a contract was strengthened and not impaired by the statutory changes.

The committee also showed what it had done to prevent harm coming from the enormous flood of cancellations, both by foreign and American buyers, which set in at that time.

In 1922 the committee still further stressed the subject of cancellations in foreign and domestic trade and its work with the United States Department of Commerce and with other chambers of commerce and trade associations in the United States and in foreign countries.

In dealing with foreigners your committee has suceeded in impressing them that difference in nationality does not operate against them in the slightest degree, nor does size, importance or complexity of the transaction affect the issue. In its endeavor to uphold the fair name of the American merchant it has striven to eliminate the latent, rankling feeling in many foreigners of being dealt with unjustly, which all too frequently finds expression in their correspondence.

Impressed with the existing difficulties in foreign trade the committee strenuously urged the negotiation of foreign arbitration treaties.

In 1923 the committee quoted from the report of the Manchester, England, Chamber of Commerce as follows:

The small number of arbitrations relatively to the vast number of arbitration clauses points to the fact that the existence of the clauses in general use is a great deterrent to avoidable disputation.

In 1924 the committee reported that in one instance a case had been brought to their notice where one party was leaving town, necessitating immediate action. An award was made before 4 o'clock P.M. on the next day, with which both parties were perfectly satisfied.

A referendum in relation to the desirability of arbitration, conducted by the Merchants Association, brought 864 favorable ballots and four unfavorable.

B. *The committee's labors in arbitration, conciliation, mediation and fact finding.*

During the past sixteen years the committee on arbitration, with its hundreds of experts in every line of business as official arbitrators, has passed on commercial disputes involving technical points in grading, condition, methods of dealing in, deliveries, etc., concerning the following among other articles: beans, honey, cheese, butter, sugar, sugar beet seed, coffee, cocoa and cocoa beans, shelled and unshelled peanuts, prunes, flour, walnuts, peas, potatoes in bulk and dehydrated, tobacco, rice, curry powder, canned salmon, cotton, poppy seeds, indigo paste, pineapples, dye stuffs, explosives, chemicals, caustic soda, quinine, carbon black, soda ash, ergot of rye, malt, insect powder, camphor, perfumes, oils, French costumes, hosiery, United States flag material, textiles, cotton goods, sail duck, rubberized materials for rain coats, woolens, woolen gloves, silks, knee pants, clothing, new and worn, artificial silk, knit goods, linen and jute padding, ribbons, worsted and other yarns, lace goods, silk goods, cotton, wool, jute twist, underwear, umbrellas, embroidered linens, coats, tapestries, textile silk, pearl buttons, hair nets, rabbit skins, leather, hides, Belgian hares, sheep gut, dried sinews, furs, goose feathers, Chinese pigtails, frozen steers, Japanese bamboo skewers, asbestos, burlaps, sugar bags, steel rails, machinery, cutlery, ball bearings, steel rods, slates, roofing, wire mesh, coal, tin plate, glass, zinc, stoves, linoleum, upholstery goods, shellac, barbed wire, razors, glass insulators, steel tanks, printing machines, light brackets, lumber, steam indicators, gold watches, silver bullion, telescopes, jewelry, eye glasses, suit cases, self-lighting gas mantles, scissors, bicycles, automobiles, automobile parts and accessories, rubber tires and tubes, lamps, phonograph needles, sewing needles, audophones, stationary engines, radio apparatus, yachts, kodaks,

NEW YORK CHAMBER OF COMMERCE

mahogany veneer, publications, stationery, dolls, manuscripts, and such intangible but important matters as trade marks, building operations, exchange and exchange rates, demurrage, commissions, interpretation of F.O.B. and C.I.F., interpretation of contracts, stock transactions, trucking charges, lawyers' and architects' fees, employment contracts, reinsurance policies, leases, advertisements, rights under patents, and banking and insurance.

These arbitrations have come from or involved transactions wholly or partly within the following among other countries besides the United States: China, Canada, Scotland, Ecuador, Italy, India, Syria, Holland, Egypt, Greece, France, Germany, Columbia, England, San Salvador, Japan, Dominican Republic, Czecho-Slovakia, Tripoli, Ireland, Austria, Mexico, Nicaragua, Cuba, Hawaii, Belgium, Australia, Norway, Philippine Islands, British West Indies, Sweden, Poland, Chile, Argentine, Brazil, Mesopotamia, Switzerland, Spain, Turkey, Madagascar, Denmark, New Zealand, Palestine, Finland, South Africa, Bermuda, West Indies, Portugal, Malta, Guatemala and Uruguay. In one instance formal arbitration was conducted at the New York Chamber between a firm in Germany and a corporation in the City of Mexico. The unanimous decision of the arbitrators was accepted and complied with by the defeated party.

Yet notwithstanding the great variety of matters arbitrated and the great number of countries involved, the Chamber can furnish from its members arbitrators who are experts in every phase of any dispute referred to it.

Along with such a diversified arbitration activity has gone conciliation, of which the committee says:

The settlements by conciliation are the invisible products of the committee's most effective work. . . . The mere instituting of negotiations before the committee tends to lower the temperature—if we may use this as a figure of speech—of the contending parties, makes each see the other's side with more reasonableness, and actually produces an honorable and mutually satisfactory settlement. Here is realized one of your committee's aims to prevent arbitration, no less than litigation.

Mediation is that phase of conciliation in which the parties cannot be gotten together in person, but the work must be done by correspondence with parties separated by long distances.

Before 1920 the committee was compelled to adopt a new agency which often prevented formal arbitration.

A fact determining board is appointed, composed preferably of members of the Chamber—men whose standing in the community in the particular line of business involved is beyond question—who are asked to state in writing over their respective signatures, to your committee, certain required facts or trade customs, as the case may be. The committee on arbitration then, over its own signature, certifies to these facts—presenting a certificate to the parties raising the issue.

It was fortunate that the committee had time to get well settled in its work before the beginning of the World War in 1914. Many questions then arose between contractors and foreign governments and afterwards our own government. These matters usually involved technical trade customs and terms and business methods. Many such disputes were submitted to the committee and its decisions respected by both parties.

C. *Necessary changes in the law and rules governing intrastate, interstate and international disputes.*

From the outset the committee on arbitration knew that

its work must be more or less futile unless it could change, by statute or treaty or reversal of court decisions, the old common law rules that either party to an arbitration might withdraw before the award was actually made and that agreements to arbitrate future disputes were not enforceable. This problem presented three forms:

1. Intrastate disputes, in which the differences were between citizens of the same state, and could not be brought in or removed to the federal courts, and where only state laws were applicable;

2. Interstate and admiralty disputes, to be adjudicated in the federal courts and be governed by the United States laws or the rules of the federal courts;

3. International disputes, where it was probable that neither the state nor the federal courts would be able to acquire jurisdiction of all the parties.

The difficulties in intrastate controversies must be met by changes in the state statutes and the rules of state courts. Those in interstate or admiralty disputes by corresponding changes in federal statutes and court rules. International commercial controversies must be covered by treaties with the various foreign governments.

Many advisers insisted that the common law rules would be changed by the courts themselves if the facts and the decision in Scott *vs.* Avery and other later English cases were duly brought to their attention. This was done in a few instances, but Mr. Bernheimer from the beginning has insisted that really adequate reforms could be obtained only through changes by statutes and court rules; and this position has been fully sustained.

To accomplish such results, the committee first established the most cordial relations with the local bar, and the state and American bar associations. Every proposed change in statute or court rule or in treaties has had the previous approval of the proper bar associations or of the American Bar Association. Indeed the relationship fostered by the New York Chamber of Commerce between bar and business became so intimate that the legislative measures were invariably drafted by the bar with the collaboration of the Chamber's committee.

In its labors, the committee sought, obtained and made use of the influence and coöperation of many other chambers of commerce, of trade and similar associations, and of every organization or public spirited individual whose aid could be enlisted.

In 1917, Illinois passed an arbitration law making a submission to arbitration of an existing dispute irrevocable, providing for judgment upon an award, and carefully regulating the practice under arbitrations, but not specifically validating written agreements to arbitrate future disputes. This is hereafter referred to as the narrow form of statute.[1]

In 1920 New York passed its Arbitration Law, which provided that not only the submission of an existing dispute, but any written agreement to submit a future controversy to arbitration was valid, enforceable and irrevocable, and the court practice was amended so as to favor arbitration in every way. The New York law is in the nature of a uniform statute to be followed in other states to take care of intrastate commerce, and is hereafter spoken of as the broad form.[2] It has been embodied in the laws of New Jersey,[3]

---

[1] See Appendix No. IV, which includes also the rule of the Municipal Court of Chicago governing arbitrations.
[2] See Appendix No. V, which includes also Article 24 of the New York Civil Practice Act governing arbitration, and the rules of the Municipal Court of the City of New York governing arbitration and conciliation.
[3] See Appendix No. VI.

NEW YORK CHAMBER OF COMMERCE 109

and is likely soon to be duplicated in several other states. Oregon and Massachusetts modernized their arbitration laws during 1925.[4]

The most important step on the program of the committee on arbitration of the Chamber of Commerce of the State of New York was the enactment of a federal arbitration law to take care of interstate, foreign trading and admiralty disputes. Heretofore there had been no arbitration law whatever in the federal statutes.

The United States Arbitration Act, which is in the broad form, was drafted by the American Bar Association's committee on commerce, trade and commercial law, and approved by the Association in 1922, 1923 and 1924. After failing in the Sixty-seventh Congress for lack of time, the act had to pass the Sixty-eighth Congress—that body of warring blocs, ragged parties and quasi majorities—and it seemed at times impossible that any public act of real importance and merit could pass both houses of that Congress. But Mr. Bernheimer so handled the enormous business forces of the country which he had marshaled to support the bill, that it passed both houses unanimously at the very time when the fight was at its hottest on all other measures. The United States Arbitration Law was signed by President Coolidge on February 12, 1925.[5]

The approval of the American Bar Association had great weight with the lawyers. The sponsorship of scores of chambers of commerce and trade associations in all parts of the United States, and of the American Farm Bureau Federation, and other similar bodies took the measure out of politics, and into the realm of the things that "all the people at home" everywhere wished to see enacted; and so the bill

---
[4] See Appendices Nos. VII, VIII. [5] See Appendix No. IX.

unanimously passed both houses of a Congress two-thirds of whose members were lawyers.

The form of commercial treaties with foreign nations for the arbitration of disputes between subjects of the United States and other nations was submitted to Secretary of State Charles E. Hughes, who expressed himself as in sympathy with the principle. Much work remains to be done with our Department of State.

During all the time that these efforts were made the New York Chamber of Commerce sought repeatedly to get the courts to change their old common law rulings upon arbitration, and to this end it has appeared by its own counsel as the friend of the court in the United States Supreme Court and in lower tribunals.

Thus the Chamber has carried out its sense of its responsibility and duty to serve as the "big brother." Its primary object has not been arbitration in the narrow sense, but to spread and to cause other organizations to spread the gospel of

good-will between men—business honor—the elimination at the source of unnecessary business friction—the elimination of waste —the saving to the merchant of time, trouble and expense—the application of common sense and equity to business misunderstandings.

At the same time the Chamber has sought out and acceleratingly cut out causes likely to provoke business disputes. This has been done, in part, by urging the adoption of uniform and standardized contracts, and in part by doing everything in its power to raise the standard of business honor throughout the country.

For the past sixteen years Mr. Bernheimer has increasingly devoted his time to his duties as chairman of the committee on arbitration of the New York Chamber of Commerce, and to the correspondence and addresses, here and abroad, and other matters connected with this great civic duty. For this purpose he has maintained at his own office a skilled secretariat. More and more he has turned over his duties and some of his emoluments as president of his company to his younger associates, so that he might devote more of his time to his arbitration activities.

In appreciation of his labors, and in order that there might ultimately be a fund to provide for the expenses of the committee on arbitration, 146 members of the Chamber of Commerce of the State of New York in 1924 contributed a fund sufficient to pay for $324,000 of ten year endowment insurance upon Mr. Bernheimer's life, so that in 1934, or before that time in case of his death, that principal sum will be realized and its income made available for the continuance of the work of the committee on arbitration. The policies have been placed in the custody of the trustees of the New York Community Trust, through which agency the fund will have assurance of perpetual administration.

In 1925, there was incorporated The Arbitration Foundation, Inc., with Mr. Bernheimer as president and with a distinguished board of directors. The purposes of the Foundation were to spread the use of arbitration, mediation and conciliation throughout this and other countries, to coöperate with bar associations, international, American, state and local, in the proper delimitation of the fields for arbitration, mediation and conciliation, and the coördination with the administration of the law of the machinery and systems of arbitration, mediation and conciliation, and to obtain further legislation upon these subjects. Associated with the Foundation were about twenty-five international chambers of commerce, including the Association of British Chambers of Commerce, London, England, whose membership includes about 116 local chambers of commerce throughout the British Empire.

It is extremely fortunate that all these great reforms have been conducted under the leadership of an old and influential association of merchants, many of whose most active members also belong to the New York Stock and Produce and other exchanges, or are connected with the New York Clearing House Association, where the finest examples of strict commercial arbitration are to be found; and that the movement has been under the immediate and continuous leadership of a sagacious merchant to whom better business ethics, the carrying out of contracts and the development of higher and better business standards and methods were the chief ends.

This upward movement in organized business has been distinctively by business men, and not by statesmen, legislators or lawyers—although all these have helped. It has been of, by and for business; and its primary results have been first felt by organized business, and then by the public at large.

One of the greatest accomplishments of the Chamber of Commerce of the State of New York, in its long history of commercial and civic usefulness, has been the revelation to America of the fine ethical and friendly spirit which must be at the very foundation of commerce and business. More and more the Chamber has made plain, through the unselfish labors of its committee on arbitration, that a bargain is a bargain—a single complete contract—until it is finished in every particular; that the bargain itself may provide how any disputes arising under it shall be settled; that it is to be carried through in the same spirit that prevailed when the price, deliveries and other terms were originally agreed upon. It has been made perfectly clear that in properly organized and conducted commercial dealings, especially between business acquaintances and friends, litigation should be made impossible, arbitration avoidable and even conciliation unnecessary, because a difference in regard to the performance of a contract will be met in the same spirit of fairness which prevailed in the original fixing of the purchase price, dating, delivery and other details.

As a result of the Chamber's work and the interest which has been stirred up by it (a) many exchanges, boards of trade and trade associations have added compulsory or voluntary arbitration provisions to their working rules and regulations, or provided them through uniform trade contracts; (b) many chambers of commerce and other business organizations, whose members do not do a homogeneous business with each other, have provided arbitration tribunals and arbitration facilities for members and nonmembers; (c) there has been a very great improvement in the prevalence and application of business ethics.

In *Current History* for March, 1926, Judge Elbert Gary, chairman of the United States Steel Corporation, has an article upon "Higher Standards Developing in American Business." He begins his article with the following words:

Sometimes I hear men ask if the world really has improved in the last twenty-five years. In my opinion it has improved immeasurably within a decade, and I believe the next ten years will witness an even broader and surer movement toward higher ethics in business, in private life and in public affairs.

114   ARBITRATION AND BUSINESS ETHICS

Judge Gary says that when he first came to New York about twenty-five years ago he encountered a code of practice which has almost disappeared, although there were then a few exceptions to the rule:

The managers of some large institutions apparently believed that so long as their conduct came within the strict, technical rules of law it was immune from public or private attack. With them the conception of moral duty did not extend beyond the belief that if no provision of public law was violated a corporation should be permitted to earn unlimited profit and might treat indifferently its customers, employes, competitors and even the body politic as a whole. Too often there were officials, actuated by this reasoning, who recognized no barriers when profits were in the making for themselves or their companies.

So far as these men were concerned—and I might say they were sufficiently numerous to constitute a definite group—the Golden Rule received no thought and had no place in the practice of that school and period. Competition was tyrannical and destructive. Weaker competitors were forced to quit business as the big combinations arose, sometimes by means not only unethical but brutal as well. The graves of insolvents were strewn along the paths of industrial development. The financially strong grew richer and stronger. Instead of competition existing as the life of trade and a very necessary element of progress, it was made the instrument of death in trade. Instead of monopoly being destroyed, it was thus encouraged. Instead of preventing increasing combinations of capital, such combinations were brought into being by the pressure of destructive competition.

There are many documents furnishing indisputable evidence of the practice prevailing in the period of which I speak. Let me say again that this was not universal, but unquestionably it dominated business to a regrettable degree, to the everlasting humiliation of industrialism. The men responsible had inherited wrong ideals—false ethics—from the past. It would be possible to build up a condemning indictment against them. They failed to give employes just consideration. Wage rates were adjusted strictly in accordance with the laws of supply and demand and with no thought whatever of results to the thousands concerned. The welfare of the typical workman was decided almost entirely from the standpoint of utility and profit.

Such reasoning resulted in a similar stand by employes. Many of them assumed an unreasonable and wholly unethical position with regard to employers. Their forced partnership was marked by secret enmity bordering upon open hostility. And this situation resulted in hardship to the public, the third and most important partner, since costs of production, transportation and delivery necessarily were increased by the turmoil of industry and inevitably were paid by the consumer.

But I think none of these purely material reasons led to a change for the better. On the contrary, I believe we improved our methods when we obtained a new glimpse, a finer conception of ethics. . . .

We need but look around us to see evidences on all sides of the new day in business. Operations are conducted under a stricter rule of ethics than ever before. Undoubtedly the world is growing better. It may be asserted with the fullest confidence that in the period of which I write business has undergone a moral overhauling without precedent. To my personal knowledge many men of big affairs have completely changed their opinions and methods concerning ethical questions in business. A host of others unknown to me, men of great interests and small, conducting their affairs in many parts of the country, have adopted this example, consciously or unconsciously. Men who once believed that the subject of ethics in business had little bearing upon their conduct, now assert that a proper code is the controlling element.

No doubt a very large part of the improvement in ethical conditions in connection with the conduct of corporations is due to the influence exerted by President Theodore Roosevelt while he was in the White House. Many other factors have contributed to the same result. Certainly not the least of these has been the sixteen years of enlightened, persistent and consistent efforts of the Chamber of Commerce of the State of New York and of its committee on arbitration, and the twenty-five years of Judge Gary's own fight for better business ethics and practice.

PART IV
INDUSTRIAL ARBITRATION

CHAPTER XIV

THE ENGLISH INDUSTRIAL REVOLUTION OF 1760; THE GROWTH AND MEANING OF TRADE UNIONS

THE English Industrial Revolution of 1760 was the beginning of a complete change in English industrial and agricultural conditions so far, among other things, as they related to the employment of labor. For almost 1,000 years before 1760 the English people had lived under the feudal system in which all lands were held under military tenure, and the lord and the churl alike paid their rentals and taxes in voluntary military service. Readiness for war was the chief function of society, and prowess in war, the most valued personal characteristic in nobleman or yeoman.

The hereditary military captain, who was also the hereditary LANDlord, valued his tenants more as members of his bodyguard than as artisans or laborers. At first the nobility were almost the only employers of skilled labor, which rendered personal and lifelong service to its lord in war as well as in peace. Often lands were held for centuries upon the further condition that the tenant should render free to his lord a certain number of days' work per year—as "ten days' work at Michaelmas." In the universal business, agriculture, there was keen competition between lord and vassal in the public markets. There were no middlemen or contractors. The great landowner produced most of his raw materials from his own lands and hired his own tenants or outside artisans to work under his immediate direction or that of his steward.

A law of Elizabeth provided that every cottage should have at least four acres attached to it, and all cottagers had important rights in common—of pasture, fuel, wood and waste. The apprentice, journeyman and guild systems built up a close personal touch in the various handicrafts, whose workers, nevertheless, might by law be drafted into the fields at harvest time. Servants were hired by the quarter or year rather than by the hour or day or week. For centuries successive generations of masters and servants grew up together in the same villages as lifelong friends and neighbors and comrades in arms. As a result of this agelong intimate personal and military relationship the thought was fixed in the national mind that a man, no matter how noble or ignoble, was to be judged by his manhood value to his master, his local community and the state; and a predominant English racial characteristic was intense personal loyalty between master and servant, who were bound together by the close mutual neighborhood and military allegiance of liege and liegeman.

Out of all this grew an important rule of English law: that a servant of any kind, who received pay for his services, was bound to observe with care and diligence the interest of his master and to exert the same diligence and care as his master would have shown. Notwithstanding the many buffetings which it has received in the house of its friends, the desire for personal loyalty between master and servant, based upon manhood and man-to-man values, is still an ideal of the Anglo-Saxon race in all parts of the world.

The English Industrial Revolution of 1760 marked the beginning of the change in these relations, as England commenced to turn from a strictly agricultural and trading country to the first modern industrial nation, and from a feudal system which valued servants for their manhood value and sedulously respected their manhood rights to one which considered only their labor value, and thought of them merely as mill hands. The economists of that day asserted that employers were justified in insisting that labor was only a commodity—to be bought in the cheapest market, and often a drug on the market. The early invention of the steam engine made the increasing development and use of machinery inevitable. Under the crude political, social and economic conditions then prevailing, the use of machinery tended inevitably to the degradation of the human workers; and as inevitably forced them to combine to combat the malign forces that were attacking their manhood rights.

Of the first seventy-five years of the English Industrial Revolution, Toynbee says:

We now approach a darker period—a period as disastrous and as terrible as any through which a nation ever passed—disastrous and terrible, because, side by side with a great increase of wealth, was seen an enormous increase of pauperism; and production on a vast scale, the result of free competition, led to a rapid alienation of classes and to the degradation of a large body of producers.

The facts have been preserved to us in the voluminous reports put out by the Parliamentary commissions which, during the second quarter of the nineteenth century, constantly investigated industrial and housing conditions in Great Britain. Bad agricultural conditions and the comparatively large mill wages caused an inrush to the industrial centers where, however, there were no adequate housing facilities and but little new building to care for the newcomers, who were herded into foul and vile quarters, which had not been fumigated or disinfected since the time of the Great Plague.

In Liverpool 13 per cent of the whole population, or 30,000 persons, occupied 8,000 cellars, few of which, from the absence of drains and sewers, were entirely free from damp, while some were almost inundated after a fall of rain. In Manchester about 12 per cent of the population lived in such cellars and in Salford 8 per cent.

In London the great bulk of the people were compelled to crowd in districts undrained, in perishing houses ill-ventilated, in pestilential courts and alleys from which typhus, especially, and every form of contagious and epidemic disease never departed.

There were houses in which squalid families were lodged in the proportion of twenty-four adults and thirty children to nine small rooms. There were lodging houses in which sixty persons occupied nightly a pestilential den of filth and depravity.

There were no sewers or water systems, the population depending upon occasional wells. The Poor Law Commission of 1840 reported that it found that

the habits of filth and intemperance induced by the total unfitness of many tenements for healthful occupation caused the death rate of the poor to be twice that of the rest. Inclosed courts where the sunshine never penetrated, where a breath of fresh air never circulated, where noxious vapors filled every corner from the horrible cesspools, where the density of population was so excessive as in itself to be sufficient to produce disease, where a single room was often occupied by a whole family without regard to age or sex—the wonder is how the poor lived at all, uncared for by the rich who knew them not—neglected by their employers, who in some trades exposed them to labor in workshops not far superior in ventilation to the Black Hole of Calcutta.

Factory conditions were almost on a par with the housing. It was shown that

sixty to eighty workingmen were huddled close together, nearly knee to knee, in a room fifty feet long by twenty feet broad, lighted from above, where the temperature in summer was thirty degrees higher than the temperature outside. Young men from the country fainted when they were first confined in such a life-destroying prison; the maturer ones sustained themselves by gin till they perished from consumption, typhus and delirium tremens.

The working conditions of certain trades for women in London were so bad that more than one-half of the operatives died of lung diseases before they attained the average age of twenty-eight. There was a total ignorance of anything like modern economics, sociology, business ethics, sanitation, or the handling of factory and urban conditions.

Furthermore, her political, financial and economic situation prevented England from giving proper attention to her novel industrial problems, and thus played into the hands of her newly rich and ignorant profiteers. From about 1755 till 1815 the nation was engaged in almost unceasing foreign warfare, with all of evil and chaos which that implied—then as now. Her debt increased 2,400 per cent between 1714 and 1815, when her net taxes amounted to over £72,000,000 and her budget failed to balance by about £20,000,000. In 1817 about 60 per cent of her net receipts were used in paying the interest upon her funded and unfunded debts. Taxation was higher than ever before or since, and the public debt almost exceeded the value of the property in the kingdom. Toynbee says that "even as late as 1834 half the laborer's wages went in taxes."

The political condition was equally bad. Only one person in forty could vote. The House of Commons had 556 members, of whom one-ninth were elected by 354 persons and one-half by 5,723. This left the political power in the hands of the waning agrarian aristocracy, who by the rotten borough system maintained their majority in Parliament long after they had become a minority in the country, and for almost a century fought the growing power of the waxing aristocracy of trade, commerce and industry, opposed any improvement in industrial conditions, and retained the iniquitous Corn Laws upon the statute books. An attempt to make the poor laws of the feudal period applicable to the new industrial crises in the cities pauperized the ordinary laborer, and heavily handicapped those who had unusual skill or strength; with the result that in 1815 one person in every fifteen in England and Ireland was officially classed as a pauper and was receiving aid from the poor rates.

As is almost always the case, the purchasing power of wages lagged behind the cost of living, even without allowing for the scale of living which is constantly on the rise in modern times. Between 1760 and 1820 wages estimated in money had risen 100 per cent; estimated in commodities, and regardless of the rising scale of living, they had fallen 33 per cent. In some parts of England the agricultural laborers' wages were less in 1850 than they had been in 1750. England was entirely unprepared to understand or to solve and handle the scores of terrific questions of human welfare which constantly sprouted in the path of her Industrial Revolution. The better class of her citizens were afraid to help, for the French Revolution of 1789, at their very doors, had been a terrible shock to the landed gentry and *bourgeoisie* of England, many of whom honestly believed that if the common people were given any political power the scenes of the French Revolution would be reënacted on English soil.

The combination of these affirmative and negative forces soon undermined the age-old allegiance between master and servant and inevitably tended to reduce the English workingman to an industrial serf. As a result, he was forced, quite contrary to his racial habit of thought, to organize against his employers in order to retain and conserve some of his manhood rights and to avoid absolute industrial slavery. In point of time, the first combinations in this struggle were those of the masters, who by lockouts strove to starve their hands into accepting a reduction in their paltry wages. The first strikes were to resist these reductions and then to improve working conditions. The trade unions were formed, first to accumulate funds to prevent the workingman from being reduced to pauperism by the deliberate action of their own masters, and then to consolidate and marshal the forces of labor against industrial oppression. Thereupon the loyalty which had been given to the English master in feudal times was transferred to these new militant leaders.

The heroic side of this early struggle through the trade unions must not be forgotten. Never before in history was greater persistence and willingness to sacrifice and bear hardships shown than by those who believed that only through these organizations could the very lives and health of themselves and their families be saved. As early as 1867 an eminent authority said:

> The strikes occurring in Great Britain and in other countries within a few years are piteous and terrible exhibitions of the devotion and desperation of the laboring classes to principles accepted as true and luminous with good to themselves.

Under these conditions the trade union system developed rapidly in England, and naturally took the form which was familiar to the English mind, viz: loyalty to the clan and a solid front against the enemy, and probably a fight to the finish.

Arbitration was and almost invariably has been banned by the trade unions, which have insisted upon taking up and settling by collective bargaining each dispute as it arose.

Naturally many of the English ideas in regard to the rules which should govern the relations between master and servant and capital and labor found root in America; but there they met other forces, among which was that of the equality of the individual before the law, unaffected by the caste system which was so strongly entrenched in England. Here the trade unions developed later, less quickly and in a less tyrannical manner, and the understanding between labor and capital was greater because of the fact that in this country the journeyman of to-day, whether a member of a union or not, might be the employer of to-morrow. In this respect the conditions in America more closely resembled those of the earlier craft guilds of England.

It is probably because of these distinctive features of American trade unionism that the nation-wide and international American Federation of Labor has had a longer and more successful continuous history and power than almost any combination of capital and employers that is not merely local in its scope.

Then there is the Red element in labor which must be dealt with. But we must not forget that the American Federation of Labor has done more than all other influences to crush out Bolshevism in this country. Organized labor was the first section of the people to sense the possible ruin to be wrought by boring from within the labor ranks because these were assumed to correspond to the European proletariat. If organized labor had been friendly to this boring-from-within process, it is probable that it would have been impossible to stop it until it had done terrible harm.

Possibly no one has done more for the country during the past eight years than the late Samuel Gompers when he gathered his forces and staked his all on the struggle with Bolshevism in which success did not seem very near or certain.

The Associated Press cabled from Moscow, Russia, on March 24, 1926, that:

> Unless the discords and disputes within the American Communist party are soon composed Gregory Zinovieff believes it may disappear altogether. Addressing a plenary session of the executive committee of the Communist International, of which he is chairman, Zinovieff admitted frankly that the prospects in the United States were not bright. The precarious position of the American Communist party demanded that all the energies of the parent body should be concentrated upon it.
>
> "If we tolerate factions within the American party, our growth will be arrested," he added. "The American party is faced by the mighty enemy of American capitalism and the American Federation of Labor.
>
> "The leaders of the American Federation of Labor are pupils of the notorious Gompers. They represent a group of audacious servants of capitalism. They are bitter enemies of Communism. They will in time become Fascists."

CHAPTER XV

COLLECTIVE BARGAINING AND INDUSTRIAL ARBITRATION

IN Birdseye's Abbott's Encyclopædia [1] will be found about fifty-five contracts under the general headings of agreements upon closed shop union basis, inside union shop, preferential shop, open shop, company's union, and agreements upon the representation plan by companies with their unorganized employees.

An examination of these contracts will disclose the following, among other facts, in regard to collective bargaining as distinguished from pure or strict industrial arbitration, and in addition will show that industrial arbitration is closely following the course of the commercial type, and, although in a far different field of human activity, has almost the same life history, characteristics and ethical basis.

(*a*) Many labor agreements are still modeled upon the earlier practice, and are merely written statements, signed by the representatives of the respective parties, setting out the terms arrived at by collective bargaining as to working conditions and wages, usually for a fixed period, and with or without provision for further collective bargaining for the renewal or extension of the agreement. Frequently such collective bargainings have been arrived at during a period of cessation of work because of a strike or lockout.[2]

---

[1] Birdseye's Abbott's *Encyclopædia of General Business and Legal Forms*, Ch. XLIX, pp. 1302-1518.   [2] *Ibid.*, pp. 1358-1389.

(b) The change from mere collective bargaining without provisions for arbitration to an honest desire to bring about an adjustment of future disputes without the cessation of work has come through a new appreciation and plain statement of the mutual ethical rights of the parties and an expression of the desire to recognize and respect such rights, and in some instances the rights of the public.[3]

(c) In labor agreements which contain rules for the arbitration of future disputes, there is usually a provision for conciliation to precede and avoid arbitration. Frequently in the better agreements, this takes the form of attempted adjustments, on the spot, in the shop, by minor representatives of the management and employed; and, as usual, in all other types of arbitration, the mere bringing of the parties face to face with each other and the facts in the presence of a friendly conciliator is generally successful and formal arbitration is avoided.[4]

(d) Successive appeals to higher tribunals or officials are provided for, until an impartial final board or arbitrator is reached whose decisions are to be binding on all parties.[5]

(e) As this form of machinery is extensively used over a considerable period of time, its defects and frailties are detected and remedied, and mutual confidence tends to take the place of mutual suspicion. Some degree of self-government sobers and satisfies the employees and makes them more conservative in their views and demands, and more reasonableness is engendered on both sides.

(f) As we have seen that, after the Industrial Revolution of 1760, it was the errors and ignorance of the industrial

---
[3] Ibid., pp. 1445, 1446, 1456-1458, 1465, 1471.
[4] Ibid., pp. 1353-1355, 1406, 1409, 1415, 1418.
[5] Ibid., pp. 1406, 1446-1449, 1459, 1460.

masters which alienated and forfeited the age-old and nation-wide allegiance of the English servants, so the growth of industrial arbitration shows that that allegiance can be won back only as the masters acknowledge their past errors, and relinquish the mistaken theory of labor units and the market value of labor, and build anew upon the older English and present American assumption of the manhood value of every worker. At least, the prolonged and bitter fights of labor for its rights have made the employer and the public realize that the servant, the worker with his hands, has an unalienable right to be treated as a man, and to protect that right and obtain its full enjoyment, as much as any other man in the community.

An outstanding characteristic of the English feudal relations of master and servant, liege and liegeman, was that, as a soldier of the realm, every man felt that he owed his prime duty to his community and the state. The new industrial employers and employees lost sight of this duty in the struggles which followed the English Industrial Revolution, but the old and better vision is gradually returning. It will pay the masters in dollars and cents to be leaders in this march back to the older and higher realization that industrialism, in return for its many civic privileges, has equally important civic duties.

Therefore any attempt to substitute true industrial arbitration instead of old-fashioned collective bargaining must be based upon new ethical proposals from the employers, who must not be surprised if for a time their efforts are met with suspicion, and that their employees say, "Beware of the Greeks bringing gifts."

(g) Reforms of this kind are best worked out by men having mutual confidence in each other based upon acts and acquaintance rather than upon any theory which may have been tried in far different fields. Any conciliatory machinery devised must prove its value in actual use, and must be more or less fool-proof and allow for the peculiarities of human nature.

From all of which it is clearly evident that it will not do to get the cart before the horse in industrial any more than in commercial arbitration. At the very foundation of each type must lie ethics, fair dealing, faith based upon works, and mutual confidence which has been justified by long experience.

As in commercial arbitration, so in industrial, there must be a wise, impartial, expert and permanent tribunal; a common interest in settling future disputes so that the crop thereof shall tend to lessen and disappear; a willingness to abide by the final award; a mutual appreciation of the higher good of the whole and of public duty; an ability to see the other fellow's side—especially, if it is also the side of the impartial arbitrator; a realization that capital and labor are partners, as so many delight to proclaim; and that, therefore, they are equals, at least so far as manhood values are concerned.

If these premises be correct the application of the rule of fair play and the best ethics and the mutual recognition of manhood values should work out like favorable results, whether tried in an open or closed shop or upon the employee representation plan. And this is precisely what we find. Apparently the most important factor is the wisdom and broadmindedness of the employer in meeting his employees more than half way, and with a perfectly open mind. We find this to be more and more true as the years go by. Substantially the same result is gotten from like conditions whether applied under the trade unions or without them.

A good example is that of the Bethlehem Steel Corporation as reported upon by John Calder in the *Iron Age* of June 14, 1923. Mr. Calder had been trained in Scotland in the steel industry and was an honor graduate of the Royal Technical College. For twenty years he had managed well-known industrial plants, including those of the Remington Typewriter Company and Cadillac Motor Car Company. He had acquired a national reputation in labor management and was the first manager of industrial relations of Swift and Company, with over 100 plants. Mr. Calder was given every facility to examine the workings of the Bethlehem Company's plan. Among other things he found that:

> The unique feature of the Bethlehem idea is that the employees of each of its plants are *trusted* to organize as a body, to meet through their collective representatives of their own choosing and to formulate their opinions or requests. In all this they have full access to the company's information, with the assistant to the president at headquarters and his special representative at each plant devoting themselves to the work and available at all times for conference. In other words, there is not the slightest attempt at the initial stage of any issue to condition the arrangements under which the whole representative body of the employees or any committee of that body may thrash out the matter among themselves.
>
> Ample provision for review by joint committees is made, should either employees or employer desire this, and also for appeals beyond that stage. But the outstanding fact is that the Bethlehem Corporation has such convictions behind its own intentions and ideals and such a grasp of the employee's psychology that it has been content for five years to trust to the good faith and common sense of large groups of English speaking and non-English speaking workers, with the happiest results. . . .
>
> One of the reasons for the atmosphere of confidence is the

fact that at the headquarters of the corporation in Bethlehem the officers are all residents and are veterans in the service of the steel company whose joint terms cover nearly four hundred years, and average twenty-one years of service.

The democratic attitude and feeling of the big chiefs has become the equally genuine practice of the managers, superintendents and foremen in its many plants and is a pleasing contrast to the traditional autocracy of the "boss" in various industries. Every genuine conversion to "leading" instead of "driving," to "understanding" instead of "aloofness," is an aid to employees' representation and every camouflage of sympathy and interest is a nail in its coffin. The workman cannot be fooled and pretense or ulterior motive is soon uncovered. The Bethlehem official family are all sincere boosters of the plan and genuine exponents of its virtues and its moral implications. . . .

What about the employees? How do they perform when left unfettered to "make their own mistakes"? Well, whether a Bethlehem plant has fifteen thousand or one thousand men, the writer has found that they take their representation responsibilities most seriously, consider office an honor to be sought, and elect only able fellow-workmen with years of experience. As a matter of fact over ninety per cent of the employees take part in elections. In the Bethlehem main plant the average service period of the 98 elected workmen is twelve years and the average over all plants is eight years, though one year qualifies for office. Rome was not built in a day; neither was the Bethlehem plan "sold" to the corporations' employees by a few fine gestures. Nevertheless it has been thoroughly sold to 70,000 workers who remember the old bad days of "catch 'em young, treat 'em rough and tell 'em nothing." These workers appreciate the new spirit and recollect how much better the plan functioned than the wartime committees when they operated simultaneously, how it weathered the steel strike, the slump of 1920 and the succeeding boom, with harmony, mutual respect and satisfaction in all the adjustments that were necessary.

The Bethlehem Company considers its industrial relations department as necessary as its manufacturing, purchasing, treasury and selling bureaus, and it is organized just as completely. President Eugene G. Grace, in speaking to the employees, said:

> We are all employees . . . there is no difference whatever except that I have to do one part of the work while you men have your individual tasks in the shops and mills, but my work is not any more important than yours and I regard myself just as much an employee as you men.

The Bethlehem plan calls for conciliation in the largest sense; that is, an attempt to settle matters on the spot in the shop where the dispute arises, with three successive appeals ending in the president, and if necessary in arbitration on mutual consent. In the first five years there were, in the four original plants, 2,400 disputes, not one of which came to final arbitration, and only one, a purely personal issue, reached the president. Yet there was a full knowledge in the president's office, through his assistant, of every dispute as it arose.

These disputes were classified as follows: employment and working conditions, 612; wages, piece-work, bonuses and tonnage conditions, 570; safety and prevention of accidents, 298; practice, method and economy, 298; health and works sanitation, 184; employees' transportation, 162; pensions and relief, 122; housing, domestic economies and living conditions, 50; education and publication, 22; athletics and recreation, 12; rules, ways and means, 35. Of the total, 1,682 cases were settled in favor of the employees, 330 against them, 103 were withdrawn by the employees, 201 were compromised and 49 were pending settlement at the time the report was made.

There have been the same favorable results under strict union conditions in such instances as Hart, Schaffner and

Marx, or the Council of Industrial Relations for the Electrical Construction Industry of the United States and Canada, where the original collective bargaining agreements provide for conciliation on the spot and arbitration thereafter in the few cases in which it will be necessary.[6]

The following additional quotations from Mr. Calder's article show that he understood the sources of difficulty usually found in dealing with ordinary labor.

All who know the American workman through years of contact with him are well aware that his desires do not take the form which many who merely theorize about him have prescribed. What does successful employee representation in the Bethelem Steel Corporation and other industries reveal? First, that the worker is initially strictly self-regarding in his desires; that he is little interested in any form of long-deferred reward; that profit-sharing is little in his mind and loss-sharing not at all; that he has no wish to share the burdens of administration and only occasionally has the capacity, but that he is entirely competent to discuss his own economic relationships.

Five things are first in his mind, and all progress in broadening his conception of industry and his intelligent coöperation in it depends upon these primary satisfactions. They are, in the order of their importance: A steady job; adequate real wages; a good supervisor; an individual and collective voice about all of his conditions; and a chance to rise on his merits. Where he can be vocal about these within his plant, without discrimination, without espionage, and apart from any external affiliations, it is found that regardless of nationality, religion, language or politics, he plays in loyally with his fellow workmen. The craft jealousies so diligently fostered outside gradually disappear in a real brotherhood in which the common laborer at last comes into his own.

The writer found one group of employee representatives in a Bethlehem Steel Corporation plant presided over by a worker

---

[6] *Ibid.*, pp. 1445-1454, 1353-1358.

high in the councils of one of the oldest and most successful unions in the country. He had been chosen unanimously by his fellow-workers—8,000 of them—through their representatives to be their chairman. He told the writer that he had been astonished at the things that are on the minds of the workers, which the rules and practices of no union, not even his own finely organized one, could satisfy. He said that his chairmanship was a liberal education in the true inwardness of business, its risks and adventure, its penalties and its meager rewards, which could never have been acquired in any other way.

In the ordinary closed shop union contracts there is usually no provision for arbitration, although the Council on Industrial Relations for the Electrical Construction Industry of the United States and Canada is a marked exception to this rule. Its agreement, with the preamble and principles, organization and rules, will be found in Birdseye's Abbott's Encyclopædia.[7] It has a board of conciliation as well as an appellate tribunal in the nature of a board of arbitration. The agreement is a continuing one, and provides that there shall be no interruptions of work pending the settlement of disputes.

The weakness of the best of labor agreements is that they lack on the one hand the power of a self-governing business organization to enforce its awards by expelling or disciplining its members, and, second, the right under statutory arbitration to enter a judgment upon an arbitration award and enforce it by the ordinary machinery of the law. Still, the fact that the railway unions have continued for decades with practically no strikes, and that this is getting to be the rule in some other lines, shows that it is possible for organized labor and capital to so modify and improve their collective bargaining that it may have many of the

---
[7] *Ibid.*, pp. 1353-1358.

NATURE OF INDUSTRIAL ARBITRATION   137

advantages and purposes of strict commercial arbitration in providing for the settling of disputes which may arise in the future. The arbitration laws of New York and New Jersey are comprehensive enough to include labor disputes; the United States Arbitration Act expressly excludes them.

Also there has grown up, especially in the needle and clothing trades, a form of arbitration which closely resembles commercial arbitration, especially in those agreements which are on the preferential shop basis. In general, these underlying contracts resemble the underlying rules and regulations of an exchange, which set forth the conditions under which members may join and how dealings between members are to be carried on.[8]

The Hart, Schaffner and Marx labor agreement [9] shows: (1) an entire revolution within a century in the ethical relations between master and servant as they were worked out in England in the eighteenth and nineteenth centuries; (2) it defines by a set of rules the technical conditions under which the work is to be carried on; (3) it vests the administration of the contract in a board of arbitration and a trade board, together with certain deputies, officials and representatives of the respective parties whose powers and duties are carefully set forth. Complaints and grievances are to be made in the first instance in each shop to a shop representative, who is

a duly accredited representative authorized by the Joint Board. . . .[10]

It is characteristic of this agreement that it applies to future disputes, is under certain fixed rules, has provisions

---

[8] *Ibid.*, pp. 1445-1471.
[9] See Appendix No. X.
[10] *Ibid.*, No. X, Sec. I (pars. 17-22), Sec. II.

for conciliation, covers substantially all the relations between the corporation and its union employees, and that the ultimate decision lies with the impartial chairman who is a strict outsider appointed beforehand by both parties.[11]

Where employers of large numbers of men have refused to recognize the unions they have frequently made formal agreements with their nonunion employees, who for this purpose have been given a form of representative government. Naturally this movement has been opposed by the trade unions and the American Federation of Labor, but nevertheless it does cover large numbers of workmen, especially in the steel and iron industries and some of the craft employees of some of the railroads.

The plans of the Bethlehem Steel Corporation, already referred to, the Standard Oil Company of New Jersey, the coal and iron mines of the Colorado Fuel and Iron Company of Colorado and Wyoming, Armour and Company, and the Association of Shop Craft Employees of the Eastern Region, Pennsylvania System, Excluding Shops, are found in Birdseye's Abbott's Encyclopædia.[12] In general, these plans contain a set of working rules which, so far as possible, provide for the conciliation of any dispute upon the spot between minor representatives of the company and the employees, and for successive appeals to higher officials in case of inability of the parties to agree.

It is evident that there is a great drawing together of labor and capital and a decided tendency to understand that they are a part of a great system in which the public or consumer is the third party, and that this *rapprochement* is marked by an increasing growth in cordiality, better understanding and

---

[11] Birdseye's Abbott's *Encyclopædia of General Business and Legal Forms*, p. 1446.   [12] *Ibid.*, pp. 1480-1518.

ethics. In this connection there is also a decided tendency to formulate the rules which shall govern working conditions and wages, and provide for conciliation by minor officials in the early stages of any dispute, and, only in case these fail to agree, for arbitration by an expert board usually presided over by an impartial chairman or umpire.

On the contrary, the scale agreements covering anthracite and bituminous coal mining [13] are examples of thoroughly bad, old-fashioned collective bargaining. These agreements leave out entirely the consuming public, and the parties have seemingly sought by newspaper notoriety and by criminations and recriminations to get the best bargain possible regardless of equity and justice. Yet notwithstanding the protestations that the miners would not consent to arbitration in any form, the joint agreement of February 17, 1926, for resuming work after the strike of five and a half months in 1925 and 1926, provides for an unusual and comprehensive form of arbitration.[14]

A wonderful advance would be made in settling labor troubles, if the employers, individually and collectively, would realize that pure industrial arbitration is much more akin to pure commercial arbitration than is any other type.

Therefore let them study carefully the ethical fundaments and the spirit of fair play and broadmindedness of the best exchanges and boards of trade, and then strive to make their employee friends, whether trade unionists or not, fully understand that this change of viewpoint has come to stay. In many cases it will not be easy; for the scars of the Industrial Revolution cut deep in this country, and far deeper in England. The memories of some of the terrible fights which labor and its loved ones have been through in the past, in

---

[13] *Ibid.*, pp. 1358-1389.   [14] See Appendix No. XI.

order to maintain their rights to be treated as men rather than as serfs or labor units, are burned deep into the souls of those who led and suffered in those tragic years.

Finally, industrial like commercial arbitration has many gyroscopic advantages. With little cost it constantly steadies the craft and makes it more safe and comfortable for employer and employee in ways that are not noticed at the time. It is peculiarly adapted to work wonders in the great and difficult psychological field of industrial employment.

PART V

OTHER EXAMPLES OF ARBITRATION; MISCELLANEOUS; CONCLUSIONS

CHAPTER XVI

OTHER EXAMPLES OF ARBITRATION

It is desirable to consider some concrete instances of arbitration not referred to in the preceding pages. They will illustrate the principles already laid down and show how they apply to any instance of arbitration which may arise.

Chamber of Commerce of the United States

The Chamber of Commerce of the United States, which was incorporated December 3, 1915, has persistently worked for the spread of arbitration (a) among its own members; (b) under and through other chambers of commerce and similar bodies throughout the United States; (c) for the success of conciliation (good offices) and arbitration through the International Chamber of Commerce; and (d) for the arbitration of disputes in trade arising between parties in the United States and the Argentine Republic, Brazil, Colombia, Ecuador, Panama, Paraguay, Uruguay and Venezuela respectively. The agreements and procedure are practically identical as to all these countries.

(a) The rules which the United States Chamber of Commerce has provided for arbitration under its own auspices are found in Birdseye's Abbott's Encyclopædia.[1] (b) The rules which it has proposed to be adopted by other similar organizations are found in the same volume.[2] (c) Also the

---

[1] Birdseye's Abbott's *Encyclopædia of General Business and Legal Forms*, pp. 211-213. [2] *Ibid.*, pp. 213-215.

agreement between the Chamber of Commerce of Buenos Aires and the United States Chamber of Commerce for arbitration;[3] and the rules of arbitration thereunder;[4] also, the rules for dealing with merchandise affected by the arbitration agreements;[5] and the form for the appointment of a representative of the parties.[6] (d) The rules of conciliation (good offices) and arbitration of the International Chamber of Commerce can be had upon application to the United States Chamber of Commerce in Washington, D. C.

Since the Argentine agreement became effective, April 10, 1916, but five cases have actually reached formal arbitration. Two of these were held in Argentina and two in the United States, and terminated in definite awards which were promptly satisfied. The fifth case was terminated by the failure of one party to assent to the proceedings.

Meantime the United States Chamber of Commerce has been called upon to consider informally and unofficially many cases involving disputes between American business men and merchants and traders in the other countries. The secretary of the Chamber writes:

> The existence of facilities for arbitration has called attention to the possibility of adjusting disputes in an amicable manner with resulting benefits to trade and commerce generally. Just how much has been accomplished by such arrangements in preventing the introduction of technical objections and other matters of little importance to excuse the performance of contract obligations it is, of course, impossible to say. The realization that a tribunal exists which will look through such objections to the real merits of the matter in controversy must necessarily influence the conduct of a party who is seeking grounds to terminate his contract.

---

[3] *Ibid.*, pp. 215-218.
[5] *Ibid.*, pp. 221, 222.
[4] *Ibid.*, pp. 218-221.
[6] *Ibid.*, p. 222.

In this respect the international experience of the United States Chamber of Commerce corresponds with that of the New York Stock Exchange, New York Clearing House Association and other examples of commercial arbitration already cited.

Throughout the United States, more and more chambers of commerce and similar bodies are offering conciliation and arbitration facilities—usually along the lines suggested by the Chamber of Commerce of the State of New York. There has not been developed, however, any such close relations and interworkings between these chambers of commerce as exist between the Association of British Chambers of Commerce and its 116 local chambers scattered throughout the British Empire.

Arbitration Under Rules of Court

Under statutory authority, the municipal courts of New York City and Chicago provide arbitration in addition to court trials of the ordinary type. The rules governing this form of arbitration are found in Appendices, Nos. IV and V.

Jewish Court of Arbitration

In January, 1920, the Jewish Court of Arbitration was formed in New York City, to divert, so far as possible, litigation between Jews and Jewish institutions from the civil and criminal courts to a court peculiarly adapted to deal with questions arising under Hebraic laws and customs. In addition to the Old Testament, as it is known to the gentile world, the orthodox and other Jews are governed by the Talmud and by a mass of rabbinical interpretations thereof and rules founded thereupon which are fully known only to the learned rabbis of the Jewish religion.

The Jews who founded the Court of Arbitration felt that it was impossible for non-Jewish legal or other authorities to understand fully the racial and religious rules and customs by which the Jew governs his life and his relations with his religious fellows, and that a court of arbitration strictly under the control of Jews would save them from much misunderstanding, undesirable publicity and unfair criticism. It was possible to conduct this unofficial court under the very broad and liberal laws of New York relating to arbitration.

After the court had been formed the Sinking Fund Commission of New York City set aside for its sessions a small grand jury room in the Criminal Courts Building, and later one of the court rooms in the Madison Street Municipal Courthouse. The sessions are held in the evening and are always presided over by three arbitrators, a judge or a lawyer, a rabbi and a business man, thus insuring fair decisions based upon a complete grasp of the problems which are presented. The proceedings may be in Yiddish or English. As the arbitrators give their time gratuitously and there is no charge for rent, there is no fee for the services of the court, whose motto is "Truth, Law and Peace."

Since the first formal session, on February 18, 1920, the court has been presided over at various times by judges of the Supreme Court of the State of New York, the county judge of Bronx County, and justices of the City Court and Municipal Court of the City of New York, as well as well-known lawyers, rabbis and business men.

The court has become a potent force among Jews in New York, but those from neighboring cities have come to it to seek redress and obtain justice at the hands of Jews who understand the underlying historical and religious causes that bring about their various disputes. The number of cases actually tried and disposed of at formal sessions of the court in its first six years, was 875, but 5,236 complaints, or about six times the number of actual trials, filed with the executive secretary, were settled without trial.

The following table will show how wide has been the court's scope, dealing with legal, equitable and quasi criminal cases:

Number of synagogues, benevolent societies, community centers, and other institutions that were the subject of litigation 343
Number of Hebrew schools against which complaints were filed and cases tried.................................. 135
Number of domestic relation cases submitted, tried or settled without a trial.................................. 172
Number of complaints affecting the internal affairs of relief committees, donations or pledges promised but not fulfilled. (A happy thought for other religious denominations and charitable organizations!)........................ 47

This Jewish Court of Arbitration presents many of the better features of the commercial type. It is a permanent tribunal, presided over by experts. While not attached to a self-governing business body whose members do a homogeneous business, it does deal with a homogeneous class of questions, since it is a court "for the trial and settlement of cases involving Jewish life, Jewish traditions, Jewish interests." It was started because

it was felt then, as now, that quarrels between various factions of Jewry should not be permitted to be aired in public courts, before unfriendly tribunals, in an atmosphere charged with misunderstanding and prejudice against the old customs and traditions of the Jew, but on the contrary should be submitted to our fellow men, to our own rabbis, learned and steeped in the ancient

Hebraic law, to our own judges, thoroughly versed in the American laws, to our own merchants and men of affairs, thoroughly familiar with the common faults and frailties of man.

The record of this court also emphasizes one of the great advantages of commercial arbitration and of statutory arbitration before a business tribunal, and also indicates one of the unfortunate shortcomings of American courts of justice. Conciliation as forestalling and avoiding arbitration is an outstanding feature of commercial arbitration. That it may be made applicable to a court is proved by the fact that there were six times as many conciliations in this Jewish tribunal as there were trials. This has been accomplished largely through the unceasing efforts of Louis Richman, a lawyer, who has gratuitously acted as the executive secretary from the beginning. In six years, Mr. Richman has settled 5,000 cases by applying the great principle of conciliation, which is to bring the parties face to face with each other and the facts, in the presence of a respected and experienced official who does not claim to act as an arbitrator.

Frequently the court hears an action to reinstate a member who claims to have been unlawfully expelled from his Jewish society or congregation. If such a litigant should desire to obtain redress by the ordinary procedure of the New York courts he would be compelled, through an attorney specially familiar with such highly technical special proceedings, to bring mandamus proceedings in the Supreme Court. These are usually held in the equity part, and involve a trial of special issues of fact before a jury, after which the case is again returned to the equity part for final disposition. After the judgment, which involves intricate written findings of fact and law, the defeated party may appeal to the Appellate Division and to the Court of Appeals—all at a large expense of time and money.

In the Jewish Court of Arbitration the aggrieved party lays his claim before the executive secretary. The other parties are notified by an ordinary letter to appear for trial, and after their signing the arbitration agreement the case is heard in a short time and judgment is rendered, reinstating the member or deciding against him.

In one instance there was involved a large Jewish relief association in Palestine, with branches in the United States for the collection of funds. Many disputes grew out of factions within the organization, involving not only actions for money had and received and replevin and attachment proceedings, but also criminal charges of grand larceny, fraud and deceit. These various legal proceedings, commenced in Europe as well as in this country, had seriously handicapped the work of the organization. Within a few hours after the case finally came before the Jewish Court of Arbitration all the various disputes were amicably adjusted and the association enabled to continue the excellent work that it was doing.

Although the New York law provides for the entry of a regular judgment upon the award of the court, Mr. Richman writes:

> We have never had occasion actually to enter judgment in the Supreme Court, and so far as we know all the decisions have been respected and complied with by the respective parties.

The American Arbitration Association

The American Arbitration Association is a legal consolidation, under the Membership Corporations Law of the State of New York, effective on January 29, 1926, of the Arbitration Foundation, Inc., already mentioned,[7] the Arbitration Society of America, Inc., organized in 1922, and the Arbitration Conference, organized in 1925 by representatives of various trade and professional groups. The Association is supported by dues from its membership and by contributions. Its primary purposes are to promote knowledge of arbitration and its application to the settlement of disputes. At its office in New York City, the Association provides arbitration facilities for existing disputes at a small cost before arbitrators suggested by the Association or selected by the parties. The Association also maintains a research and publication division which issues a monthly information bulletin and furnishes information to those interested in arbitration; and generally the Association seeks to forward the cause of arbitration in the commercial, statutory and other fields.

---

[7] See *Ante*, pp. 111, 112.

CHAPTER XVII

OFFICIAL ADMINISTRATIVE ARBITRATION BY NONJUDICIAL FUNCTIONARIES

THERE were many disputes which, under the laws of the thirteen colonies and of the present states, have always been settled outside of the courts by locally constituted agencies which were in fact and in principle nothing but arbitration by official nonjudicial arbitrators.

For example, in our early colonial days and even after the Revolutionary War, settlers' lands, situated in an uncharted wilderness, were purchased from or assigned by the authorities of the colonies or by the land boards of the states. It was not customary to fence in such lands, as a whole, but merely to fence out intruders, trespassers and wild game from the fields which were cultivated or in which cattle were kept. When these fences extended across roads or trails, the owners were bound to provide bars or gates that could be opened by passers-by. We are told that in one instance in northeastern Connecticut, on an ordinary trip to church, it was necessary to take down twelve pairs of bars which crossed the highway.

Under these circumstances disputes as to boundary lines between the lots and farms of colonists and settlers and the maintenance of fences upon such lands were to be determined by fence-viewers—different local officials being given these functions at various times and in different localities.

The fence-viewers were, immediately upon the submission of the dispute to them, to view the premises and call witnesses, and their decision was conclusive.[1] They were also to determine the damages done by beasts trespassing upon property.[2]

The provisions for wreck masters, for opening and closing public and private roads, and for tax assessments usually follow this early procedure of having disputes settled on the spot in an orderly way by recognized nonjudicial authorities.

Whether these officials are elected, appointed or selected by the disputants, the principle is the same—that well-qualified citizens, who are not members of the judiciary, but who are presumed to be well acquainted with local customs and rules—experts therein—are designated by the statutes to act in a judicial capacity, and often as judge, jury and sheriff.

This phase of our administrative government was brought by our forefathers from England where there was very little local legislation. Most rights as to real or personal property were to be determined by the neighboring landholding squires, who were laymen, and under local customs which had the force of our local or state legislation, but which often had to be proved as matters of fact by testimony as to such customs by the oldest inhabitants, "from the time when the memory of man runneth not to the contrary." Evidently in the colonies such customs could be best interpreted and applied by locally elected or appointed officials, trusted by their neighbors and personally acquainted with surrounding conditions.

As already shown [3] the English Parliament is increasingly

---

[1] 2 R. L. of N. Y., 1813, p. 133.   [2] *Ibid.*, p. 134.   [3] See *Ante*, p. 81.

putting into effect this feature of administrative government wherever possible, so that questions arising under departmental rules and regulations shall be decided by the department head or by some branch devoted to such work. The same tendency is seen in this country, in the quasi judicial powers conferred on our insurance, banking and other departments. It is only an extension to bureaucracy of the fundamental principle of commercial arbitration—that a permanent tribunal of fair minded experts is the natural and necessary forum to decide technical questions with which they are thoroughly familiar.

CHAPTER XVIII

CONCILIATION

FREQUENT reference has been made to the importance of conciliation as a substitute for formal arbitration. All proper systems for the arbitration of future disputes should provide for their conciliation as a means of avoiding formal arbitration. This is well shown in the reports of the committee on arbitration of the New York Chamber of Commerce referred to above:

Through its good offices the disputants were enabled to continue amicable personal relations leading to an adjustment.[1]

The very existence of the Chamber's system, the very presence of a committee elected to administer it, and the mere offer of arbitration were sufficient in many cases to bring the disputants together, and an otherwise expensive and irritating litigation turned into a friendly settlement. . . .[2]

The settlements by conciliation are the invisible products of the committee's most efficient work. . . . The mere instituting of negotiations before the committee tends to lower the temperature—if we may use this as a figure of speech—of the contending parties, makes each see the other's side with more reasonableness, and actually produces an honorable and mutually satisfactory settlement. Here is realized one of your committee's aims—to prevent arbitration, no less than litigation.[3]

In fact, the attitude of the committee on arbitration is to offer arbitration but to effect conciliation.

---

[1] See *Ante*, p. 98.   [2] *Ibid.*, p. 98.   [3] *Ibid.*, p. 106.

CONCILIATION

The same is true of all other systems for the arbitration of future disputes. In some instances the rules of exchanges and other bodies provide for formal efforts at conciliation before arbitration; but whether so provided or not, any well developed system will have and use the machinery for conciliation so that the actual arbitrations are very much reduced in number.

In the Jewish Court of Arbitration the proportion of conciliations to arbitrations was six to one. It is impossible to state exactly the similar proportions in such bodies as the New York Stock Exchange or the New York Produce Exchange—for there the conciliations are very informal and not matters of record, and even conciliation is largely displaced by amicable settlement between members.

The same rule applies in industrial arbitration for we find that where the system of conciliation is provided for, the actual arbitrations become negligible in number, and usually relate to highly technical questions which require interpretation, or to the construction of the underlying rules or agreements. Thus, under the Bethlehem Plan [4] only one out of about 2,400 disputes reached the president, and not one got to the formal board of arbitration.

The very existence and working of a system of arbitration and an impartial board or committee or chairman in itself tends to reduce the desire of the parties to go to that length in their disputes.

In litigation there is the same tendency to conciliation. In a sense lawyers, as a class, are the greatest conciliators, for probably ten disputes are settled (conciliated) to every one that is actually tried in court.

---

[4] See *Ante*, p. 134.

It is desirable to adopt any proper means for relieving the courts from the mass of litigation which is now swamping them and making it impossible for them to render justice promptly and efficiently. Then why not adopt legal conciliation as an efficient aid for this purpose? Conciliation has shown its value in all fields of formal arbitration, and has also been successful in the few instances where it has been applied in ordinary court procedure. Why should not the law and the courts take the next logical step and provide all necessary facilities for statutory conciliation as well as statutory arbitration?

Legal conciliation has been defined as follows:

> Conciliation is an informal proceeding by which two disputants are enabled to discuss the issue between them in private before a trained and impartial third person having the dignity of official position, representing the state, who explains to them the rules of law applicable, informs them of the uncertainty and expense of litigation, tries to arouse their friendly feelings and suppress their fighting instincts. If an adjustment agreeable to the parties is reached, the official draws up a proper agreement, has it signed, and certifies it so that it may be entered in court as a judgment. There are no pleadings. There are no rules of evidence. The parties tell their stories in their own words. There are no lawyers—plaintiff and defendant appear in person.[5]

This definition should also provide that thereafter nothing that any party or witness says or that the conciliator hears may be admitted as evidence in a subsequent suit, and that the conciliator may not act as a lawyer in any subsequent litigation.

It is not a new thought that there should be courts of conciliation, or else such a change in court procedure as will

---

[5] *American Bar Association Journal,* November, 1923, Vol. IX, p. 746.

interpose an opportunity for an official conciliation before the beginning of actual litigation.

In Norway and Denmark, official conciliators or members of the conciliation court are appointed or elected in local jurisdictions, and in most instances there must be an unsuccessful attempt at conciliation and a certificate thereof before an action can be brought. Between 1846 and 1851 the constitutions of New York, Wisconsin, California, Michigan, Ohio and Indiana, in the order named, authorized their legislatures to establish tribunals of conciliation. Apparently nothing came of these provisions and they were overlooked in the struggle of the Civil War. Courts of conciliation or conciliation proceedings in certain courts have existed in Denmark for over 130 years, in North Dakota since 1921, and in certain lower courts in Minneapolis, Cleveland, Milwaukee and the municipal courts of the City of New York. This form of conciliation is confined to the inferior courts and limited to actions involving small amounts.

The law and practice usually take the following forms:

(*a*) No suit may be brought unless the conciliation facilities of the court have been first tried and a certificate to that effect granted. This is sometimes modified where it is necessary to have attachment, replevin or other provisional remedies, or upon application to the court in particular cases.

(*b*) Noncompulsory—and often nonsuccessful—conciliation, in which the defendant may be informally cited, although he is not compelled to appear. At first this form of conciliation is not likely to be very successful, but if the procedure is wisely followed under an astute and fair conciliator, the people gradually gain confidence and the facilities are increasingly used.

(*c*) The important thing is the personality of the conciliator. He should be a wise counselor, probably a common-sense lawyer, whose personality breeds respect and wins regard. Undoubtedly an unfortunate selection of an official conciliator might ruin the success of the best possible plan. It is claimed that in some courts the clerk and conciliator have been able to dispose of 100 cases a day by letting the respective parties state their claims briefly and then suggesting a fair disposition of the case.

For years the New York Legal Aid Society has successfully employed conciliation in adjusting the disputes that come to it. The late Arthur von Briesen, for twenty-five years president of the Society, said:

It brings antagonists together, inculcates the spirit of compromise and adjustment, under authority of the searching legal mind, expert in resources, yet in the persuasive and kindly attitude of a lover of humanity unselfishly seeking to render unto every one his own.

It is not proposed to discuss this matter at length or to do more than to suggest that at this point the experience of commercial and all other types of arbitration distinctly points the way to a far-reaching legal reform. Enlightening discussions upon this subject will be found in the Survey Graphic of April, 1923,[6] and in the American Bar Association Journal of November, 1923.[7]

---

[6] *Survey Graphic,* Vol. III, No. 1.
[7] *American Bar Association Journal,* Vol. IX, No. 11.

CHAPTER XIX

COMPULSORY AND VOLUNTARY ARBITRATION

As a general rule compulsory arbitration is applicable only in self-governing business organizations trading in homogeneous products. Stock exchanges deal chiefly in stocks and bonds and similar securities. Produce and other exchanges and boards of trade cover various wholesale transactions upon the floor or in the pit, in regard to grain, sugar, coffee, meats and other food products, or in cotton, wool and other commodities. The members of trade associations deal with each other in lumber, rubber and other articles, usually under very carefully drawn uniform contracts prepared by the best lawyers, under the supervision of clients thoroughly acquainted with the facts. The trading between the members of such organizations can be, and usually is, subject to compulsory arbitration before their own permanent and expert tribunals.

Where such members deal with outsiders, there may be voluntary arbitration under the rules of the organization, as in the New York Stock Exchange or other like organizations.

The rule, however, is different with chambers of commerce and other similar bodies, which are rather in the nature of clubs whose membership includes those who are engaged in various kinds of business, finance or transportation, and who do not deal with each other in homogeneous commodities or products, under the rules of the organization.

Chambers of commerce have no floor rules or other technical regulations of business such as those of exchanges, boards of trade and trade associations. The members, as such, do not belong to the organization for the purpose of making contracts between themselves; and, therefore, arbitration is not a necessity in enforcing the agreements between members of the chamber. Any disputes would be likely to come before the governing or house committee.

Nevertheless, more and more chambers of commerce and other similar business organizations are providing recognized, permanent and honored arbitration tribunals before which their members and outsiders may arbitrate disputes upon complying with the prescribed rules; but it must be clearly understood that this form of arbitration is entirely different from the compulsory type possible under a self-governing exchange, board of trade or trade association. Awards by arbitration committees of the latter form of organizations can be enforced between members under their own rules, while those by arbitration committees of chambers of commerce and similar associations can be enforced only if a statute provides therefor, or where public sentiment or business ethics, as is usually the case, induce the losing party voluntarily to comply with the award.

Furthermore, the rules of exchanges, boards of trade and trade organizations almost exclusively relate to future dealings, and are formed to dispose of future disputes. Thereby, as already shown, they tend to prevent such disputes, because, in a friendly atmosphere, they clearly define the rights of the parties under all circumstances; and if this is not sufficiently done by the existing rules, these can be readily amended to cover future contingencies. This future element is lacking in most disputes under common law or statutory or voluntary arbitration or those which come before the arbitration committees of chambers of commerce. These latter facilities provide rather for the disposition of existing disputes then pending between the parties. Few men would join a chamber of commerce if they knew that its rules provided for compulsory arbitration between members; for such disputes would not arise under trade rules to which they had mutually subscribed. Yet, if a dispute should arise, they might very gladly agree to submit it to the arbitration committee of their chamber.

Hence it may be laid down as a general rule that compulsory arbitration is possible and desirable only between members of a self-governing business organization whose members deal with each other in homogeneous securities, commodities or products, under rules or standardized contracts which provide for arbitration of any future disputes which may arise thereunder, and before a permanent and expert arbitration tribunal composed of honored fellow members, whose awards can be and are enforced by the organization itself.

CHAPTER XX

COMMERCIAL COURTS AND SMALL CLAIMS COURTS

THE history and philosophy of arbitration upon the continent of Europe, in the British Empire and in the United States vary as widely as do their customs and laws. As has been already shown, the compulsory arbitration of the medieval merchants in the continental European countries took the form of the merchants' own consular courts, which functioned like the arbitration committees of our exchanges, and developed the *lex mercatoria*. Therefore the settlement of disputes between merchants in these continental jurisdictions tended to assume a permanent legal form covering all commercial questions, rather than that of separate informal tribunals to decide disputes between the members of a trade association.

At first these consular courts were voluntary tribunals instituted and maintained by the merchants themselves for their own particular uses, but recognized and acquiesced in by the several states. Among the nations upon the continent, following Roman precedents, the tendency has always been to reduce the law to codes and written statutes, rather than have a large body of common law, which consisted of decisions of the courts. In all these nations, within modern times, the consular courts have been taken over by the government, incorporated in the general court organization, and their general powers and duties regulated in the codes or statutory law.

No attempt will be made here to trace this history upon the Continent because, in a sense, it is materially different from the American pattern of arbitration as heretofore discussed. In general it may be said that the commercial courts of Europe, as the direct successors of the consular courts, have, in the main, the jurisdiction and powers of their consular predecessors, and are considered as the keepers and interpreters of the law merchant as it developed many centuries ago.

In England the growth of commercial arbitration was rapid after 1855, and was fully recognized and regulated by Parliament in the Act of 1889. Nevertheless there was still a feeling that there should be either a separate commercial court or a branch of the High Court of Justice which should deal exclusively with commercial questions somewhat along the line of the commercial courts upon the continent of Europe. Many endeavors were made to cover this by an act of Parliament, but finally it was developed through the inherent powers of the High Court of Justice, which assigned a particular justice to hear this class of cases. As most of such disputes are disposed of under the arbitration provisions of the various trades associations, very few cases reach the courts, and usually only those which involve novel and important questions of law which will probably go to the highest court of appeal in England, the House of Lords.

The decisions in this quasi commercial court are published in a special set of reports known as the Court of Commerce Cases, started in 1894, and which in thirty-one years have run into thirty slim volumes.

There have been practically no commercial courts in the United States with the exception of the Court of Arbitration for the Port of New York, under the auspices of the

Chamber of Commerce of the State of New York mentioned in Chapter XII; but it seems evident from the history of organized business as heretofore referred to that there is a place in some of the large commercial centers in this country for commercial courts devoted to the trial of such commercial disputes as are not or cannot be disposed of by the ordinary arbitration tribunals. This is not the place to discuss such a broad and important subject, but it is clear that this matter should receive careful consideration by those interested in a solution of the problems of organized business.

In a sense, our United States district courts deal very largely in commercial cases and, as a whole, probably approximate, more than any class of state courts, to tribunals dealing in commercial cases.

It is evident that any growth and development of commercial courts in the United States must be upon lines radically different from those of continental Europe, with their basis of the Roman law, codification and the law merchant, and from those of England with its comparatively simple and single judicial system under the laws of Parliament.

There is a large class of cases involving wages and other small claims which should be brought on for trial on short notice or "before the third turn of the tide," as in ancient days. Provision should be made for the wide distribution of small claims courts or for the adoption of such procedure as would allow a special calendar for such claims in the lower civil courts of the cities. In such instances conciliation would play a large part and would dispose of much unnecessary litigation and should be provided for in such courts.

CHAPTER XXI

CONCLUSIONS

The following conclusions may properly be drawn from the foregoing:

Commercial Arbitration

First, the field of strict commercial arbitration, covering the enormous and intricate transactions under the rules of self-governing exchanges and trade associations whose members deal with each other in homogeneous securities or commodities, vastly exceeds that of all the other types. It is impossible to estimate accurately its extent or the amounts directly and indirectly involved. The underlying purposes of such organizations are better business ethics and methods, with arbitration in the background and applicable mainly if not wholly to future disputes. As the ethics and methods improve and the business machinery works more smoothly, the resort to arbitration becomes less and less necessary. It largely gives way to the amicable settlements and more or less formal and official conciliations which have many advantages over it, just as it has advantages over litigation. There is a great possibility that its applications in cases of disputes may finally come to involve, in most cases, mere official interpretations of the rules and regulations of the organization as applied to current transactions, made by an expert executive or standing committee. In this sense and form, commercial arbitration is the *ultima Thule;* the last word; less and less used, yet always an indispensable part of the machinery of the business. In many respects its honored and permanent expert tribunals are the finest and most successful courts in the world, judged by economy of time and money, fairness of results, absence of rancor, and reflex action in discouraging and lessening disputes in the future. They are free from the great faults which characterize the so-called administration of justice under the cumbersome methods of modern procedure, and especially in our crowded cities. They represent trial by a man's peers far more than a trial by an inexpert judge or a petit jury.

So far as may be, commercial arbitration should be much extended in this country to correspond with the field which it fills in England and the British Empire. Wonders have been accomplished during the past sixteen years, but much remains to be done.

Hence commercial arbitration is the only fair and adequate standard by which to compare and judge the advantages, faults and shortcomings of common law, statutory and industrial arbitration and also the value and performance of litigation.

Common Law Arbitration

Second, strict common law arbitration is as bad as commercial arbitration is good. It applies only to existing disputes. It is not based on better ethics or business methods, but, on the contrary, often lends itself to unethical and unworthy practices. It does not presuppose a permanent, fair and expert tribunal. Too frequently it is not an honest and fair trial of the issues, but is rather an attempt to jockey with issues or compromise on the best terms obtainable. It grew up in an uncongenial soil, which had none of the fructifying elements of commercial ethics. Its fair name was blasted centuries ago by the adverse decisions of some of England's greatest jurists, and it never can and never will recover from those blows. Its chief importance lies in the harm it is capable of doing. Its deserved ill repute tarnishes the fair name and thus affects the usefulness of the other types.

R. I. P.

Statutory Arbitration

Third, admittedly statutory arbitration is an attempt to eliminate the faults of the common law type and to grasp as many as possible of the advantages of the commercial variety. With these ends in view, certain things should be kept in mind.

The statute should be made to apply to all disputes, future as well as present. Otherwise one chief advantage of commercial arbitration will be lost and one grave fault of common law arbitration retained. The right of trade associations, and of business organizations which have not the power to enforce their own rules, to insert provisions for arbitrating future disputes may be greatly curtailed by a statute which does not specifically validate contracts to submit future disputes to arbitration. The chief argument for thus narrowing the statute is "the danger of allowing persons to contract away their right to go into court." This is suspiciously like the arguments of the English courts of three centuries ago; only then it was the judges who had no salaries and needed a grist of litigation from which they might get their fees. Now it seems as though some lawyers felt that their grist and fees needed protection.

Also this is a purely academic view which is contradicted by the fact that all commercial arbitration, which covers transactions vastly larger than those which can ever come before the courts, relates entirely to future disputes. Of this, the Honorable Harlan S. Stone, now associate justice of the United States Supreme Court, said:

> That two merchants of full age and mental competency should not be permitted by the laws of their country to stipulate for the adjustment and settlement of controversies between them exclusively by the arbitration of a fellow merchant would seem incredible to a layman. It would seem incredible to most lawyers did we not actually know that such at one time was the law of England and that until the recent adoption of the arbitration statute in New York it was the law of our greatest commercial state, as well as that of most of the states of the Union. There could be no better example of the vitality and persistence of a false doctrine when it is once lodged in the body of our common law than the history of the common law view of the invalidity of arbitration agreements.

Furthermore, the United States Arbitration Act, passed unanimously by the Sixty-eighth Congress, and the New York, New Jersey and Massachusetts laws provide that agreements to arbitrate future disputes shall be valid, irrevocable and enforceable, save upon such grounds as exist at law or in equity for the revocation of any contract. It is reasonably certain that these provisions will never be abrogated in either of these four great commercial jurisdictions. The narrower statute has been passed in Illinois and Oregon. Here arises an unnecessary and unfortunate conflict of laws so common in the United States.

Why not exercise plain common sense and business sense

in this matter? The wonderful scope, simplicity and success of commercial arbitration and its direct and indirect superiority over statute-made and court-made litigation has already been demonstrated overwhelmingly. If business men, largely unaided by lawyers, legislators or courts, have been able to work out their own salvation in such an amazing way, why not trust them, without interference from the lawyers, to decide whether the proposed statutes shall or shall not apply to future disputes?

In the first place, they certainly know what they wish, what is best for them and their business needs. This is a business and not a legal question, and they are more competent to decide it than their legal advisers, who have not been very successful in the fifty-seven varieties of legal procedure and practice within our national borders.

In the second place, business men have already most emphatically expressed their opinion upon this subject.

The sixteen years of continuous and arduous labors of the committee on arbitration of the Chamber of Commerce of the State of New York have been largely devoted to obtaining statutory arbitration which applied to future disputes, to the adoption of uniform standardized contracts providing for the arbitration of future disputes, and to getting chambers of commerce and other similar commercial bodies to provide expert tribunals before which those future disputes might be expertly conciliated or arbitrated. The efforts of the committee and of the other commercial bodies which it marshaled have resulted in the United States Arbitration Act, and the New York, New Jersey and Massachusetts arbitration laws. Through the efforts of this committee and of the vast public opinion which it organized to aid the passage, the United States Arbitration Act unanimously passed the Sixty-eighth Congress, two-thirds of whose members were lawyers. This was accomplished only after the Congress had been made to realize that there was an equal unanimity of commercial interests in favor of the passage of a law which applied to future disputes. The New York and New Jersey laws were also unanimously passed. This history of the passage of these three great and practically identical acts shows what the great commercial, financial, manufacturing, transportation and merchandising interests of the country wish, and what they are ready to fight for.

It is true that the New York Chamber of Commerce and other similar bodies have felt that half a loaf was better than no bread and that, therefore, it was desirable to accept the narrower statutes of Illinois and Oregon as a step in the right direction and as covering one of the two outstanding flaws in common law arbitration, rather than have no legislation at all. Yet all commercial experts regard the narrower statutes as only a partial achievement and not as a rounded-out whole.

In the third place and most important of all, it must not be forgotten that, as already shown, the philosophy of organized business shows that commercial arbitration always has and must apply to future disputes, just as in the English craft guilds and medieval international merchants.

Statutory arbitration may be regarded from two diametrically opposite viewpoints. It may be considered, in a narrow way, as an endeavor to improve common law arbitration methods. From this standpoint any change must be for the better. On the contrary, it may be advocated as a means of spreading the intrinsic advantages of commercial arbitration to those who are not members of self-governing commercial bodies whose members do a homogeneous business with each other. This larger view is that which has always been advocated by Mr. Bernheimer and by all the other great merchants and business men who have worked so hard for the best form of statutory arbitration, and who have so enthusiastically sponsored the United States Arbitration Act and the New York and New Jersey arbitration laws. Their object has not been the simple improvement of common law arbitration procedure in regard to existing disputes. Their tremendous and persistent efforts would not have been put forth for so trivial a gain, which was largely a matter of procedure.

Probably every one of these men was a member of an exchange, or of a trade association using uniform contracts providing for the arbitration of future disputes. They knew the relations between business ethics and commercial amicable settlements, conciliations and arbitrations. They advocated the broad statute because they knew its greater value by reason of constant contact with its principles in the conduct of their everyday business.

Then why not let the business men rather than the lawyers decide as to whether any new arbitration statutes should cover future disputes? Why thwart their universal desire for the broader statute because of "the danger of allowing persons to contract away their right to go into court"?

Expert Tribunals and Simplified Procedure

Fourth, the laws of all the states should, so far as possible, encourage the formation of expert and permanent tribunals, skilled in getting at the true rights of the parties, ready to enforce all fair contracts in the spirit of business ethics, and determined to cut out all chicanery and unethical practices. Such a tribunal is furnished by the New York Chamber of Commerce with its 650 official arbitrators who are skilled experts in 175 different commercial activities.

Also the statutes of every state should provide simple and fair rules of procedure as a substitute for the cumbrous practice and practices of the courts. Otherwise the simplicity and directness of commercial arbitration will be "sicklied o'er with the pale cast" and drawbacks of litigative methods.

Statutory arbitration has many disadvantages to overcome as compared with its commercial prototype. It should be approached with this thought in view, and everything should be done to assure the broadest and most enlightened liberality in enactment by the legislature and in construction by the courts.

Industrial Arbitration

Fifth, industrial arbitration is very likely to be misinterpreted and misunderstood, although it closely resembles the commercial type.

The foundation of commercial arbitration is the underlying charter or rules of a voluntary or incorporated business body organized, in most cases, to set up machinery for dealing in homogeneous commodities or securities. Arbitration is provided as a part of the machinery necessary to carry out the greater objects of the organization.

In the same way, collective bargaining provides the underlying agreement which is to govern the future relations between employer and employed. As part of the machinery necessary to insure the faithful and ethical interpretation and carrying out, by all parties, of the terms of this underlying contract, industrial conciliation and arbitration may be—but usually are not—provided to settle future differences as to the operations of or under the collective bargaining agreement, or even as to its variation or continuance. We shall think much more clearly on the subject if we will think of the collective bargaining as only the main underlying basic contract, and of industrial conciliation and arbitration only as means of carrying out, in an ethical and agreed manner, the objects of that agreement. There have been comparatively few instances of the successful framing and adoption of this pure form of industrial arbitration, but some of these are shown in this volume.[1]

Viewed from this standpoint, the true field of industrial arbitration is relatively very important—possibly in some ways more important than that of any of the other types. Its potential field covers the livelihood, the working conditions and wages of the majority of our wage earners and should be considered chiefly from this standpoint, and as to its possible mental, moral and financial effects upon them and upon the rest of the country, whose fate and interests are inextricably commingled with theirs.

It may be argued *ad nauseam* as to whether or not the true prosperity of a country depends upon the relative prosperity of its working classes; but it must not be forgotten that at the present time our greatest national affluence is contemporaneous with the greatest prosperity of the working classes—that is the highest average wage with a high buying capacity.

Therefore it may be well to consider whether all employers should not think of making liberal and eminently fair collective bargainings with their employees, which shall embody conciliation, arbitration and investigation machinery

---

[1] See Chapter XV; Appendix No. X.

to take a broad-minded view of the common interests of all affected by the original agreement, just as the New York Stock Exchange and other similar bodies provide machinery for the protection of the public and the improvement of business conditions affecting their members.

More and more, collective bargainings should be ethical and broad-minded basic contracts which should progressively have regard to the interest of both of the immediate parties and the customer and the public, and which should provide adequate machinery to insure their smooth and continued working and the orderly and amicable conciliation or arbitration of subsequent disputes. The value of such agreements has been demonstrated by the wonderful success of the comparatively few instances where this thought has been persistently and consistently carried out.

Therefore successful industrial arbitration will closely follow the objects and methods of the purest form of commercial arbitration. It will be founded upon a broad-minded underlying contract, binding on all parties, intended to draw them together for the mutual good, recognizing the manhood value of every person, putting a premium upon good team work and providing for orderly amendment, revision and extension whenever necessary.

It will be a function of the machinery to eliminate unethical aims and practices; to breed increasing mutual confidence; to encourage amicable adjustments of differences on the spot, or provide for their conciliation or arbitration; to be applicable to the weak and the strong alike, playing no favorites; and to build up the *esprit de corps* which gives zest to the common work and makes for the common good.

It is perfectly evident to any one who will study our labor agreements as a whole that in most of the trades and crafts this higher ethical view is constantly gaining ground because it is being more widely and intelligently studied and applied.

Conciliation

Sixth, the business value and power of conciliation, whether of the official, unofficial or legal type, should be constantly borne in mind. The recognized methods of settling disputes rank, in relative value as follows: amicable settlement, conciliation (mediation), arbitration and litigation. Legal conciliation should be developed as fast and as surely as possible so that it may, under proper laws or court rules, assume a like relation towards litigation that it now occupies toward arbitration.

Seventh, there are several ways in which the ordinary courts can be aided and their calendars relieved, if that is the object sought: (*a*) by the formation and spread of commercial courts of the European type, in our commercial centers, to deal exclusively with commercial disputes; (*b*) by the adoption of small claims courts to give speedy justice in many urgent cases; (*c*) by the formation, wherever possible, of local permanent arbitration courts, usually meeting in the evening in some public building, presided over by well-known attorneys and business men, who shall serve without compensation, and with ample facilities for conciliation; (*d*) by broad arbitration laws and the proper court or other rules for conducting and enforcing arbitration to be passed in as many states as possible; (*e*) so far as possible all classes of trade and business should be organized, like those in England, into exchanges, boards of trade, trade associations or similar bodies whose members shall deal in homogeneous securities, products or commodities, under rules or standardized contracts which provide for compulsory conciliation and arbitration of all future disputes. Then we may hope, in this class of business, to follow, at a considerable distance, the example of England where substantially no commercial disputes are tried in courts but are disposed of under the rules of the proper trade bodies; (f) in classes of commercial disputes to which compulsory arbitration is not ordinarily applicable, the will to arbitrate must be cultivated, the use of arbitration clauses must be encouraged, and special care must be taken to provide permanent and expert arbitration tribunals which will win the confidence of business men, and act, not as compromisers, but as those who believe in enforcing contracts and upholding and spreading better business ethics by encouraging all proper facilities for official, unofficial and legal conciliation.

Eighth, there are two inherently different kinds of arbitration tribunals. The first and higher type is a permanent committee, board or other tribunal, composed of absolutely disinterested experts, in whose selection the disputants have no voice. The second kind is where the arbitrators are chosen by the parties to an existing dispute, with or without an umpire. This is an unfortunate survival of the earlier common law attorney-in-fact-compromiser type of tribunal. It is pretty sure not to be quite as disinterested as the first kind, or to be so regarded. The permanent form of tribunal gains much valued experience and a prestige which a transient set of arbitrators, picked for the occasion, cannot be expected to have. This distinction should be borne in mind in drafting any rules or agreements for the arbitration of future disputes.

Ninth, finally there should be cultivated and inculcated a public and private sentiment for peaceful relations with our neighbors, competitors and those with whom we deal in business. There should be fostered a will to avoid disputes in every possible way; but if they arise, to settle them amicably, or by resort to conciliation or arbitration, with litigation only as a *dernier ressort*. This would mean merely that the present organization of business has required the seeking out and adoption of better business ethics—which is but another name for the Golden Rule. Certainly no one who has been in active business for half a century and whose studies on the subject carry him even further back can doubt that better business ethics are gaining by leaps and bounds, and that the will to litigate is correspondingly losing force.

APPENDICES

APPENDIX I

Ordinaunces of the Arte or Mystery of Clothworkers of the City of London

2nd July, 29 Elizabeth, A.D. 1587

1. Preamble.
2. An Ordinaunce that the Companye maye assemble together.
3. An Ordinaunce for the choyse of the Master of the Companye.
4. An Ordinaunce for the choise of the Wardenes.
5. An Ordinaunce that every new Master and Warden shalbe sworne within Fourteene daies after their election.
6. An Ordinaunce that everie one y^t hath beene Master or Warden shalbe Assistaunt.
7. An Ordinaunce y^t the Master Wardenes and Assistauntes shall rule and governe the Company.
8. An Ordinaunce for the olde Master and Wardenes to give attendaunce to sweare the newe.
9. An Ordinaunce that the yongest Warden shalbe Rentgeatherer and Receyver for the Companie.
10. An Ordinaunce for the choice of ye Auditors and Auditinge of Accompts.
11. An Ordinaunce for the paym^t of suche money as shall come to the handes of the Master and Wardenes to the use of the Companye.
12. An Ordinaunce for the choise of the Wardennes of the Yomanrye.
13. An Ordinaunce for the choise of Twoe Stewards against the Maiores feaste.
14. An Ordinaunce for the choise of one Steward or more upon occasion.

APPENDICES

15. An Ordinaunce for the cho[i]se of ye Clerk of the Companye.

16. An Ordinaunce for the choyse of the Beadles of the Companye.

17. An Ordinaunce for the Master and Wardenes overleaping any rowme to paye Fower Pounds for a fine.

18. An Ordinaunce for a notorious or vicious liver to be removed from his office.

19. An Ordinaunce to have a Cheste or Counting-house with keyes for keepinge their Bookes.

20. An Ordinaunce for keepinge of Assemblies and Fower Quarter-daies.

21. An Ordinaunce for the Quarter-Warden to deliver the goods by inventorie to the newe Warden.

22. An Ordinaunce for the choise of the Lyverey everie thirde or fourth yeare and a decent Lyverey.

23. An Ordinaunce for the whole Liverie to attende at the Election of the Master and Wardeñs.

24. An Ordinaunce for the Liverie to goe to the buriall of any of the Liverey or their wives.

25. An Ordinaunce for the Lyverey to keepe twoe lyverey gownes for the Companeyes worshipp.

26. An ordinaunce for certen poore housholders of the Company to be releeved and buryed by ye Company.

27. An Ordinaunce for the Master and Wardeñs to procure a searche everie quarter at the leaste.

28. An Ordinaunce for the searche to be made everie quarter at the leaste or oftenner.

29. An Ordinaunce y^t none of the Companie change their freedome Uppon payne of an Hundred Marks.

30. An Ordinaunce y^t none shall hyre an other mannes house tenter or soyle over his head.

31. An Ordinaunce that no Forener be sett on worke before a Free Jorneyman.

32. An Ordinaunce that none shall set an other mannes Jorneyman on worke without a certificate.

33. An Ordinaunce to occupie true workmanshippe in Roweinge Shearinge and Cottoninge.

APPENDICES

34. An Ordinaunce that none shall collour any forreners goodes or teach them theyr trade.

35. An Ordinaunce that none shall buye clothes for any straunger or forener in Blackwell Hall.

36. An Ordinaunce y^t none of ye Company shall suffer his Servingman Jorneyman or Apprentice to beare clothes from Blackwell Hall but Porters onelie.

37. An Ordinaunce that none shall dye or kallender Fustyanes before they be shorne throughe.

38. An Ordinaunce for the Clerke of ye Company to make all ye Indentures.

39. An Ordinaunce y^t everie personn upon his admission into the Company to be sworne.

40. An Ordinaunce for everie person to be contributarie to the chardges of the Company.

41. An Ordinaunce that no person of ye Company shall worke on the Sabaothe daie.

42. An Ordinaunce y^t ye Master and Wardennes maye take in any personne by redemption.

43. An Ordinaunce for all apprentices to be bounde within one moneth and presented after.

44. An Ordinaunce that none shall entice awaie an other mannes servaunte.

45. An Ordinaunce for the Master of the Company in divers respectes to substitute a Deputie.

46. An Ordinaunce for controversies to be decided by the Master Wardennes and Assistauntes.

47. An Ordinaunce that none shall take apprentices but housholder admitted.

48. An Ordinaunce to avoyde misrule of servauntes uppon the Saboth daies and holy-daies.

49. An Ordinaunce y^t ye apprentices of men of other Companies usinge Clotheworkinge to be bounde to one of the Clotheworkers Company.

50. An Ordinaunce for none to joyne in partnershipp excepte the one be olde or a widowe.

51. An Ordinaunce for the apprentices of the dead to be ordered by the Master and Wardens.

52. An Ordinaunce for none to sett upp house before he be worth Tenne Poundes and thereto admytted.

53. An Ordinaunce for no hoseholder to sett an Apprentice on worke after his terme expired before he be allowed.

54. An Ordinaunce that none shall have but Twoe apprentices at one tyme excepte he keepe one Jorneyman.

55. An Ordinaunce for none to lende out his Apprentice to worke with any other.

56. An Ordinaunce for none to lende out their apprentices to beare Burthenes.

57. An Ordinaunce for noe Merchaunte Straunger or Englishe to sett any Forrener to worke in theyr houses to Tack Fowlde Muster or Cancell Clothes.

58. An Ordinaunce for every newe housholder in the Twooe firste yeares to have but one Apprentice.

59. An Ordinaunce for the Indentures of the Apprentices runnynge awaye to be broughte to the Hall.

60. An Ordinaunce that every Master Wardene or Assistant usinge the handycrafte maye keepe three Apprentices.

61. An Ordinaunce that none of the Company shall sett over his Apprentice to any Forrener without lycence.

62. An Ordinaunce for every personne to appeare uppon his warninge Uppon a payne.

63. An Ordinaunce for punishing of such as shalbe obstynate and unrulye.

64. An Ordinaunce that none of the Company shall use any undecente fowle or uncomlye speaches or wordes of slander to the Master or Wardens of the Companye.

65. An Ordinaunce that none of the Companye shall doo the lyke as aforesaide to any inferyour personne of the sayde Companye.

66. An Ordinaunce that none of the Companye shall stryke make an assaulte or an affraye uppon any of the same Companye.

67. An Ordinaunce that every Jorneyman and Servingeman shalbe of good behavioure and keepe good order.

68. An Ordinaunce for none to resiste the Master and Wardennes in theyr Searche.

69. An Ordinaunce for everye personne Englishe Aliante Den-

izon or Forreyner within the Citye or Three myles compasse usinge the arte and Mysterye of Clotheworkynge to be contributorie to the Chardges of the Companye.

70. An Ordinaunce that noe Forreyner using the saide Mysterye shall keepe above Towe Apprentices at the moste and those Apprentices to be borne within the Queenes Dominiones.

71. An Ordinaunce for noe Apprentice to be sette over to an other Master but that he be first recorded in the Clothworkers Hall.

72. An Ordinaunce for no Jorneyman of the Companye to worke with any of an other Fellowshipp when he maye have reasonable wages with any of his owne Companye.

73. An Ordinaunce that if any Master or Warden be remisse perciall or carlesse in the xecutinge of Justice to have a fyne set on his heade.

74. An Ordinaunce for no Apprentice to be presented to the Chamberlayne of London to be made free but that he be firste examyned and tryed of his sufficiencie by the Master and Wardenes or some of them.

75. An Ordinaunce for no Apprentice to paye for his entry into the Fellowshipp above Three Shillings Fower Pence.

76. An Ordinaunce that none of the Company that worketh in any other trade shall make or use any false workmanshipp but that he shalbe punnyshed.

77. An Ordinaunce that everye Jorneyman and Servingman being at his Master or Mystres fyndinge shall gyve due attendance uppon them.

78. An Ordinaunce that everye Jorneyman and Servingman beinge at his owne fyndinge shall gyve suche attendaunce as hath byne accus[om]ed and kepe his howers at worke.

79. An Ordinaunce for noe Jorneyman uppon any Breache to departe before the matter be hearde by the Master and Wardennes.

80. An Ordinaunce for paymente of Quarteredge by Houshoulders and Jorneymen.

81. An Ordinaunce for dysclosinge any secretts of the Company.

82. An Ordinaunce for the Master Wardens and Assistaunts

to appoynte Sessors to taxe the Company upon any occasion and to appoynte Collectors.

83. An Ordinaunce to declare the number of the Assistaunts.

84. An Ordinaunce to declare howe the Penalties and fynes to be due by these Ordynaunces shalbe levyed.

84^2. An Ordinaunce or Provyso for the penalties and fynes.

85. An Ordinaunce to declare to whome the Fynes and Penalties herein mentioned shalbe due and appertayne.

86. An Ordinaunce for all matters orders decrees and judgments concerninge the Companye to be made passed and decreed by the Master Wardens and Assistauntes.

87. An Ordinaunce that the Master Wardennes and As[sis]tauntes maye pardon or myttygate Fynes.

88. An ordinaunce what the othes shalbe.

89. An Ordinaunce for the Othe of the Master and Wardennes.

90. An Ordinaunce for the Othe of the Assistauntes.

91. An Ordinaunce declaring the Othe of Supremacy for the Master Wardenes and Assistauntes.

92. An Ordinaunce for certen other Othes.

93. An Ordinaunce for the Othe of every one which commethe in by Redemption of a Jorneyman and of an Apprentice.

94. An Ordinaunce for the Othe of the Clerke.

95. An Ordinaunce for the Othe of the Bedell.

96. An Ordinaunce for the Othe of the Free-denizon.

97. An Ordinaunce for the mynystryng of the Othe of Supremacye.

98. An Ordinaunce that every Jorneyman upon sommons foure tymes in the yeare shall come to the Hall to heare specially that belongeth to them the Ordynaunces readde and that done they maye departe.

99. An Ordinaunce that none shall occupy the sayde Arte or Mystery unlesse he be free of the sayde Companye.

100. The Conclusion of observinge of all the Ordynaunces and for alteratyon as shall seeme meete to the Lorde Chaunceller of Englande Lorde Keeper of the Greate Seale Lorde Treasurer of Englande the Chief Justices of both the saide Benches for the tyme beinge or any Three of them.

APPENDIX II

Objects of Organized Business

New York Stock Exchange

Article I. Title—Objects.

The title of this Association shall be the "New York Stock Exchange." Its objects shall be to furnish exchange rooms and other facilities for the convenient transaction of their business by its members; to maintain high standards of commercial honor and integrity among its members; and to promote and inculcate just and equitable principles of trade and business.

New York Produce Exchange

The objects of this Association are to provide and regulate a suitable room or rooms for a Produce Exchange in the City of New York; to inculcate just and equitable principles in trade and enforce observation of same among its members; to establish and maintain uniformity in commercial usages; to acquire, preserve and disseminate valuable business information, and to adjust controversies and misunderstandings between its members,

Rubber Association of America

Article 2. The purposes for which said corporation is formed are as follows, to wit: to promote in all lawful ways the commercial interests of its members and to secure the advantages to be obtained by mutual coöperation; to acquire and disseminate information concerning trade conditions at home and abroad, credits and other matters of interest; to stimulate social intercourse among those connected with the rubber industry and commerce and in general to promote the welfare of the rubber industry.

Interstate Cotton Seed Crushers' Association

Article II. The objects and purposes for which this corporation is formed are stated and declared to be as follows, to wit:

First: To secure coöperation among the edible oil millers of North America in lawfully furthering and protecting the interests and general welfare of the industry.

Second: To afford a means of coöperating with the Federal and State Government in all matters of general concern to the industry.

Third: To promote and foster domestic and foreign trade in edible oil mill products.

Fourth: To promote the mutual improvement of its members and the study of the arts and sciences connected with the edible oil milling industry.

Fifth: To inform and interest the public as to the economic worth of the edible oil mill industry.

Sixth: To encourage coöperation with growers, producers and distributors of edible oil mill products.

APPENDIX III

Arbitration Clause from Standard Exhibition Contract Used by Members of Motion Picture Producers and Distributors of America, Inc.

TWENTIETH: The parties hereto agree that before either of them shall resort to any court to determine, enforce or protect the legal rights of either hereunder, each shall submit to the Board of Arbitration (established or constituted pursuant to rules and regulations now on file in the office of the Motion Picture Producers and Distributors of America, Inc., bearing date of March 1, 1926, and identified by the signature of its President, a copy of which will be furnished to the Exhibitor upon request) in the city wherein is situated the Exchange of the Distributor from which the Exhibitor is served or if there be no such Board of Arbitration in such city then to the Board of Arbitration in the city nearest thereto (unless the parties hereto agree in writing that such submission shall be made to a Board of Arbitration located in another specified city), all claims and controversies arising hereunder for determination pursuant to the rules of procedure and practice adopted by such Board of Arbitration.

The parties hereto further agree to abide by and forthwith comply with any decision and award of such Board of Arbitration in any such arbitration proceeding and agree and consent that any such decision or award shall be enforceable in or by any court of competent jurisdiction pursuant to the laws of such jurisdiction now or hereafter in force; and each party hereto hereby waives the right of trial by jury upon any issue arising under this contract, and agrees to accept as conclusive the findings of fact made by any such Board of Arbitration, and consents to the introduction of such findings in evidence in any judicial proceeding.

In the event that the Exhibitor shall fail or refuse to consent to submit to arbitration any claim or controversy arising under this or any other film service contract providing for arbitration which the Exhibitor may have with the Distributor or any other distributor or to abide by and forthwith comply with any decision or award of such Board of Arbitration upon any such claim or controversy so submitted, or if the Exhibitor shall be found by such Board of Arbitration in any such arbitration proceeding to have been guilty of such a breach of contract as shall in the opinion of such Board of Arbitration justify the Distributor or any other distributor in requiring security in dealings with the Exhibitor the Distributor may, at its option, demand, for its protection and as security for the performance by the Exhibitor of this and all other existing contracts between the parties hereto, payment by the Exhibitor of an additional sum not exceeding $500 under each existing contract, such sum to be retained by the Distributor until the complete performance of all such contracts and then applied, at the option of the Distributor, against any sums finally due or against any damages determined by said Board of Arbitration to be due to the Distributor, the balance, if any, to be returned to the Exhibitor; and in the event of the Exhibitor's failure to pay such additional sum within seven (7) days after demand, the Distributor may by written notice to the Exhibitor suspend service hereunder until said sum shall be paid and/or terminate this contract.

In the event that the Distributor shall fail or refuse to consent to the submission to arbitration of any claim or controversy arising under this or any other film service contract providing for arbitration which the Distributor may have with the Exhibitor, or to abide by and forthwith comply with any decision or award of such Board of Arbitration upon any such claim or controversy so submitted, or if the Distributor shall be found by such Board of Arbitration in any such arbitration proceeding to have been guilty of such a breach of contract as shall in the opinion of such Board of Arbitration justify the Exhibitor in refusing to deal with the Distributor, the Exhibitor may at his option terminate this and any other existing contract between the Exhibitor and the Distributor by mailing notice by registered mail within two (2) weeks after such failure, refusal or finding, and in addition the Distributor shall not be entitled to redress from such Board of Arbitration upon any claim or claims against any exhibitor until the Distributor shall have complied with such decision, and in the meanwhile the provisions of the first paragraph of this Article Twentieth shall not apply to any such claim or claims.

Any such termination by either party, however, shall be without prejudice to any other right or remedy which the party so terminating may have by reason of any such breach of contract by the other party.

The provisions of this contract relating to arbitration shall be construed according to the law of the State of New York.

APPENDIX IV

Arbitration Law and Court Rules of Illinois

Section 1. *Be it enacted by the People of the State of Illinois, represented in the General Assembly:* That all persons having requisite legal capacity may by an instrument in writing to be signed by them submit to one or more arbitrators to be named in the manner indicated by such writing, any controversy existing between them, and may, in such submission agree that a judgment of any court competent to have jurisdiction of the subject matter of such instrument, shall be rendered upon the award made pursuant to such submission.

Section 2. The parties to such submission may by such submission designate the number of such arbitrators, which number may be one or more as the parties shall agree; the manner in which they may be appointed in the first instance and vacancies caused by the refusal, incapacity or death of an appointee filled; the time and place of the hearing and the rules for the hearing of such controversy, not in conflict with the provisions of this Act; the parties to such submission may include by reference in said written submission the published rules of any organization or association which rules shall thereby become a part of the contract of submission.

Section 3. A submission to arbitration shall, unless a contrary intention is expressed therein, be irrevocable.

Section 4. Said arbitrators or any of them shall have the power to administer oaths, subpoena and examine witnesses, to issue subpoenas *duces tecum* requiring the production of such books, papers, records, and documents as may be evidence of any matter under inquiry and to examine and inspect the same; service of such subpoena shall be made by any sheriff or constable or other person; the fees of witnesses for attendance and travel shall be the same as the fees of witnesses before the circuit courts of this State; any court of this State, having jurisdiction of the subject matter of the submission or any judge thereof upon the application of such arbitrators or any of them, either in term time or vacation may compel attendance of witnesses, the production of books and papers and giving of testimony before said arbitrators by attachment for contempt or otherwise in the same manner as the production of evidence may be compelled before said court.

Section 5. The said arbitrators may authorize the taking of depositions without a commission in the same manner as may be provided by law for the taking of depositions in suits pending in courts of record of this State.

Section 6. The arbitrators may, of their own motion and shall by request of a party,

(*a*) At any stage of the proceedings submit any question of law arising in the course of the reference for the opinion of the court stating the facts upon which the question arises and such opinion when given shall bind the arbitrators in the making of their award.

(*b*) State their final award as to the whole or a part of the reference in the form of a conclusion of fact for the opinion of the court on the questions of law arising and such opinion shall finally conclude the proceeding, except as by this Act otherwise provided.

Section 7. The award of the arbitrators, or a majority of them, shall be drawn up in writing and signed by the arbitrators or a majority of them; the award shall definitely deal with all matters of difference in the submission requiring settlement, but the arbitrators may, in their discretion, make a partial award or awards, which shall be enforceable in the same manner as the final award; upon the making of such award, the arbitrators shall deliver a true copy thereof to each of the parties thereto without delay.

Section 8. If either of the parties neglect to comply with any partial or final award, made by the arbitrators, the other party may, at any time within one year from the time of such failure, file such award, together with the submission in court.

Section 9. The party filing such award may, by giving ten days' notice of his intention to the opposite party, and if no legal exceptions are taken to such award, have judgment thereon, as on the verdict of a jury; upon any legal exceptions taken, the findings of fact by the arbitrators shall be conclusive; successive judgments in the same case may be entered on successive awards of the arbitrators on the subject matter of the submission together with the costs of arbitration and the court, and execution may issue as in other cases.

Section 10. When the award requires the performance of any act other than the payment of money, the court rendering such judgment shall enforce the same by rule, and the party refusing or neglecting to comply with such rule may be proceeded against by attachment or otherwise as for a contempt.

Section 11. If any legal defects shall appear in the award or other proceedings, or if it shall appear that the award is not sustainable under the opinions of the court upon questions of law under section 6 of this Act, the court may set aside such award, or remit the matters contained in the said award to the reconsideration of the said arbitrators; or, if it shall appear, on oath or affirmation, that said award was obtained by fraud, corruption or other undue means, or that such arbitrators misbehaved, said court may set aside such award.

Section 12. If there be any evident miscalculation or misdescription, or if the arbitrators shall appear to have awarded upon matters not submitted to them, not affecting the merits of the decision upon the matters submitted, or where the award shall be imperfect in some matters of form, not affecting the merits of the controversy, and where such errors and defects, if in a verdict, could have been lawfully amended or disregarded by the court, any party aggrieved may move the court to modify or correct such award.

Section 13. Applications to set aside, modify or amend or remit such award, as provided in the sections 11 and 12 of this Act, must be made before the entry of final judgment on such award: *Provided,* nothing herein contained shall be so construed as to deprive courts of chancery of their jurisdiction, as in other cases.

Section 14. Writs of error and appeals may be taken from any decision of the court upon questions of law under section 6 of this Act, or matters arising in the course of the proceedings, by the party feeling himself aggrieved, as in other cases; and if the case shall be upon such writ of error or appeal remanded, such further proceedings shall be had as the nature of the case may require.

Section 15. The parties may, in the submission, agree upon the amount of compensation to be paid to the arbitrators and the terms of the payment of the same; unless so agreed, each arbitrator shall be allowed, for every day's attendance to the business of his appointment $3.00, to be paid in the first instance by the party in whose favor the award shall be made, but to be recovered of the other party with the other costs of suit, if the award or final decision shall entitle the prevailing party to recover costs. Sheriffs, constables, the bailiff of the Municipal Court of Chicago, clerks and justices of the peace shall be entitled to the same fees for services performed in relation to any arbitration, as shall be allowed by law for the like services in their respective courts.

Section 16. Arbitrators may be compelled, by order of the court, to proceed to a hearing of the submission and to make report without unnecessary delay.

Section 17. In this Act unless the context or subject matter otherwise requires,

"Court" means the court named in the submission, and if no court be named, any court having jurisdiction of the subject matter, to which application is made or proceedings had on a submission.

"Submission" means a written agreement to submit differences to arbitration, whether such differences be in whole or in part in suit or not in suit.

Section 18. (*Repeal*.) An Act to revise the law in relation to arbitrations and awards, approved April 29, 1873, in force July 1, 1873, except as herein reënacted, is hereby repealed, but this section shall not be construed so as to affect any right, actions or causes of action that may have accrued or be pending when this Act shall take effect. (Approved June 11, 1917.)

Municipal Court of Chicago; Rule Governing Arbitrations

Rule 22. Upon the filing in this court of any instrument of submission to arbitration of any controversy existing between the parties thereto, with the written consent of the parties to such filing, the court shall take jurisdiction of the parties and subject-matter of such submission without the filing of any *praecipe,* statement of claim, statement of set-off, affidavit of claim, answer, affidavit of merits or other pleading. From time to time during the pending of such suit, either before or after award, any party or arbitrator may submit to the court any matter of law arising in the proceedings before the arbitrators or on the award, and the court shall thereupon give such directions or enter such order affecting matters of law as shall appear to be in accordance with law.

Form of Submission to Arbitration Used in the Municipal Court of Chicago

The Municipal Court } Submission to Arbitration
State of Illinois } ss.
City of Chicago } In The Municipal Court of Chicago.

and } —Submission to Arbitration. No.

Whereas, a controversy exists between   and parties to this instrument, which briefly stated is as follows:

Now, therefore, this agreement, made this   day of A.D. 19 , by and between   and

Witnesseth: That the parties hereto submit the above mentioned controversy to arbitration, and to that end they appoint arbitrator   as follows:
Said arbitrator shall, after having taken the oath as arbitrator in the form attached to this instrument, proceed with all convenient speed to hear the allegations, evidence and arguments

of the respective parties hereto. Said arbitrator shall conduct proceedings in all things pursuant to the laws of the State of Illinois and the practice of The Municipal Court of Chicago, Rule 22 of said court being hereby, by reference, included in this submission and made a part hereof.

It is further agreed that this instrument of submission to arbitration may be filed in The Municipal Court of Chicago either by the arbitrator of his own motion or by one of the parties to this instrument, notice thereof being given to all parties to this submission and to said arbitrator, and such filing in said Municipal Court of Chicago shall be deemed a filing with the written consent of the parties to this submission in accordance with law and the practice of said court, and the court shall thereupon take jurisdiction of the parties and subject-matter of this submission without written pleadings, in accordance with the practice of said court.

It is further agreed that a judgment or successive judgments of said Municipal Court shall be rendered upon any award or awards made pursuant to this submission.

It is further agreed that the compensation of said arbitrator shall be as follows:

Said compensation shall be taxed as costs and made a part of said judgment in favor of the successful party and against the unsuccessful party.

IN WITNESS WHEREOF the parties hereto have hereunto set their hands and seals the day and year first above written.

[Seal]
(Corporations must attach their corporate seals.) [Seal]

THE SAME; OATH OF ARBITRATOR

State of Illinois ⎫
County of Cook ⎬ ss.
City of Chicago ⎭

I   who have been appointed arbitrator by the above instrument of submission to arbitration, being duly sworn, on oath say that I will faithfully and fairly hear, examine and determine the cause and controversy mentioned in the foregoing instrument of submission to arbitration, according to the principles of equity and justice, and make a just and true award according to the best of my understanding.

Subscribed and sworn to before me this
    day of   , A.D. 19 .   [*Signature.*]

APPENDIX V

ARBITRATION LAW AND COURT RULES OF NEW YORK

(L. 1920, ch. 275, amended, L. 1921, ch. 14, constituting chapter 72 of the Consolidated Laws. Birdseye, C. & G. Cons. Laws, 2nd Ed., Vol. 10, pp. 82-85, and Supp. of 1921, pp. 32-34.)

ARTICLE I

Section 1. *Short title.*—This chapter shall be known as the "Arbitration Law."

ARTICLE II. GENERAL PROVISIONS

Section 2. *Validity of arbitration agreements.*—A provision in a written contract to settle by arbitration a controversy thereafter arising between the parties to the contract, or a submission hereafter entered into of an existing controversy to arbitration pursuant to title eight of chapter seventeen of the code of civil procedure, or article eighty-three [renumbered article eighty-four by Act of 1921] of the civil practice act, shall be valid, enforcible and irrevocable, save upon such grounds as exist at law or in equity for the revocation of any contract.

Section 3. *Remedy in case of default.*—A party aggrieved by the failure, neglect or refusal of another to perform under a contract or submission providing for arbitration, described in section two hereof, may petition the supreme court, or a judge thereof, for an order directing that such arbitration proceed in the manner provided for in such contract or submission. Eight days' notice in writing of such application shall be served upon the party in default. Service thereof shall be made in the manner provided by law for personal service of a summons. The court, or a judge thereof, shall hear the parties, and upon being satisfied that the making of the contract or submission or the failure to comply therewith is not in issue, the court, or the judge thereof, hearing such application, shall make an order directing the parties to proceed to arbitration in accordance with the terms of the contract or submission. If the making of the contract or submission or the default be in issue, the court, or the judge thereof, shall proceed summarily to the trial thereof. If no jury trial be demanded by either party, the court, or the judge thereof, shall hear and determine such issue. Where such an issue is raised, any party may, on or before the return day of the notice of application, demand a jury trial of such issue, and if such demand be made, the court, or the judge thereof, shall make an order referring the issue or issues to a jury in the manner provided by law for referring to a jury issues in an equity action. If the jury find that no written contract providing for arbitration was made or submission entered into, as the case may be, or that there is no default, the proceeding shall be dismissed. If the jury find that a written contract providing for arbitration was made or submission entered into, as the case may be, or that there is no default, the proceeding shall be dismissed. If the jury find that a written contract providing for arbitration was made or submission was entered into and there is a default in the performance thereof, the court, or the judge thereof, shall make an order summarily directing the parties to the contract or submission to proceed with the arbitration in accordance with the terms thereof.

Section 4. *Provision in case of failure to name arbitrator or umpire.*—If, in the contract for arbitration or in the submission, described in section two, provision be made for a method of naming or appointing an arbitrator or arbitrators or an umpire, such method shall be followed; but if no method be provided therein, or if a method be provided and any party thereto shall fail to avail himself of such method, or for any other reason there shall be a lapse in the naming of an arbitrator or arbitrators or umpire, or in filing a vacancy, then, upon application by either party to the controversy, the supreme court, or a judge thereof, shall designate and appoint an arbitrator or arbitrators or umpire, as the case may require, who shall act under the said contract or submission with the same force and effect as if he or they had been specifically named therein; and unless otherwise provided, the arbitration shall be by a single arbitrator.

Section 5. *Stay of proceedings brought in violation of an arbitration agreement or submission.*—If any suit or proceeding be brought upon any issue otherwise referable to arbitration under a contract or submission described in section two, the supreme court, or a judge thereof, upon being satisfied that the issue involved in such suit or proceeding is referable to arbitration under a contract containing a provision for arbitration or under a submission described in section two, shall stay the trial of the action until such arbitration has been had in accordance with the terms of the agreement.

Section 6. *Applications to be heard as motions.*—Any application to the court or a judge thereof, hereunder shall be made and heard in the manner provided by law for the making and hearing of motions, except as otherwise herein expressly provided.

Sections 7, 8 and 9 repeal and amend certain acts and make sections 1448 to 1469 of the New York Civil Practice Act, so far as practicable and consistent with this chapter, applicable to an arbitration agreement under this chapter, and for such purpose the arbitration agreement is to be deemed a submission to arbitration. Wherever in such sections reference is made to the court specified in the submission, the supreme court shall have jurisdiction of the subject matter if no court be specified in the arbitration agreement.

THE CIVIL PRACTICE ACT OF NEW YORK, ARTICLE 84

(As renumbered by Laws of 1921, ch. 199. In effect October 1, 1921)

Section 1448. *Submission to arbitration.*—Except as otherwise prescribed in this section, two or more persons may submit to the arbitration of one or more arbitrators any controversy existing between them at the time of the submission, which may be the subject of an action.

A submission of a controversy to arbitration cannot be made, either as prescribed in this article or otherwise, in either of the following cases:

1. Where one of the parties to the controversy is an infant, or a person incompetent to manage his affairs by reason of lunacy, idiocy or habitual drunkenness.

2. Where the controversy arises respecting a claim to an estate in real property, in fee or for life.

But where a person capable of entering into a submission has knowingly entered into the same with a person incapable of so doing, as prescribed in subdivision first of this section, the objection on the ground of incapacity can be taken only in behalf of the person so incapacitated.

The second subdivision of this section does not prevent the submission of a claim to an estate for years, or other interest for a term of years, or for one year or less, in real property; or of a controversy respecting the partition of real property between joint tenants or tenants in common; or of a controversy respecting the boundaries of lands or the admeasurement of dower.

Section 1449. *Contents of submission.*—A submission authorized by the last section shall be in writing, duly acknowledged or proved, and certified, in like manner as a deed to be recorded. The submission may provide that a judgment of a specified court of record shall be rendered upon the award made pursuant to the submission. If the supreme court is thus specified, the submission may also specify the county in which the judgment shall be entered. If it does not, the judgment may be entered in any county.

Section 1450. *Appointment of additional arbitrator or umpire.*—Where a submission is made as prescribed in this article, an additional arbitrator or an umpire cannot be selected or appointed unless the submission expressly so provides. Where a submission, made either as prescribed in this article or otherwise, provides that two or more arbitrators therein designated may select or appoint a person as an additional arbitrator, or as an umpire, the selection or appointment must be in writing. An additional arbitrator or umpire must sit with the original arbitrators upon the hearing. If testimony has been taken before his selection or appointment, the matter must be reheard, unless a rehearing is waived in the submission or by the subsequent written consent of the parties or their attorneys.

Section 1451. *Hearings by arbitrators.*—Subject to the terms of the submission, if any are specified therein, the arbitrators selected as prescribed in this article must appoint a time and place for the hearing of the matters submitted to them, and must cause notice thereof to be given to each of the parties. They, or a majority of them, may adjourn the hearing from time to time upon the application of either party for good cause shown or upon their own motion, but not beyond the day fixed in the submission for rendering their award, unless the time so fixed is extended by the written consent of the parties to the submission or their attorneys.

Section 1452. *Oath of arbitrators.*—Before hearing any testimony, arbitrators selected either as prescribed in this article or otherwise must be sworn, by an officer authorized by law to administer an oath, faithfully and fairly to hear and examine the matters in controversy and to make a just award according to the best of their understanding, unless the oath is waived by the written consent of the parties to the submission or their attorneys.

Section 1453. *Power of arbitrators.*—The arbitrators selected either as prescribed in this article or otherwise, or a majority of them, may require any person to attend before them as a witness; and they have, and each of them has, the same powers with respect to all the proceedings before them which are conferred upon a board or a member of a board authorized by law to hear testimony. All the arbitrators selected as prescribed in this article must meet together and hear all the allegations and proofs of the parties; but an award by a majority of them is valid unless the concurrence of all is expressly required in the submission.

Section 1454. *Fees and expenses of arbitrators.*—Unless it is otherwise expressly provided in the submission, the award may require the payment, by either party, of the arbitrators' fees, not exceeding the fees allowed to a like number of referees in the supreme court; and also their expenses.

Section 1455. *Requirements as to award.*—To entitle the award to be enforced, as prescribed in this article, it must be in writing; and, within the time limited in the submission, if any, subscribed by the arbitrators making it; acknowledged or proved, and certified, in like manner as a deed to be recorded; and either filed in the office of the clerk of the court in which, by the submission, judgment is authorized to be entered upon the award, or delivered to one of the parties or his attorney.

Section 1456. *Motion to confirm award.*—At any time within one year after the award is made, as prescribed in the last section, any party to the submission may apply to the court specified in the submission for an order confirming the award; and thereupon the court must grant such an order unless the award is vacated, modified or corrected, as prescribed in the next two sections. Notice of the motion must be served upon the adverse party to the submission, or his attorney, as prescribed by law for service of notice of a motion upon an attorney in an action in the same court. In the supreme court, the motion must be made within the judicial district embracing the county where the judgment is to be entered.

Section 1457. *Motion to vacate award.*—In either of the following cases, the court specified in the submission must make an order vacating the award, upon the application of either party to the submission:

1. Where the award was procured by corruption, fraud or other undue means.

2. Where there was evident partiality or corruption in the arbitrators or either of them.

3. Where the arbitrators were guilty of misconduct in refusing to postpone the hearing upon sufficient cause shown, or in refusing to hear evidence pertinent and material to the controversy; or of any other misbehavior by which the rights of any party have been prejudiced.

4. Where the arbitrators exceeded their powers, or so imperfectly executed them, that a mutual, final and definite award upon the subject-matter submitted was not made.

Where an award is vacated, and the time within which the submission required the award to be made has not expired, the court, in its discretion, may direct a rehearing by the arbitrators.

Section 1458. *Motion to modify or correct award.*—In either of the following cases, the court specified in the submission must make an order modifying or correcting the award, upon the application of either party to the submission:

1. Where there was an evident miscalculation of figures, or an evident mistake in the description of any person, thing or property referred to in the award.

2. Where the arbitrators have awarded upon a matter not submitted to them, not affecting the merits of the decision upon the matters submitted.

3. Where the award is imperfect in a matter of form not affecting the merits of the controversy, and, if it had been a referee's report, the defect could have been amended or disregarded by the court.

The order may modify and correct the award so as to effect the intent thereof and promote justice between the parties.

Section 1459. *Notice of motion and stay.*—Notice of a motion to vacate, modify or correct an award must be served upon the adverse party to the submission, or his attorney, within three months after the award is filed or delivered, as prescribed by law for service of notice of a motion upon an attorney in an action. For the purposes of the motion, any judge who might make an order to stay the proceedings in an action brought in the same court may make an order, to be served with the notice of the motion, staying the proceedings of the adverse party to enforce the award.

Section 1460. *Costs on vacating award.*—Where the court vacates an award, costs, not exceeding twenty-five dollars and disbursements may be awarded to the prevailing party; and the payment thereof may be enforced in like manner as the payment of costs upon a motion in an action.

Section 1461. *Entry of judgment on award and costs.*—Upon the granting of an order confirming, modifying or correcting an award, judgment may be entered in conformity therewith, as upon a referee's report in an action, except as is otherwise prescribed in this article. Costs of the application and of the proceedings subsequent thereto, not exceeding twenty-five dollars and disbursements, may be awarded by the court in its discretion. If awarded, the amount thereof must be included in the judgment.

Section 1462. *Judgment-roll.*—Immediately after entering judgment, the clerk must attach together and file the following papers, which constitute the judgment-roll:

1. The submission; the selection or appointment, if any, of an additional arbitrator, or umpire; and each written extension of the time, if any, within which to make the award.

2. The award.

3. Each notice, affidavit or other paper used upon an application to confirm, modify or correct the award, and a copy of each order of the court upon such application.

4. A copy of the judgment.

The judgment may be docketed as if it was rendered in an action.

Section 1463. *Effect of judgment and enforcement.*—The judgment so entered has the same force and effect, in all respects as, and is subject to all the provisions of law relating to, a judgment in an action, and it may be enforced as if it had been rendered in an action in the court in which it is entered.

Section 1464. *Appeals.*—An appeal may be taken from an order vacating an award, or from a judgment entered upon an award, as from an order or judgment in an action. The proceedings upon such an appeal, including the judgment thereupon and the enforcement of the judgment, are governed by the provisions of statute and rule regulating appeals in actions as far as they are applicable.

Section 1465. *Death or incompetency of party.*—Where a party dies after making a submission either as prescribed in this article or otherwise, if the submission contains a stipulation authorizing the entry of a judgment upon the award, the award may be confirmed, vacated, modified or corrected, upon the application of, or upon notice to, his executor or administrator, or a temporary administrator of his estate; or, where it relates to real property, his heir or devisee who has succeeded to his interest in the real property. Where a committee of the property or of the person of a party to a submission is appointed, the award may be confirmed, vacated, modified or corrected, upon the application of, or notice to, a committee of the property, but not otherwise. In a case specified in this section, a judge of the court may make an order extending the time within which notice of a motion to vacate, modify or correct the award must be served. Upon confirming an award, where a party has died since it was filed or delivered, the court must enter judgment in the name of the original party; and the proceedings thereupon are the same as where a party dies after a verdict.

Sections 1466, 1467 and 1468 repealed.

Section 1469. *Application of this article.*—This article does not affect any right of action in affirmance, disaffirmance, or for the modification of a submission, made either as prescribed in this article or otherwise, or upon an instrument collateral thereto, or upon an award made or purporting to be made in pursuance thereof. And, except as otherwise expressly prescribed therein, this article does not affect a submission made otherwise than as prescribed therein, or any proceedings taken pursuant to such a submission, or any instrument collateral thereto.

Municipal Court of the City of New York; Rules for Arbitration

Pursuant to subdivision six of section six and subdivision six of section eight of the Municipal Court Code, the Board of Justices of the Municipal Court of the City of New York, hereby establish a system of arbitration and adopt the following rules:

Rule I. The parties to any controversy, except infants and incompetents, may submit the same for arbitration to a justice of this court, or to any other person upon whom they shall agree.

Rule II. The persons desiring an arbitration shall sign a consent which shall contain the name of the arbitrator, a brief recital of the nature of the controversy to be determined and a statement that they will abide by these rules. The consent must be filed with the clerk of one of the districts, which district shall be the proper district for all further proceedings, and a copy thereof shall be given by the parties to the arbitrator.

Rule III. The arbitrator shall forthwith proceed to hear the controversy. He shall not be bound by the rules of evidence, but may receive such evidence as seems to him equitable and proper. Either party may be represented by counsel, but no record of the proceedings before the arbitrator shall be kept. No expense shall be incurred by him except upon the consent in writing of the parties.

Rule IV. After the first hearing neither party may withdraw from the arbitration unless both parties consent to, or the arbitrator directs a discontinuance of the proceedings.

Rule V. The arbitrator shall make his award in writing and file the same forthwith, together with his opinion, if any, with the clerk of the proper district. Unless both parties file a request in writing not to enter judgment, the clerk shall within two days after the filing of the award enter judgment in accordance therewith, provided the award has been filed within thirty days from the date of filing the consent. The time within which the clerk shall enter judgment may be extended by a stipulation in writing for a further period of not to exceed thirty days.

Rule VI. The clerk in each district shall keep a docket wherein proper entries of all proceedings shall be made.

Rule VII. No fees or disbursements of any kind shall be demanded or received, except as hereinabove provided.

Forms.—The consent, award and judgment must be in substantially the following form, the blanks being properly filled:

Consent.—Municipal Court of the City of New York, Borough of   ,   District.

We,   , residing at   , and   , residing at   , hereby designate   as arbitrator to hear and determine the following controversy existing between us, viz:

We agree that the arbitrator proceed in accordance with the rules of the Municipal Court of the City of New York, and do hereby declare that we know said rules and that we will abide by them.

Dated   , 19   .

Award.—I,   , the arbitrator appointed pursuant to a consent signed by   and   , and filed in the office of the Clerk of the Municipal Court for the   District, Borough of   , on the   day of   , 19   , to hear and determine the controversy therein specified, do hereby certify that I have heard the parties to said controversy and the evidence submitted by them and find and decide that

Dated, New York, , 19 .
Judgment.—Upon the consent filed on the day of , 19 , and the award of , arbitrator, filed on the day of , 19 , judgment is entered [or insert other judgment in accordance with the award] in favor of against , for the sum of Dollars ($).
Dated , 19 .

MUNICIPAL COURT, CITY OF NEW YORK; RULES ON CONCILIATION

Pursuant to sub-division six of section six and sub-division five of section eight of the Municipal Court Code, the Board of Justices of the Municipal Court of the City of New York hereby establish a system of conciliation and adopt the following rules:

Rule I. Any person having a claim which in his opinion may be adjusted without resort to an action at law may apply to the clerk in any district for the issuance of a notice of conciliation.

Rule II. The clerk shall immediately fix a date for hearing and inform the applicant of such date when the request for the notice is presented and shall forthwith mail the notice to the adverse party at the address given by the applicant. At least three days' notice shall be given, exclusive of the day of mailing. The hearing shall be had in any district which the applicant may specify.

Rule III. Hearings of conciliation shall be had in each district on such day or days of each week as the Justices of the district may designate. Where there is more than one part of the court established, the hearing shall be had at Part I.

Rule IV. The cases in conciliation shall be heard informally. The justice hearing the case shall endeavor to effect an amicable and equitable adjustment between the parties. He may, in his discretion, permit either party to be assisted by counsel, but no record of the proceedings before him shall be kept. He shall not be bound by the rules of evidence, but may receive such evidence as seems to him equitable.

Rule V. The Justice shall direct the Clerk to make an entry in the docket hereinafter referred to, of the terms of the settlement or of the failure thereof. No judgment or order enforceable by process of law shall be rendered or made by the Justice.

Rule VI. The Justice before whom the hearing in conciliation was had shall not take part in any trial between the same parties involving the same controversy.

Rule VII. The clerk of each district shall keep a docket wherein proper entries of all proceedings shall be made. Such record may not be offered in evidence or referred to upon any subsequent trial of the controversy.

Rule VIII. If the hearing is to be had in a district other than wherein the notices has been issued, the clerk issuing the notice shall forthwith notify in writing the clerk of the district in which the hearing is set, of the names of the parties, and the dates of mailing the notice and of the hearing.

Rule IX. Parties appearing voluntarily may submit their controversy to a Justice for conciliation without the issue of a notice, but otherwise subject to these rules.

MUNICIPAL COURT OF THE CITY OF NEW YORK

BOROUGH OF————————, ————————DISTRICT

To————————————————————

————————————————residing at————————
having presented a claim against you for————————
amounting to————————Dollars, you are hereby requested to appear before a Justice of this Court at the Court House of ————————District, Borough of————————, situated at ————————————, on the————day of————————191 , at————M., for the purpose of an amicable adjustment of the controversy.

Clerk

Dated New York,————————————19

APPENDIX VI

Arbitration Law of New Jersey
Chapter 134, Laws of 1923

AN ACT CONCERNING ARBITRATION AND AWARDS

BE IT ENACTED *by the Senate and General Assembly of the State of New Jersey.*

1. A provision in a written contract to settle by arbitration a controversy thereafter arising out of the contract or the refusal to perform the whole or any part thereof or an agreement in writing to submit an existing controversy to arbitration pursuant to section two hereof, shall be valid, enforceable and irrevocable, save upon such grounds as exist at law or in equity for the revocation of any contract.

2. Two or more persons may submit in writing to arbitration any controversy existing between them at the time of the agreement to submit, which arises out of a contract or the refusal to perform the whole or any part thereof or the violation of any other obligation. They may also so agree that a judgment of a court of record, specified in writing, shall be rendered upon the award, made pursuant to the submission. If the court is thus specified they may also specify the county in which the judgment shall be entered. If the writing does not specify, the judgment may be entered in any county.

3. A party aggrieved by the failure, neglect or refusal of another to perform under an agreement in writing providing for arbitration may petition any justice of the Supreme Court or judge of a Circuit Court, holding court for the county where either party resides, for an order directing that such arbitration proceed in the manner provided for in such agreement. Five days' notice in writing of such application shall be served

personally upon the party in default. The justice or judge shall hear the parties, and upon being satisfied that the making of the agreement or such failure to comply therewith is not in issue, shall make an order directing the parties to proceed to arbitration in accordance with the terms of the agreement. If the making of the agreement or the default be in issue an order shall be made directing a summary trial thereof. Where such an issue is raised, the party alleged to be in default may, on or before the return day of the notice of application, demand a jury trial of such issue, and if such demand be made, said justice or judge shall make an order referring the issue or issues to a jury called and impanelled in the manner provided for the trial of actions at law. If no jury trial be demanded said justice or judge shall hear and determine such issue. If the finding be that no agreement in writing providing for arbitration was made, or that there is no default in proceeding thereunder, the proceeding shall be dismissed. If the finding be that a written provision for arbitration was made and there is a default in proceeding thereunder, an order shall be made summarily directing the parties to proceed with the arbitration in accordance with the terms thereof.

4. If, in the agreement, provision be made for a method of naming or appointing an arbitrator or arbitrators or an umpire, such method shall be followed, but if no method be provided therein, or if a method be provided and any party thereto shall fail to avail himself of such method, or for any other reason there shall be a lapse in the naming of an arbitrator or arbitrators or umpire, or in filling a vacancy, then, upon application by either party to the controversy, any justice or judge as aforesaid shall designate and appoint an arbitrator or arbitrators, or umpire, as the case may require, who shall act under the said agreement with the same force and effect as if he or they had been specifically named therein; and unless otherwise provided, the arbitration shall be by a single arbitrator.

5. If any suit or proceeding be brought upon any issue arising out of an agreement providing for the arbitration thereof, any justice or judge as aforesaid, upon being satisfied that the issue involved in such suit or proceeding is referable to arbitra-

tion, shall stay the action until an arbitration has been had in accordance with the terms of the agreement; *provided*, that the applicant for the stay is not in default in proceeding with such arbitration.

6. Any application made under the authority of this act shall be heard in a summary way in the manner provided by law for the making and hearing of motions, except as otherwise herein expressly provided.

7. When more than one arbitrator is agreed to all the arbitrators shall sit at the hearing of the case, unless, by consent in writing, all parties shall agree to proceed with the hearing with a less number. The arbitrator or arbitrators so sitting may require any person to attend before him or them as a witness and in a proper case to bring with him any book or written instrument. The fees for such attendance shall be the same as the fees of witnesses before masters. Summons shall issue in the name of the arbitrator or arbitrators, or a majority of them, and shall be signed by the arbitrator or arbitrators, or a majority of them, and shall be directed to the said person and shall be served in the same manner as subpoenas to testify before a court of record of this State; if any person or persons so summoned to testify shall refuse or neglect to obey said summons upon petition any justice or judge as aforesaid may compel the attendance of such person or persons before said arbitrator or arbitrators, or punish said person or persons for contempt in the same manner now provided for the attendance of witnesses or the punishment of them in the courts of this State.

8. At any time within three months after the award is made, unless the parties shall extend said time in writing, which award must be in writing and acknowledged or proved in like manner as a deed for the conveyance of real estate, and delivered to one of the parties or his attorney, any party to the arbitration may apply to any justice or judge aforesaid, for an order confirming the award; and thereupon said justice or judge must grant such an order, unless the award is vacated, modified or corrected, as prescribed in the next two sections. Notice in writing of the motion must be served upon the adverse party or his attorney five days before the hearing thereof.

9. In either of the following cases the justice or judge must make an order vacating the award, upon the application of any party to the arbitration:

(*a*) Where the award was procured by corruption, fraud or undue means.

(*b*) Where there was evident partiality or corruption in the arbitrators, or either of them.

(*c*) Where the arbitrators were guilty of misconduct, in refusing to postpone the hearing, upon sufficient cause shown, or in refusing to hear evidence, pertinent and material to the controversy; or of any other misbehaviors, by which the rights of any party have been prejudiced.

(*d*) Where the arbitrators exceeded their powers, or so imperfectly executed them, that a mutual, final and definite award, upon the subject matter submitted, was not made.

Where an award is vacated and the time, within which the agreement required the award to be made, has not expired, the court may, in its discretion, direct a rehearing by the arbitrators.

10. In either of the following cases the court must make an order modifying or correcting the award, upon the application of any party to the arbitration:

(*a*) Where there was an evident miscalculation of figures, or an evident mistake in the description of any person, thing or property, referred to in the award.

(*b*) Where the arbitrators have awarded upon a matter not submitted to them, unless it is a matter affecting the merits of the decision upon the matters submitted.

(*c*) Where the award is imperfect in a matter of form, not affecting the merits of the controversy.

The order must modify and correct the award, so as to effect the intent thereof, and promote justice between the parties.

11. Notice of a motion to vacate, modify or correct an award must be served upon the adverse party, or his attorney, within three months after award is filed or delivered as prescribed by law for service of notice of a motion in an action. For the purposes of the motion any judge who might make an order to stay the proceedings, in an action brought in the same court, may make an order to be served with the notice of motion

staying the proceedings of the adverse party to enforce the award.

12. Upon the granting of an order confirming, modifying, correcting an award, judgment may be entered in conformity therewith in the court wherein the justice or judge making the same sits.

13. The party moving for an order confirming, modifying or correcting an award shall at the time such order is filed with the clerk for the entry of judgment thereon, also file the following papers with the clerk:

(*a*) The submission; the selection or appointment, if any, of an additional arbitrator or umpire, and each written extension of the time, if any, within which to make the award.

(*b*) The award.

(*c*) Each notice, affidavit or other paper used upon an application to confirm, modify or correct the award, and a copy of each order made upon such an application.

The judgment may be docketed, as if it was rendered in an action.

14. The judgment so entered has the same force and effect in all respects, as, and is subject to all the provisions of law relating to, a judgment in an action; and it may be enforced as if it had been rendered in an action in the court in which it is entered.

15. An appeal may be taken from an order confirming, modifying, correcting or vacating an award, or from a judgment entered upon an award, as from an order of judgment in an action.

16. All acts and parts of acts inconsistent with this act are hereby repealed, and this act shall take effect on and after the fourth day of July next after its enactment, but shall not apply to contracts made prior to the taking effect thereof.

Approved March 21, 1923.

APPENDIX VII

Arbitration Law of Oregon

General Laws of Oregon, 1925, Chapter 186

AN ACT to provide for arbitration and award, and to prescribe the procedure, and to make awards effective.

BE IT ENACTED *by the People of the State of Oregon:*

Section 1. All persons desiring to settle by arbitration any controversy, suit or quarrel, except such as respect the title to real estate, may submit their differences to the award or umpirage of any person or persons mutually selected.

Section 2. Said agreement to arbitrate shall be in writing, signed by the parties, and may, at the option of the parties, be by bond in any sum, conditioned that the parties entering into said submission shall abide by the award.

Section 3. If any suit or proceeding be brought upon any issue arising out of an agreement which contains a provision for arbitration of the same matter in controversy in such suit or proceeding, then, upon application, any judge of a court of record, upon being satisfied that the issue involved in such suit or proceeding is referable to arbitration, shall abate the action so that arbitration may be had in accordance with the terms of the agreement; said application to be heard similarly to hearings on motions.

Section 4. If, in the arbitration agreement, no provision be made for the manner of selecting the arbitrators, or if, for any reason, there be a failure to act or a vacancy, and no provision in the agreement for the filling thereof, then, upon application of either party to the agreement, any court of record shall appoint such arbitrator or arbitrators or fill such vacancy, which appointee or appointees shall act under the said arbitration agreement with the same force and effect as if he or they had been specifically named therein.

Section 5. The said arbitrators shall be sworn to try and determine the cause referred to them and an award make out under the hands and seals of a majority of them, agreeable to the terms of the submission. Said award, together with the written agreement to submit, shall be delivered to the clerk of any court of record of the county wherein said arbitration is held, who shall enter the same of record in his office. A copy of the award, signed by said arbitrators, or a majority of them, shall also be delivered to each of the parties interested in the award, and if no exceptions be filed against the same within twenty (20) days after such service, judgment shall be entered as upon the verdict of a jury, and execution may issue thereon, and the same proceedings may be had upon said award with like effect as though said award were a verdict in a civil action.

Section 6. The compensation of arbitrators in all cases shall be governed by agreement between the parties to the arbitration, or in case of their inability to agree, then by any judge of a court of record.

Section 7. Within the period specified in section 5 the party against whom an award shall have been made may except in writing thereto for any of the following causes:

(*a*) That the arbitrators or umpire misbehaved in the case;

(*b*) That the arbitrators or umpire committed error in fact or law;

(*c*) That the award was procured by corruption or other undue means.

Section 8. If, upon exceptions filed, it shall appear to the court that the award should be vacated or modified, the court may refer the cause back to said arbitrators with proper instructions for correction or rehearing, and upon failure of the arbitrators to follow said instructions, the court shall have jurisdiction over the case and proceed to its determination.

Section 9. Whenever no objection is made to the entering of judgment after award, judgment shall be entered according to the award and shall have all the force and effect of a judgment obtained in a court of record in this state after default, but whenever any judgment is entered after objection on the part of any party by the order of such court, such judgment shall be subject to appeal to the same extent as if said judgment had been obtained after trial by a court of law.

Section 10. Arbitrators, or a majority of them, shall have power:

(*a*) To compel the attendance of witnesses duly notified by either party, and to enforce from either party the production of all such books, papers and documents as said arbitrators may deem material to the cause;

(*b*) To administer oaths or affirmations to witnesses;

(*c*) To adjourn their meetings from day to day, or for a longer time, and also from place to place, if they think proper;

(*d*) To decide both the law and the fact that may be involved in the cause submitted to them.

Section 11. Whenever, on motion of any arbitrator or party in interest, it shall be made to appear to the county or circuit court of the county in which any arbitration proceedings are pending, that any witness or party has refused to answer a subpoena or obey any lawful order of said arbitrator or arbitrators, said court may require such witness or party to show cause why he should not be punished for contempt of court, to the same extent and purpose as if the said proceedings were pending before said court.

Section 12. Unless otherwise agreed upon, the costs of witness fees and other fees in the case shall be taxed against the losing party, and such fees shall be indorsed upon the award, and when the award is confirmed as the judgment of the court of record, execution shall issue therefor as for costs in civil actions.

Section 13. All acts and parts of acts inconsistent with this act are hereby repealed.

Approved by the governor February 24, 1925.

Filed in the office of the secretary of state February 25, 1925.

APPENDIX VIII

Chapter 251 of the General Laws of Massachusetts as Amended by Chapter 294, Acts of 1925

An Act Relative to the Arbitration of Controversies between Parties to Contract

Section 1. Controversies which might be the subject of a personal action at law or of a suit in equity may be submitted to the decision of one or more arbitrators, as provided in this chapter.

Section 2. The parties in person or by their lawful agents or attorneys shall sign an agreement in substance as follows:

Know all men that   of hereby agree to submit the demand, a statement whereof is hereto annexed, (and all other demands between them, as the case may be), to the determination of   and   , the award of whom, or of a majority of whom, being made and reported within one year from this day to the superior court for the county of   , the judgment thereon shall be final; and if either of the parties neglects to appear before the arbitrators, after due notice given to him of the time and place appointed for hearing the parties, the arbitrators may proceed in his absence.

Dated this   day of   in the year

_____

_____

Section 3. If a specific demand is submitted to the exclusion of others, it shall be set forth in the statement annexed to the agreement, otherwise it shall not be necessary to annex any statement of a demand, and the submission may be of all demands between the parties or of all demands which either has against the other. The submission may be varied in this respect in any other manner, according to the agreement of the parties.

Section 4. An agreement to submit all demands shall include only such as might be the subject of a personal action at law or of a suit in equity.

Section 5. The time within which the award shall be made and reported may be varied according to the agreement of the parties, but no award made after the time fixed by the agreement shall have any legal effect, unless made upon a recommitment by the court to which it is reported.

Section 6. Neither party may revoke the submission without the consent of the other; and if either neglects to appear after due notice, the arbitrators may hear and determine the cause ex parte.

Section 7. All the arbitrators shall meet and hear the parties, but an award by a majority of them shall be valid, unless the concurrence of all is expressly required in the submission. In the case of the death of an arbitrator or of his inability or refusal to serve, the superior court shall, upon the application of either party, name an arbitrator in his stead.

Section 8. The award shall be delivered by one of the arbitrators to the court designated in the agreement, or shall be enclosed and sealed by the arbitrators and transmitted to the court, and shall remain sealed until opened by the clerk.

Section 9. The award may be returned at any time limited in the submission and the parties shall attend without any express notice for that purpose; but the court may require actual notice to be given to either party before it acts upon the award.

Section 10. The court shall have cognizance of the award in the same manner, and may proceed thereon, as if it had been made by referees appointed by a rule of court, and may accept, reject, or recommit it to the same arbitrators for a rehearing. When accepted and confirmed by the court, judgment shall be rendered thereon as upon a like award by referees.

Section 11. If there is no provision in the submission relative to costs and expenses, the arbitrators may make an award relative thereto, including compensation for their own services; but

APPENDICES

the court may reduce the charge for compensation. All expenses of arbitration under this chapter shall be borne by the parties.

Section 12. An appeal founded on matter of law apparent upon the record shall be allowed from any order or judgment of the superior court on an award made under this chapter; or a party aggrieved may bring a writ of error for any error in law or fact as in other cases. The supreme judicial court shall thereupon render such judgment as the court below ought to have rendered.

Section 13. Fees in court shall be the same as for like services relative to an award made under a rule of court.

Section 14. The parties to a contract may agree in writing that any controversy thereafter arising under the contract which might be the subject of a personal action at law or of a suit in equity shall be submitted to the decision of one or more arbitrators.

Section 15. Such an agreement may either name the arbitrator or arbitrators or may define the method by which an arbitrator or arbitrators may be chosen. In case of the death, inability or refusal to serve of any person so named, or in case the method of choosing arbitrators prescribed by the parties becomes impossible of performance because of the default of one of the parties or otherwise, or in case such agreement fails either to name or to provide a method for choosing an arbitrator or arbitrators, the superior court shall upon the application of either party, name an arbitrator or arbitrators.

Section 16. If a party to the contract be named as arbitrator, or the agent or agents or employee or employees of any one party to the contract be named in the contract or selected by the method therein defined as sole arbitrator or as a majority of the arbitrators under such an agreement, the provisions of sections fourteen to twenty-two, inclusive, shall not apply.

Section 17. The submission shall be made within six months, unless otherwise stipulated by the parties, but in no event within less than a reasonable time, after due notice by any party to the contract claiming the arbitration of any controversy thereunder.

Section 18. If any one of the parties neglects to appear before the arbitrators after due notice is given to him of the time and place appointed for hearing, the arbitrator or arbitrators shall proceed in his absence.

Section 19. The award of the arbitrator, or of a majority of the arbitrators, being made and reported to the superior court within one year from the date of the submission or within such further time as the court may upon the application of the arbitratrator or arbitrators allow, the judgment thereon shall be final.

Section 20. Any question of law may, and upon the request of all parties shall, be referred by the arbitrator or arbitrators to the court to which the report is to be made. Upon application by a party at any time before the award becomes final under section nineteen, the superior court may in its discretion instruct the arbitrator or arbitrators upon a question of substantive law.

Section 21. If any suit or proceeding be brought upon any issue referable to arbitration under an agreement in writing for such arbitration, the court in which such suit is pending, upon being satisfied that the issue involved in such suit or proceeding is referable to arbitration under such an agreement, shall on application of either the plaintiff or defendant stay the trial of the suit or proceeding until such arbitration has been had in accordance with the terms of the agreement; provided, that the applicant for the stay is ready and willing to submit to arbitration.

Section 22. Proceedings under sections fourteen to twenty-one, inclusive, shall be governed by the provisions of sections six to thirteen, inclusive, not inconsistent therewith.

Section 23. This act shall not apply to contracts made prior to the taking effect hereof. Approved April 29, 1925.

APPENDIX IX

UNITED STATES ARBITRATION ACT

PUBLIC—NO. 401—68TH CONGRESS

AN ACT TO MAKE VALID AND ENFORCEABLE WRITTEN PROVISIONS OR AGREEMENTS FOR ARBITRATION OF DISPUTES ARISING OUT OF CONTRACTS, MARITIME TRANSACTIONS, OR COMMERCE AMONG THE STATES OR TERRITORIES OR WITH FOREIGN NATIONS.

BE IT ENACTED *by the Senate and House of Representatives of the United States of America in Congress assembled,* That "maritime transactions," as herein defined, means charter parties, bills of lading of water carriers, agreements relating to wharfage, supplies furnished vessels or repairs to vessels, collisions, or any other matters in foreign commerce which, if the subject of controversy, would be embraced within admiralty jurisdiction; "commerce," as herein defined, means commerce among the several States or with foreign nations, or in any Territory of the United States or in the District of Columbia, or between any such Territory and another, or between any such Territory and any State or foreign nation, or between the District of Columbia and any State or Territory or foreign nation, but nothing herein contained shall apply to contracts of employment of seamen, railroad employees, or any other class of workers engaged in foreign or interstate commerce.

Section 2. That a written provision in any maritime transaction or a contract evidencing a transaction involving commerce to settle by arbitration a controversy thereafter arising out of such contract or transaction, or the refusal to perform the whole or any part thereof, or an agreement in writing to submit to arbitration an existing controversy arising out of such a contract, transaction, or refusal, shall be valid, irrevocable, and enforceable, save upon such grounds as exist at law or in equity for the revocation of any contract.

Section 3. That if any suit or proceeding be brought in any of the courts of the United States upon any issue referable to arbitration under an agreement in writing for such arbitration, the court in which such suit is pending, upon being satisfied that the issue involved in such suit or proceeding is referable to arbitration under such an agreement, shall on application of one of the parties stay the trial of the action until such arbitration has been had in accordance with the terms of the agreement, providing the applicant for the stay is not in default in proceeding with such arbitration.

Section 4. That a party aggrieved by the alleged failure, neglect, or refusal of another to arbitrate under a written agreement for arbitration may petition any court of the United States which, save for such agreement, would have jurisdiction under the judicial code at law, in equity, or in admiralty of the subject matter of a suit arising out of the controversy between the parties, for an order directing that such arbitration proceed in the manner provided for in such agreement. Five days' notice in writing of such application shall be served upon the party in default. Service thereof shall be made in the manner provided by law for the service of summons in the jurisdiction in which the proceeding is brought. The court shall hear the parties, and upon being satisfied that the making of the agreement for arbitration or the failure to comply therewith is not in issue, the court shall make an order directing the parties to proceed to arbitration in accordance with the terms of the agreement: *Provided,* That the hearing and proceedings under such agreement shall be within the district in which the petition for an order directing such arbitration is filed. If the making of the arbitration agreement or the failure, neglect, or refusal to perform the same be in issue, the court shall proceed summarily to the trial thereof. If no jury trial be demanded by the party alleged to be in default, or if the matter in dispute is within admiralty jurisdiction, the court shall hear and determine such issue. Where such an issue is raised, the party alleged to be in default may, except in cases of admiralty, on or before the return day of the notice of application, demand a jury trial of such issue, and upon such demand the court shall make an order referring the issue or issues to a jury in the manner provided by law for referring to a jury issues in an equity action, or may specially call a jury for that purpose. If the jury find that no agreement in writing for arbitration was made or that there is no default in proceeding thereunder, the proceeding shall be dismissed. If the jury find that an agreement for arbitration was made in writing and that there is a default in proceeding thereunder, the court shall make an order summarily directing the parties to proceed with the arbitration in accordance with the terms thereof.

Section 5. That if in the agreement provision be made for a method of naming or appointing an arbitrator or arbitrators or an umpire, such method shall be followed; but if no method be provided therein, or if a method be provided and any party thereto shall fail to avail himself of such method, or if for any other reason there shall be a lapse in the naming of an arbitrator or arbitrators or umpire, or in filling a vacancy, then upon the application of either party to the controversy the court shall designate and appoint an arbitrator or arbitrators or umpire, as the case may require, who shall act under the said agreement with the same force and effect as if he or they had been specifically named therein; and unless otherwise provided in the agreement the arbitration shall be by a single arbitrator.

Section 6. That any application to the court hereunder shall be made and heard in the manner provided by law for the making and hearing of motions, except as otherwise herein expressly provided.

Section 7. That the arbitrators selected either as prescribed in this Act or otherwise, or a majority of them, may summon in writing any person to attend before them or any of them as a witness and in a proper case to bring with him or them any book, record, document, or paper which may be deemed material as evidence in the case. The fees for such attendance shall be the same as the fees of witnesses before masters of the United States courts. Said summons shall issue in the name of the arbitrator or abitrators, or a majority of them, and shall be signed by the arbitrators, or a majority of them, and shall be directed to the said person and shall be served in the same manner as subpœnas to appear and testify before the court; if any person or persons so summoned to testify shall refuse or neglect to obey said summons, upon petition the United States court in and for the district in which such arbitrators, or a majority of them, are sitting may compel the attendance of such person or persons before said arbitrator or arbitrators, or punish said person or persons for contempt in the same manner now provided for securing the attendance of witnesses or their punishment for neglect or refusal to attend in the courts of the United States.

Section 8. That if the basis of jurisdiction be a cause of action otherwise justiciable in admiralty, then, notwithstanding anything herein to the contrary, the party claiming to be aggrieved may begin his proceeding hereunder by libel and seizure of the vessel or other property of the other party according to the usual course of admiralty proceedings, and the court shall then have jurisdiction to direct the parties to proceed with the arbitration and shall retain jurisdiction to enter its decree upon the award.

Section 9. If the parties in their agreement have agreed that a judgment of the court shall be entered upon the award made pursuant to the arbitration, and shall specify the court, then at any time within one year after the award is made any party to the arbitration may apply to the court so specified for an order confirming the award, and thereupon the court must grant such an order unless the award is vacated, modified, or corrected as prescribed in the next two sections. If no court is specified in the agreement of the parties, then such application may be made to the United States court in and for the district within which such award was made. Notice of the application shall be served upon the adverse party, and thereupon the court shall have jurisdiction of such party as though he had appeared generally in the proceeding. If the adverse party is a resident of the district within which the award was made, such service shall be made upon the adverse party or his attorney as prescribed by law for service of notice of motion in an action in the same court. If the adverse party shall be a nonresident, then the notice of the application shall be served by the marshal of any district within which the adverse party may be found in like manner as other process of the court.

Section 10. That in either of the following cases the United States court in and for the district wherein the award was made may make an order vacating the award upon the application of any party to the arbitration—

(*a*) Where the award was procured by corruption, fraud, or undue means.

(*b*) Where there was evident partiality or corruption in the arbitrators, or either of them.

(*c*) Where the arbitrators were guilty of misconduct in refusing to postpone the hearing, upon sufficient cause shown, or in refusing to hear evidence pertinent and material to the controversy; or of any other misbehavior by which the rights of any party have been prejudiced.

(*d*) Where the arbitrators exceeded their powers, or so imperfectly executed them that a mutual, final, and definite award upon the subject matter submitted was not made.

(*e*) Where an award is vacated and the time within which the agreement required the award to be made has not expired the court may, in its discretion, direct a rehearing by the arbitrators.

Section 11. That in either of the following cases the United States court in and for the district wherein the award was made may make an order modifying or correcting the award upon the application of any party to the arbitration—

(*a*) Where there was an evident material miscalculation of figures or an evident material mistake in the description of any person, thing, or property referred to in the award.

(*b*) Where the arbitrators have awarded upon a matter not submitted to them, unless it is a matter not affecting the merits of the decision upon the matters submitted.

(*c*) Where the award is imperfect in matter of form not affecting the merits of the controversy.

The order may modify and correct the award, so as to effect the intent thereof and promote justice between the parties.

Section 12. That notice of a motion to vacate, modify, or correct an award must be served upon the adverse party or his attorney within three months after the award is filed or delivered. If the adverse party is a resident of the district within which the award was made, such service shall be made upon the adverse party or his attorney as prescribed by law for service of notice of motion in an action in the same court. If the adverse party shall be a nonresident then the notice of application shall be served by the marshal of any district within which the adverse party may be found in like manner as other process of the court. For the purposes of the motion any judge who might make an order to stay the proceedings in an action brought in the same court may make an order, to be served with the notice of motion, staying the proceedings of the adverse party to enforce the award.

Section 13. That the party moving for an order confirming, modifying, or correcting an award shall, at the time such order is filed with the clerk for the entry of judgment thereon, also file the following papers with the clerk:

(*a*) The agreement; the selection or appointment, if any, of an additional arbitrator or umpire; and each written extension of the time, if any, within which to make the award.

(*b*) The award.

(*c*) Each notice, affidavit, or other paper used upon an application to confirm, modify, or correct the award, and a copy of each order of the court upon such an application.

The judgment shall be docketed as if it was rendered in an action.

The judgment so entered shall have the same force and effect, in all respects, as, and be subject to all the provisions of law relating to, a judgment in an action; and it may be enforced as if it had been rendered in an action in the court in which it is entered.

Section 14. That this Act may be referred to as "The United States Arbitration Act."

Section 15. That all Acts and parts of Acts inconsistent with this Act are hereby repealed, and this Act shall take effect on and after the 1st day of January next after its enactment, but shall not apply to contracts made prior to the taking effect of this Act.

Approved, February 12, 1925.

APPENDIX X

The Hart Schaffner & Marx Labor Agreement
(Revised to 1922-1925)

PREAMBLE

BY THE CHAIRMAN OF THE BOARD OF ARBITRATION, 1916

The parties whose names are signed hereto purpose entering into an agreement for collective bargaining with the intention of agreeing on wage and working conditions and to provide a method for adjusting any differences that may arise during the term of this contract.

In order that those who have to interpret this instrument may have some guide as to the intentions and expectations of the parties when entering into this compact, they herewith make record of their spirit and purpose, their hope and expectations, so far as they are now able to forecast or state them.

On the part of the employer it is the intention and expectation that this compact of peace will result in the establishment and maintenance of a high order of discipline and efficiency by the willing co-operation of union and workers rather than by the old method of surveillance and coercion; that by the exercise of this discipline all stoppages and interruptions of work, and all wilful violations of rules will cease; that good standards of workmanship and conduct will be maintained and a proper quantity, quality and cost of production will be assured; and that out of its operation will issue such co-operation and good will between employers, foremen, union and workers as will prevent misunderstanding and friction and make for good team work, good business, mutual advantage and mutual respect.

On the part of the union it is the intention and expectation that this compact will, with the co-operation of the employer, operate in such a way as to maintain, strengthen, and solidify its organization, so that it may be made strong enough, and efficient enough, to co-operate as contemplated in the preceding paragraph; and also that it may be strong enough to command the respect of the employer without being forced to resort to militant or unfriendly measures.

On the part of the workers it is the intention and expectation that they pass from the status of wage servants, with no claim on the employer save his economic need, to that of self-respecting parties to an agreement which they have had an equal part with him in making; that this status gives them an assurance of fair and just treatment and protects them against injustice or oppression of those who may have been placed in authority over them; that they will have recourse to a court, in the creation of which their votes were equally potent with that of the employer, in which all their grievances may be heard, and all their claims adjudicated; that all changes during the life of the pact shall be subject to the approval of an impartial tribunal, and that wages and working conditions shall not fall below the level provided for in the agreement.

The parties to this pact realize that the interests sought to be reconciled herein will tend to pull apart, but they enter it in the faith that by the exercise of the co-operative and constructive spirit it will be possible to bring and keep them together. This will involve as an indispensable pre-requisite the total suppression of the militant spirit by both parties and the development of reason instead of force as the rule of action. It will require also mutual consideration and concession, a willingness on the part of each party to regard and serve the interests of the other, so far as it can be done without too great a sacrifice of principle or interest. With this attitude assured it is believed no differences can arise which the joint tribunal cannot mediate and resolve in the interest of co-operation and harmony.

Text of Agreement

SECTION I

1. *Administration.*—This agreement is entered into between Hart Schaffner & Marx, a corporation, and the Amalgamated

Clothing Workers of America, and is effective from May 1st, 1922, to April 30th, 1925. [Subsequently extended and still in force.]

2. *The Old Agreement.*—The provision of the old agreement and the decisions based thereon shall be regarded as being in force except as they may be modified by, or are not in conflict with the provisions of the present agreement. This agreement shall cover and apply only to those occupations which were covered by the former agreement and to which said agreement was applicable at the time of its expiration.

3. *Officers of the Agreement.*—The administration of this agreement is vested in a Board of Arbitration and a Trade Board, together with such deputies, officials and representatives of the parties hereto as are now or hereafter may be appointed for that purpose, whose duties and powers are hereinafter described.

4. *Board of Arbitration.*—The Board of Arbitration shall consist of a chairman who shall be the mutual choice of the two parties, and should issue arise which in the opinion of the parties to the agreement require the enlargement of the Board, two members may be appointed, either by the parties joining in the selection of such additional members or by each of the parties naming a member.

5. It shall be the function of the Board of Arbitration to hear appeals from the Trade Board, and make application of the agreement to any questions coming before it, but said Board of Arbitration shall have no power to add to the terms of the agreement or to enlarge its scope.

6. The salaries of the Chairman of the Trade Board and the Chairman of the Board of Arbitration and the other expenses incident to maintaining their offices shall be borne jointly by the two parties to the agreement.

7. The duties and jurisdiction of the Trade Board and the Board of Arbitration are fixed and limited by this agreement and neither of said Boards shall have any power to enlarge such jurisdiction, unless by mutual consent of the two parties to the agreement.

8. It shall be the duty of the Board of Arbitration to investigate, and to mediate or adjudicate all matters that are brought

before it and to do all in its power to insure the successful working of the agreement. In reaching its decisions the Board is expected to have regard to the general principles of the agreement; the spirit and intent, expressed or implied, of the parties thereto; and, especially, the necessity of making the instrument workable, and adaptable to varying needs and conditions, while conserving as fully as possible the essential interests of the parties involved.

9. The line of practice already developed by the Board shall be continued. This contemplates that questions of fact and testimony shall in the main be considered by the Trade Board while the Board of Arbitration will concern itself mainly with questions of principle and the application of the agreement to new issues as they arise.

10. *Trade Board.*—The Trade Board is the primary board for adjusting grievances, and shall have original jurisdiction over all matters arising under this agreement and the decisions relating thereto, and shall consider and dispose of all such matters when regularly brought before it, subject to such rules of practice and procedure as are now or may be hereafter established.

11. The Trade Board shall consist of a chairman who shall represent the mutual interests of both parties hereto, and especially the interest of the successful working of this agreement. He shall endeavor to mediate conflicting interests, shall hear and decide, without unnecessary delay, all petitions and complaints filed in the proper manner by the deputies of either side. He shall also act as chairman of the cutting room commission, and perform such other duties as may be required of him by the agreement or by the Board of Arbitration.

12. The chairman shall hold office during the term of the agreement, and in case of death, resignation, or inability to act, the vacancy shall be filled by the parties thereto. It is especially agreed that James Mullenbach, chairman under the former agreement, shall be retained under the present agreement.

13. *Deputies.*—The deputies are the officers having direct charge of the execution of the provisions of this agreement in the interest of their respective principals. Each of the parties hereto shall have a sufficient number of deputies to properly

take care of the work necessary to be done to keep the docket from being clogged with complaints, and to insure an efficient working of the agreement. They shall have power to investigate, mediate, and adjust complaints, and settlements made by the deputies of the parties in dispute shall be binding on their principals unless reversed or modified by either of the trial boards. In case of appeal to the Trade Board or Board of Arbitration the deputies may represent their respective principals before these Boards, and shall have power to summon and examine witnesses, to present testimony or evidence, and do such other things as may be necessary to place their case properly before the trial body, and such body shall see to it that they be given adequate opportunity and facility for such presentation, subject to the usual rules of procedure.

14. The union deputy shall have access to any shop or factory for the purpose of making investigations of complaints; but he shall in all cases be accompanied by the representative of the employer. Provided, that the latter may at his option waive his right to accompany him; also that in minor matters where convenience or expedition may be served the union deputy may call out the shop chairman to obtain information without such waiver.

15. The deputies shall be available to give their duties prompt and adequate attention, and shall be subject to the direction of the Trade Board in all matters relating to the administration of this agreement.

16. *Qualification of Deputies.*—Each deputy, in order to qualify for duty, must have a commission signed by the proper official representing the union or the company, and said commission must be countersigned by the chairman of the Trade Board. Deputies must be either employes of Hart Schaffner & Marx, or must be persons who are connected with the Chicago Joint Board of the Amalgamated Clothing Workers of America who have been employed by Hart Schaffner & Marx.

17. *Shop Representative.*—The union shall have in each shop a duly accredited representative authorized by the Joint Board who shall be recognized as the officer of the union having charge of complaints and organization matters within the shop. He may

have an alternate to act in his absence, who, when not functioning in this manner, shall have no immunity or privilege as an official.

18. He shall be empowered to receive complaints and be given sufficient opportunity and range of action to enable him to make proper inquiry concerning them. When necessary for the shop representative to leave his place to investigate complaints the foreman may, if he deems it necessary, ask to be informed of the purpose of his movements, and the representative shall comply with his request.

19. It is understood the shop representative shall be entitled to collect dues and perform such other duties as may be imposed on him by the union, provided they be performed in such manner as not to interfere with shop discipline and efficiency.

20. The head chairman of the factory and one chairman in each shop or floor shall be subject to discipline only by the Trade Board, or the Board of Arbitration. The labor department may report any misconduct or unsatisfactory behavior to the chairman of the Trade Board, who shall order an investigation or personally investigate the matter with the deputies of both parties and render a decision on the merit of each case as promptly as possible.

21. It is expected that he will represent the co-operative spirit of the agreement in the shop, and shall be the leader in promoting that amity and spirit of good will which it is the purpose of this instrument to establish.

22. The co-operative spirit enjoined on the shop representative in the foregoing paragraph shall be expected in equal degree from the shop superintendent, who shall be expected to contribute his best efforts to promote harmony and good will in the shops.

SECTION II
PROCEDURE

1. *When Grievances Arise.*—When a grievance arises on the floor of the shop, the complainant shall report it with reasonable promptness to the shop representative, who shall present it without undue delay to the shop superintendent, or to the repre-

sentative of the labor department when there is one in the shop. These two may discuss the complaint in a judicial temper, and may endeavor to agree to an adjustment. It is understood, however, that they are not a trial board, and it is not expected that they shall argue or dispute over the case. In the event that the shop representative is not satisfied with the action of the superintendent, or the representative of the labor department, he may promptly report the matter to his deputy with such information as will enable him to deal advisedly with the case. Failure to comply with these provisions for the regulation of shop transactions shall subject the offender to discipline by the Trade Board.

2. Informal oral adjustments made by shop officials are subject to revision by the Trade Board, and are not binding on their principals unless ratified by the deputies.

3. *Adjustment by Deputies.*—When the shop officers report a disputed complaint to their respective deputies, they shall give it such investigation as its nature or importance demands, either by visitation to the shop or by the taking of testimony, and shall make an earnest endeavor to reach a settlement that will be just and satisfactory to all the parties in dispute.

4. *Disagreement by Deputies.*—In the event of a failure to agree on an adjustment, the deputies shall certify the case for trial to the Trade Board, agreeing on a written statement of facts if possible. In certifying such disagreement the deputy appealing to the Board shall file a statement stating specifically the nature of the complaint alleged with the Trade Board, and shall furnish a copy to the representative of the dissenting party who shall have, at least, twenty-four hours to prepare his answer, unless otherwise agreed on; provided, that by direction of the chairman of the Trade Board emergency cases may be brought to trial at once. Where no statement has been filed in writing within a reasonable time after disagreement of the deputies, it may be assumed that the disagreement no longer exists, and the case may be considered settled.

5. *Docket and Records.*—The chairman of the Trade Board shall keep a docket in which all cases shall be heard in the order of their filing. Duplicate records shall be made by the Board,

one copy of which shall be retained by the Chairman, and copies given to the deputies representing both parties. Such records shall contain all complaints filed with the Board; orders or decisions of the Board, or of the deputies or of any committee; calendars of pending cases, and such other matter as the Trade Board may order placed upon the records.

6. It is the purpose of this agreement to provide a practicable method for the adjustment of all disputes with a minimum of disturbance of the routine of work. When any complaint or dispute arises, therefore, it is the duty of every employe to refrain from any action such as insubordination, stoppage, etc., which is likely to interfere with the routine of work; he is expected to use diligence in communicating the matter to the shop chairman.

7. *Direct Complaints.*—Complaints may be made directly by either party, without the intervention of a shop representative, whenever it desires to avail itself of the protection of the agreement; but a statement of the facts and grounds of such complaints must be filed in writing as hereinbefore provided. Unless written notice has been filed, it may be presumed, officially, that no complaint exists.

8. *Decisions, Appeals, Etc.*—All decisions of the Trade Board shall be in writing, and copies given to the representatives of each party. Should either party desire to appeal from the decision, it shall file with the Board a notice of its intention so to do within ten days of the date of the decision. Or if either party desires an amendment or modification of the decision, or a stay of execution pending the appeal, it may make a motion in writing to that effect, and the chairman shall use his discretion in granting it. In certifying the case to the Board of Arbitration, the chairman shall make a summary of the case in writing, giving the main facts and the grounds for his decision.

9. *Hearing, How Conducted.*—The chairman shall determine the time and place of meeting and shall notify all the parties in interest. Each party shall prepare the case in advance, and have its testimony, evidence, and facts in readiness for the hearing. The Board shall give each party ample opportunity to present its case, but shall be the judge of procedure and shall

direct the hearing as to its order and course. After giving an adequate hearing of the evidence and arguments the Board shall render its decision in writing, and shall furnish copies to the deputies of each party and to the chairman of the Trade Board. In the event that the Board is unable to reach a unanimous decision, the decision of a majority shall be binding.

10. *Motions for Rehearing.*—The Board may after a reasonable time grant a rehearing of any decision, if, in its judgment, there appear sufficient reasons for doing so. Decisions are to be regarded as the Board's best solution of the problem offered to it at the time of hearing, but as the problem changes with time and experience it is proper there should be afforded a reasonable opportunity for rehearing and review. Motions for a rehearing shall be made in writing, and shall set forth the reason for the request.

11. *Enforcement of Decisions.*—All decisions, whether of deputies, Trade Board, or Board of Arbitration, shall be put into execution within a reasonable time, and failure to do so, unless for explainable cause, shall convict the delinquent party of disloyalty to the agreement. The party in error shall be notified of the charge, and suitable discipline imposed by the Trade Board. The deputies of each party shall be held responsible in the first instance, for enforcement of decisions or adjustments herein referred to, and shall be held answerable, primarily, to the Trade Board.

Unemployment.—The union serves notice that it may prior to May 1st, 1923, bring up the question of unemployment, and reserves the right to terminate the agreement on that date if no mutually satisfactory understanding on the subject of unemployment, either a definite plan in detail or an agreement to arbitrate, is reached before May 1st, 1923.

SECTION III

1. *Wages and Hours.*—The standards of wages existing on and after May 1st, 1922, and hereby established by this agreement shall be effective until April 30, 1925, provided, however, that if either party shall become convinced that a change in

wage standards is warranted, it may give notice to that effect not later than ninety days prior to the anniversary of the date of this agreement, and call for a conference on such change. If any change shall be agreed upon, it shall become effective on such anniversary date. If, after a thorough canvass of the situation, the parties find themselves unable to agree on wages before the anniversary date, the matter shall be referred to the Board of Arbitration in the regular way, unless the parties shall have agreed upon a different method, and any wage either so agreed upon or so fixed shall remain effective until the next anniversary date.

2. *Hours of Work.*—The hours of work in the tailor shop shall be forty-four per week, with the Saturday half-holiday.

3. *Overtime.*—For work done in excess of the regular hours per day, overtime shall be paid to piece workers, 50 per cent in addition to their piece work rates; to the week workers at the rate of time and a half; no work shall be allowed on Sundays or the following holidays: Christmas, New Year's, Decoration Day, Fourth of July, Labor Day and Thanksgiving Day.

4. *Piece Rate Committee.*—Whenever a change of piece rate is contemplated the matter shall be referred to a specially appointed rate committee who shall fix the rate according to the change of work. If the committee disagree the Trade Board shall fix the rate. In fixing the rates, the Board is restricted to the following rule: Changed rates must correspond to the changed work and new rates must be based upon old rates where possible.

5. New rates are always provisional and temporary, unless otherwise agreed and specified and are subject to review after sufficient period of trial to determine their merit. However, they should be set as nearly equitable as possible.

6. From May 1st, 1922, all agreements, contracts or decisions made, approved or revised by the rate committee or the Trade Board, shall be in writing and shall not be altered by custom or usage, but shall be enforced at all times by the Trade Board. If any complaint arise in the application of any specification, the rate committee shall be promptly notified and shall immediately adjust it or refer it to the chairman of the Trade Board for a speedy settlement. Specifications shall be made

uniform in every detail for all the regular shops and shall so be applied as far as possible without injuring the interest of either party.

7. *Hour Rates for Piece Workers.*—In case workers are changed from piece to hour work, the hour rates for such piece workers shall be based on their earnings on piece work.

In arriving at a basis for hour work, the company shall take the nearest four full weeks of piece work from the time of price fixing as drawn by the work of the section in which the rate is to be fixed, and shall take the average of the piece-work earnings of the individual concerned during that period and base his hour work on such average piece-work earnings.

In case four full weeks of 44 hours cannot be found in the section concerned in the year next preceding the date of price fixing, then the company shall take the four fullest weeks that can be found in the section during that period, and derive the hour rate of the worker from these weeks. Provided, however, that in no case shall the weeks taken as a basis contain less than an average of 44 hours of regular work.

In case this worker has not worked for the company for a sufficient period to have established a piece-work average under the foregoing provision, his hour rate shall be based on the nearest weeks that will afford a just average, or upon his piece work in the current week.

The company shall not be required to figure a worker's hour-work rate oftener than once in three months, except in exceptional circumstances, or unless the worker has been employed by the company for less than three months.

The intention of this provision is not to institute a rigid rule, but to provide a general working scheme to afford speedy and satisfactory action for cases as they arise, and if it is found not to result in substantial justice in every case, it is expected that such cases shall be submitted to the Trade Board. The purpose is to base hour work on full time piece work, and to avoid, as far as possible, including slack work periods of piece work on the hour-work rate.

Changing Operations.—In the event a piece worker is required to change his mode of operation so that it causes him to lose time in learning, his case may be brought to the Rate Committee for its disposition.

SECTION IV
PREFERENCE

1. *The Preferential Shop.*—It is agreed that the principle of the preferential shop shall prevail, to be applied in the following manner:

Preference shall be applied in hiring and discharge. Whenever the employer needs additional workers, he shall first make application to the union, specifying the number and kind of workers needed. The union shall be given a reasonable time to supply the specified help, and if it is unable, or for any reason fails to furnish the required people, the employer shall be at liberty to secure them in the open market as best he can.

In like manner, the principle of preference shall be applied in case of discharge. Should it at any time become necessary to reduce the force in conformity with the provisions of this agreement, the first ones to be dismissed shall be those who are not members of the union in good and regular standing.

2. *Overcrowding of Sections.*—Overcrowding of sections is important in this agreement as the point at which the provision for preference becomes operative. It is agreed that when there are too many workers in a section to permit of reasonably steady employment, a complaint may be lodged by the union, and if proved, the non-union members of the section, or as many of them as may be required to give the needed relief, shall be dismissed. For the purpose of judging the application of preference the Trade Board shall take into consideraton the actual employment condition in the section, as to whether there are more people employed at the time of complaint than are needed to do the work, and whether they, or any of them, can be spared without substantial injury to the company. If it is found that the section can be reduced without substantial injury, the Trade Board shall enforce the principle of preference as contemplated in the agreement.

3. *Preference in Transfers.*—If it becomes necessary to transfer workers from one shop to another, the non-union workers

shall be the first to be transferred, unless, at the request of the foreman, union workers are willing to go.

Or if it becomes necessary in the judgment of the company to transfer a worker from a lower to a higher paid section or operation, it is agreed that union workers shall have preference in such transfers. Provided, that nothing herein shall be construed to be in conflict with the provision relating to transfer for discipline, and provided that they are qualified to perform the work required and that their departure from their section does not work to the disadvantage of that section.

4. *Avoidance of Injury.*—Among the things to be considered in the enforcement of preference are the needs of maintaining an adequate balance of sections, of the requirements of the busy season, of the difficulty of hiring substitutes, and the risk of impairing the efficiency of the organization. The claims for enforcement of preference and for avoidance of injury to the manufacturing organization are to be weighed by the Trade Board, and the interests of both claims safeguarded as far as possible, the intention being to enforce preference so far as it can be done without inflicting substantial injury on the company.

5. *Preference of Seniority.*—If in order to properly balance sections, a reduction of force be required greater than can be secured by the laying off of a non-union worker as provided for herein, then there may be laid off those who are members of the union in the order of their seniority who have been in the employ of the company for a period of six months or less, provided that any exceptionally efficient workers, or any especially valuable member of the union, may be exempted from the rule of seniority. Provided, also, the company shall give notice to the deputy of its intention to discharge under this clause, and if he fails to agree, the matter shall be referred to the Trade Board.

SECTION V

WORKING CONDITIONS

1. *Discipline.*—The full power of discharge and discipline remains with the company and its agents; but it is understood that this power should be exercised with justice and with due

regard to the reasonable rights of the employe, and, if an employe feels that he has been unjustly discharged, he may have appeal to the Trade Board, which shall have the power to review the case.

2. Every person suspended shall receive a written notice, directing him to appear at the office of the company for a decision. Every suspension notice properly presented to the discipline officer of the company must be disposed of within six working hours from the time of its presentation and a definite decision announced to the suspended person.

3. *Stoppages.*—This agreement provides for an orderly adjustment of differences, and there is no provocation for direct action. Stoppages are, therefore, prohibited. If, however, a stoppage shall occur because the person in charge shall have refused to allow the employes to continue work, he shall be ordered to give work immediately to the employes, or in case the employes have stopped work, the respective representatives of the employes shall order the employes to return to work immediately, and in case they fail to do so within one hour after being ordered, any or all of the participants in or instigators of the stoppage shall be liable to discipline.

4. *Detention in Shop.*—Workers shall not be detained in the shops when there is insufficient work for them. The company or its agent shall exercise due foresight in calculating the work available, and as far as practicable shall call only enough workers into the factory to do the work at sight. And if a greater number report for work than there is work for, those in excess of the number required shall be promptly notified and permitted to leave the shop. The work on hand shall be divided as equally as may be between the remaining workers.

The company and the deputies have agreed to co-operate together to abolish all unnecessary waiting in the shops.

5. *Transfer of Employes.*—The company has the right to transfer employes for purposes of administration or discipline, subject to review by the Trade Board. If the Board finds that any transfer is being made to lower wages, or for any discrimination or improper purpose, or if injustice is being done the worker by the transfer, the Board may adjust the complaint.

SECTION VI
General Provisions

1. *Lay-Off of Workers.*—No member of the union who is a permanent worker shall be laid off in the tailor shops, except for cause, whether in the slack or busy season, it being distinctly understood, however, that it shall be sufficient cause for a temporary lay-off if the same is due to alternation of working periods in slack times, or to reorganization of sections or lawful discipline, or any other cause provided for in this agreement, or as may be held sufficient by the Trade Board.

2. *Division of Work.*—During the slack season, if any, the work shall be divided as near as is practicable among the union employes.

3. *Abandonment of Position.*—Whenever any employe shall have absented himself from his accustomed place without giving an acceptable reason to the foreman or other officers in charge of his work before the end of the second business day of his absence, the employer may consider his position forfeited. Notice of absence and reason therefor must be given to foreman by messenger, mail or telephone.

4. *Abolishment of Section.*—When sections are abolished, the company and its agents shall use every effort to give the displaced workers employment as much as possible like the work from which they were displaced, within a reasonable time.

5. *Sickness.*—Any workers who are absent on account of sickness shall be reinstated in their former positions if they return within a reasonable time.

6. *Union Membership.*—The provisions for preference made herein require that the door of the union be kept open for the reception of non-union workers. Initiation fee and dues must be maintained at a reasonable rate, and any applicant must be admitted who is not an offender against the union and who is eligible for membership under its rules. Provided, that if any rules be passed that impose an unreasonable hardship, or that operate to bar desirable persons, the matter may be brought before the Trade Board or Board of Arbitration for such remedy as it may deem advisable.

SECTION VII
Loyalty to the Agreement

Experience suggests that there are certain points of strain which it would be wise to recognize in advance and to safeguard as far as possible. Among the points to be safeguarded are the following:

1. When dissatisfaction arises over change of price or working conditions. It is believed that the agreement provides a remedy for every such grievance that can arise, and all complainants are urged and expected to present their cases to the proper officials and await an adjustment. If any one refuses to do this, and instead takes the law in his own hands by inciting a stoppage or otherwise foments dissatisfaction or rebellion, he shall, if convicted, be adjudged guilty of disloyalty to the agreement and be subject to discipline by the Trade Board.

2. Strain may arise because of unsatisfactory personal relations between workers and officials. The company's officials are subject to the law as are the workers, and equally responsible for loyalty in word and deed (and are subject to discipline if found guilty of violation). Any complaints against them must be made and adjudicated in the regular manner. They are to respect the workers and be respected by them in their positions, and supported in the proper discharge of their duties. Any one indulging in improper language or conduct calculated to injure them or to break down their authority in the shop shall be adjudged guilty of disloyalty and disciplined accordingly.

3. Officials of the union are equally under the protection of the agreement when in the exercise of their duties as are the officials of the company, and any words or acts tending to discredit them or the union which they represent, or which are calculated to injure the influence or standing of the union or its representatives shall be considered as disloyalty to the agreement and the offender shall be subject to discipline by the Trade Board. Provided, however, that no reasonable criticism or expression of disagreement expressed in proper language shall be deemed a violation within the meaning of this section.

4. If any worker shall wilfully violate the spirit of the agreement by intentional opposition to its fundamental purposes and especially if he carry such wilful violation into action by striking and inciting others to strike or stop work during working hours, he shall, if charge is proven, be subject to suspension, discharge or fine. (Provided, that if a fine is imposed its amount shall be determined by the chairman of the Trade Board and shall not be less than $1.00 or more than $5.00 for each offense.)

SECTION VIII

Cutters.—The wages of cutters working under the standards established pursuant to the April, 1921, decision of the Board of Arbitration shall be as follows:

Group A	$47.00
Group B	45.00
Group C	43.00
Group D	41.00
Group E	39.00

If there are cutters whose production is so exceptional as to preclude classification as above, an appropriate compensation may be fixed by agreement between the parties, with reference to the Trade Board in case of disagreement. Otherwise unclassified cutters shall receive the same compensation as Class C cutters.

The length of service feature of the April, 1921, decision is discontinued.

The Board of Arbitration and Trade Board are hereby charged with the responsibility of placing cutting and trimming under standards of output and wages wherever practicable and without undue delay.

HART SCHAFFNER & MARX,
 By Earl Dean Howard, *Labor Manager*.

THE AMALGAMATED CLOTHING WORKERS OF AMERICA,
 By Sidney Hillman, *President*.

APPENDIX XI

Anthracite Agreement of February, 17, 1926 [1]

This agreement, made this 17th day of February, 1926, between Districts 1, 7 and 9, United Mine Workers of America, parties of the first part, and the Anthracite Operators, parties of the second part, covering wages and conditions of employment in the Anthracite coal fields of Pennsylvania, witnesseth:

1. Work shall be resumed at once under the terms of the expired contract which, subject to modification as hereinafter provided, shall be in force and effect until August 31, 1930.

2. At any time after January 1, 1927, but not oftener than once in any year, either party may, in writing, propose modifications in the wage scales of said contract. The parties agree within fifteen days after receipt of such written proposals, to start conferences in the usual manner in an effort to agree upon such modifications.

3. If within thirty days after starting such negotiations, the parties have not agreed, all issues in controversy shall be referred to a board of two men with full power and without reservations or restrictions; and the parties agree to abide by any decision or decisions of such Board, either on the merits of the controversy or as to procedure to be followed. Such Board shall be appointed as follows:

The Operators shall name three men and the Miners shall name three men. The Operators shall select one man from the Miners' list and the Miners shall select one man from the Operators' list, and the two men so approved shall constitute said Board. Unless otherwise agreed, the men named by the parties

---

[1] For the full terms of the agreements now covering anthracite coal mining see Birdseye's Abbott's *Encyclopædia of General Business and Legal Forms,* pp. 1358-1368. As to bituminous coal mining, see *ibid.*, pp. 1368-1389.

shall not be connected with the United Mine Workers of America or the business of mining coal. The Board shall be obligated, within ninety days after appointment, to arrive at a decision on all issues in controversy, and to that end shall formulate their own rules and methods of procedure and may enlarge the Board to an odd number, in which event a majority vote shall be binding.

4. The demands of the Operators and the Mine Workers on the question of co-operation and efficiency are referred to the Board of Conciliation, exclusive of the Umpire, which shall work out a reciprocal program of co-operation and efficiency.

5. The Board of Conciliation shall proceed to equalize wages, etc., in accordance with clause twelve (12) of the agreement dated September 19, 1923.

6. Except as modified herein, the terms and provisions of the Award of the Anthracite Coal Strike Commission and subsequent agreements made in modification thereof or supplemental thereto, as well as the rulings and decisions of the Board of Conciliation, are hereby ratified, confirmed and continued during the term of this contract, ending August 31, 1930.

IN WITNESS WHEREOF, etc.

APPENDIX XII

Suggestions to Chambers of Commerce, Trade Associations and Other Bodies for Plan for Offering Arbitration Facilities to Members and Non-Members

This subject presents itself in two forms: (1) the plan for a trade association or exchange or other commercial body whose members deal directly with each other in homogeneous commodities, products or securities; and (2) chambers of commerce, commercial or Kiwanis and similar clubs and other civic organizations that set up such tribunals for the benefit of any who may choose to use them.

(1) An exchange, board of trade or trade association usually creates an arbitration committee by its constitution or by-laws.[1]

(2) Below are given the uniform rules proposed by the New Jersey State Chamber of Commerce, 20 Clinton St., Newark, New Jersey, for the organization of a board of arbitration and the conduct of arbitrations thereby.

For submissions, awards and other forms connected with the actual conduct of the arbitration see below.

Uniform Arbitration Rules of New Jersey [2]

ORGANIZATION AND FUNCTIONS OF THE BOARD OF ARBITRATION

Recognizing that arbitration is the best method for the imme-

---

[1] For many such forms see Birdseye's Abbott's *Encyclopædia*, Forms 389-419, pp. 222-251.

[2] The name of the organization adopting these rules should be inserted on the dotted lines.

diate settlement of business disputes upon their merits, the .... establishes a Board of Arbitration.

The Board of Arbitration shall consist of five members appointed by the President of the...... with the approval of the Executive Committee. The President shall determine the term of the Board.

The Board shall have complete supervision of all matters involving arbitration referred to the...... and shall take such steps as it may deem necessary to stimulate throughout the.......... the settlement of commercial disputes by arbitration under the auspices of the.......... or other bodies.

It shall make rules and regulations for the conduct and disposition of all matters submitted to the...... in arbitration.

It shall compile a list of qualified persons willing to act as arbitrators, consisting of both members of the...... and non-members. This list shall be known as the "List of Official Arbitrators to the.........."

The...... will provide the parties with adequate rooms, all necessary papers and forms and clerical services at a nominal fee fixed by the Board; which fee shall be chargeable as decided by the arbitrators.

The Board shall select the Secretary from the staff (or membership) of the..........

The Secretary of the Board shall receive and file with the records of the Board all submissions and copies of awards, give notice of all hearings, keep a docket of all cases and the records thereof, and such books and memoranda as shall be necessary. He shall receive and disburse all fees and expenses and keep careful and accurate account thereof.

The Board of Arbitration shall have full power to amend or suspend any of its rules, or to supply new rules either generally or in relation to any particular case or cases, as it may find expedient to reach a speedy, economical, harmonious and just determination of the matter in dispute. No change or suspension of rules shall affect any case theretofore submitted, without the consent of the parties.

The services and facilities of the...... for arbitration shall be available to non-members at fee to be fixed by the Board.

RULES AND REGULATIONS OF THE BOARD OF ARBITRATION

The Arbitrators shall construe these rules as designed to secure justice and equity.

1. *Submission.*—All submissions shall be substantially in the form annexed and duly acknowledged. Two copies shall be filed with the Secretary of the Board of Arbitration. Wherever a submission is executed by a person in a representative capacity, proof of his authority shall also be filed.

2. *Selection of Arbitrators.*—The issues in controversy shall be submitted to an arbitrator or to the arbitrators named in the submission. Where two arbitrators are named in the submission with power to select a third, the choice of a third arbitrator shall be certified to the Secretary in substantially the form annexed. Where the Arbitrators fail to agree on a third arbitrator, the Board of Arbitration shall make such an appointment from the List of Official Arbitrators. The arbitrators shall elect their own chairman. Arbitrators may be appointed by the Board of Arbitrators if the parties so desire.

3. *Oath of Arbitrators.*—Before beginning the first hearing the arbitrators shall have administered to them, and shall sign, an oath substantially in the form annexed.

4. *Arbitrability.*—The Board, at its discretion, may decline to consider any matter submitted.

5. *Hearings.*—The Secretary of the Board shall arrange with the parties and arbitrators for the hearings as promptly as possible, and the proceedings shall be pressed to a speedy termination.

6. *Privacy of Hearings.*—The hearings shall be private, unless both parties agree to a public hearing.

7. *Procedure of Hearings.*—The hearings shall be conducted in the manner the arbitrators may decide most effective for settling the dispute.

8. *Statements of the Case.*—Written statements of the case may be required by the arbitrators, in their discretion.

9. *Testimony of Witnesses.*—Testimony of witnesses shall be taken under oath or informally as the arbitrators may decide.

10. *Irrelevant Matter.*—All irrelevant or unimportant matter shall be excluded from the hearings.

11. *Evidence.*—The arbitrators shall not be bound by the technical rules of evidence or court procedure.

12. *Counsel.*—If a party so desires he may be represented by his agent or counsel.

13. *Expert Testimony.*—Expert testimony may be introduced by either party. The expense of such testimony shall be borne by the party introducing it.

14. *Mitigation of Damages.*—The arbitrators may in any case direct the parties to the submission, or any or either of them, to take any step that in their judgment will mitigate or prevent the aggravation of damages; and particularly in a case involving perishable goods or merchandise which may deteriorate in value, pending arbitration, they may direct a sale of such goods or merchandise in order to mitigate damages.

15. *Scope of Awards.*—A mutual, final and definite award must be made by the arbitrators upon the subject submitted. It may award damages, make any decision and grant any remedy with respect to the controversy which shall to the arbitrators seem just and equitable.

16. *Form of Awards.*—The award shall be in writing and shall contain the decision of the arbitrators and it shall be signed by the arbitrators or a majority of them and duly acknowledged.

17. *Copies of Awards.*—A copy of the award shall be forwarded to each of the parties and two copies filed with the Secretary of the Board.

18. *Stenographic Records.*—Stenographic notes shall be taken of all proceedings unless the parties jointly request that same be dispensed with and the arbitrators assent thereto. Such notes shall be transcribed only to the extent ordered by the arbitrators.

19. *Arbitrators' Fees.*—Each arbitrator shall receive for his services a fee of ten dollars per day or part thereof, except where special arrangements shall have been made.

20. *Service Fees.*—A fee of ten dollars shall be paid by each party who is a member of the......for the services of the...... in each case submitted to arbitration.

21. *Payment of Fees.*—The arbitrators shall ascertain the

amount of fees and expenses and shall specify in the award who shall pay them.

Below are given extracts from a letter from Charles L. Bernheimer, chairman of the committee on arbitration of the Chamber of Commerce of the State of New York, to a western chamber of commerce embodying some suggestions for the conduct of arbitrations.

. . . Our Official List, which enumerates the names of those of our Chamber who have agreed to serve as arbitrators, contains, as you will readily recognize, the names of men of the highest standing and personal responsibility. Such a list, I am convinced, cannot be dispensed with; it is a very important element.

After a controversy has arisen, usually one of the disputants communicates with the chairman of the committee on arbitration, who endeavors to arrange for a joint meeting with both the plaintiff and the party against whom the grievance exists, in rare instances meeting with them separately. The chairman discusses the subject with them with a view of arriving at a definite settlement by means of mediation or conciliation. If that is not possible, he points out to them the advantages and duties of each in the event of a formal submission to arbitration; in other words, he explains the system, the laws governing it, and the rules and regulations established by our Chamber which apply.

Arbitration is very rarely demanded by both parties. Usually it is the party really aggrieved who searches for an instrument of redress other than a suit at law. The result is that the executive in charge of the arbitration system must negotiate in order to bring the two parties to the point where *both* desire or consent to arbitration. . . .

For many years prior to the enactment of our present arbitration law, formal arbitrations were held under the Chamber's auspices, and in no case was there any trouble, although the old law gave the parties the right of revocation up to the formal closing of the hearing. In the assumption that your arbitration law corresponds somewhat to our former State Law, I may be pardoned in advising you to go ahead and do the best you can, as we did, confident that a repudiation or revocation will not occur when an arbitration has been conducted under the auspices of an institution such as yours, when, as a matter of service to the public, the membership thereof gives freely of its time and the best that is in them to their fellow merchants.

After both parties have voluntarily consented to formal arbitration (unless the contract so specifically provides), the chairman must arrange to have the questions to be decided upon by the arbitrator or arbitrators worded, firstly, so that both parties can jointly sign the Submission, and secondly, that the arbitrators will be in a position to definitely answer the questions that are the cause of the irritation. This is necessary, in order to prevent the arbitrators from going beyond the questions that are submitted to them, which might, under some circumstances, nullify the arbitration proceedings.

If one arbitrator is desired, both parties must select him jointly from our "Official List." In that event our submission form "A" is used. If three arbitrators are desired, each side selects its own arbitrator, not necessarily from the official list, nor need he be even a member of the Chamber, but he must be an entirely disinterested party, and the two so chosen then meet for the selection of the third arbitrator, or umpire, who must, under our rules and regulations, be chosen from the List of Official Arbitrators. In that event form "B" is used. Form "C" is the submission blank used if it is desired to have the entire arbitration committee of the Chamber act, but we rarely have occasion for its use.

One, several, or all of the members of the committee on arbitration always attend these formal hearings, and render such assistance as is unanimously requested. This might include the decision of some vexing question as to the rules and regulations and the laws that govern arbitration.

The method is very rapid, but none the less efficient and thorough. It offers the disputants the opportunity of selecting their own court, judge and jury, and to designate the time of hearing most convenient to all concerned. In most cases even the defeated party is on record with a letter of thanks, and in no case has dissatisfaction with a settlement or award been evinced. Instead, a disposition has been shown to continue to do business by the cultivation of respect and friendly relations by the parties.

The time required for formal arbitration hearings rarely exceeds three or four hours. The fees are $10 per day, or part thereof, for each arbitrator, which is the same fee that referees get in our state. Mediatory efforts on the part of our committee are, of course, rendered without cost, and in these cases of conciliation lies the great bulk of our work. We have always endeavored to keep the cases in this class, and while we have had thousands of disputes brought to us since our system was inaugurated, we have succeeded in keeping the cases of formal arbitration at the minimum.

The cases that come to us are of the very greatest variety. Foreign governments, foreign chambers of commerce and merchants of foreign lands appeal to us for our service and receive it. Cases come to us from departments of our own government, from American consuls and chambers of commerce, commercial bodies and individual merchants and even private persons in this and other states and territories of our own country. Demands for our services come from sources that at first flush appear properly to belong to sister institutions such as Produce, Cotton, Dried Fruit and other exchanges having arbitration facilities of their own; this is generally caused by an absolutely needless fear on the part of one of the parties to the dispute that he may not receive unbiased treatment from these specialty institutions.

In order to bring the establishment of the arbitration system which you have in mind to a successful issue, I strongly urge that some member of your organization, one who feels particularly interested in the subject, be placed at the head of the movement, for the success of the arbitration system depends entirely upon the enthusiasm and energy displayed by him. He must possess patience, perseverance and determination, he must shoulder the responsibility of the administration and help bring all issues to a satisfactory conclusion.

APPENDIX XIII

Note.—The National Wholesale Lumber Dealers' Association consolidated with the American Wholesale Lumber Dealers Association under the name of the National-American Wholesale Lumber Association, Inc., and, after the manuscript of this book had been proposed, the new association adopted new by-laws governing arbitration, and new rules of arbitration procedure. Both forms are here included because the old form provided for regional procedure, and the new form has some unusual features applicable to a trade association doing business in all parts of the United States, and some novel provisions for the taking of legal counsel, etc.

NATIONAL WHOLESALE LUMBER DEALERS ASSOCIATION;
BY-LAWS REFERRING TO ARBITRATION MATTERS

Article XII

Section 1. *Arbitration.*—(*a*) The Arbitration Committee shall consist of fifteen members, seven of whom shall be chosen from the territory on a line east of Buffalo, seven from the territory west, and one from the territory at large.

(*b*) In case said Committee shall be called upon to act as herein provided, the three members of the Committee who are nearest to the locality of the dispute shall have full power to determine the matter and the decision of a majority shall stand as the decision of the full Committee.

(*c*) The locality of the dispute shall be determined by the chairman of the Committee with reference to the residence of the contesting parties or the location of the subject-matter of the dispute, as may seem most conducive to economy in the conduct of the arbitration and he shall then designate the members who are to serve, naming one of them as chairman *pro tem*, and all papers in the case shall be referred to said chairman, who shall proceed with the arbitration.

(*d*) The Arbitration Committee shall have power to establish such rules as may be necessary for the conduct of its business.

Section 2. In case of a difference between members of this Association, arising out of a business transaction, either party may demand, and shall be entitled to an arbitration of such difference by the Arbitration Committee, upon request in writing to the Secretary and upon signing the formal arbitration agreement. The party against whom the Arbitration Committee shall decide shall pay the cost of arbitration, or the Arbitration Committee may divide the costs between the two parties as they may deem just.

Section 3. Disputes amounting to $100 or less may be referred to one member of the Arbitration Committee, said member to be selected by the Secretary, and the decision of said member to be accepted as final and binding upon both parties.

Section 4. In case of a dispute between a member of this Association and a member of any other association, arising out of a business transaction, involving lumber and other forest products, and upon notice in writing to the Secretary of the Association that arbitration is desired, this Association shall, with the approval of its member, express its willingness to submit such difference to a joint arbitration committee consisting of two persons, one to be appointed by each association, and in the event of the failure of these two to agree they shall call in a third party. The joint arbitration committee thus selected shall establish its own rules of procedure. The decision and award of a majority of the Committee shall in all matters before it be final and binding.

Whenever, by notice in writing to the Secretary of this Association, application is made for arbitration, either by, or on behalf of a member of this Association or by a non-member, who is a member of another Association, or through the Secretary of any coöperating Association, the Secretary of this Association shall forthwith use his best efforts to reach an agreement between the parties to submit the dispute to arbitration. This Association shall, with the approval and consent of the member of this Association, appoint the arbitrator hereinbefore mentioned.

Section 5. In case arbitration is demanded by one member upon a dispute arising between himself and any other member of this Association, and said other member shall decline to arbitrate the same, the matter shall be referred to the Board of Trustees, who shall have power to determine whether or not arbitration shall be required, and in the event that they decide that an arbitration should be had, both parties to the dispute shall submit thereto, or in the event of the failure of either party to comply with the order of the Board of Trustees, said Board shall have power to discipline such member as they see fit, provided the transaction did not originate prior to the admission to membership of either party to the dispute.

Provided further that in any arbitration coming under this section the Arbitration Committee may consist of two members, one to be selected by each disputant, and in the event of the failure of these two arbitrators to agree that they shall call in a third member, and the decision and award of a majority shall stand as the decision of the full committee.

Article XIV

Section 1. *Misconduct of members.*—Any member of this Association who shall fail to fulfil contracts with whom he may have dealings, or shall conduct himself so as to bring reproach upon the Association, and shall be reported to the Secretary by any member of this Association shall be notified to explain to, or appear before, the Executive Committee or Board of Trustees, and should he fail to satisfactorily explain his conduct to the said Committee, he may be fined or expelled by the Board of Trustees, at their option but may have the right, within thirty days, to appeal from their decision to a full vote of the Association.

THE SAME; RULES FOR THE PRESENTATION OF EVIDENCE, ETC.

Both parties must first sign arbitration agreements as per printed forms furnished by the Association.

APPENDICES

The party demanding the arbitration must first submit his full evidence of claim through the Association to the other party to the agreement. This second party is then to submit his full evidence of counter-claim which is to be submitted to the party demanding the arbitration.

Each party to the agreement may then submit to the Arbitration Committee his argument of the case, but without any new evidence, which argument may not be seen by the other party to the agreement.

Final arguments and replies shall be placed in the hands of the Secretary within thirty days after the arbitration agreements have been signed.

THE SAME; AGREEMENT FOR ARBITRATION

Pursuant to Article 12 of the By-Laws of the National Wholesale Lumber Dealers Association, 41 East 42nd Street, New York City.

Whereas, A difference has arisen between   of   and   of   , both of said parties being members of the National Wholesale Lumber Dealers Association, and said differences having arisen out of a business transaction. And,

Whereas,   requested an arbitration of such difference by the Arbitration Committee and   signified   willingness to submit said difference to said Arbitration Committee,

Now, in Consideration of the Premises, It is hereby mutually agreed by and between the parties hereto, as follows:

First, That the difference existing between said   and   arising out of the shall be and the same hereby is submitted to the Arbitration Committee of the National Wholesale Lumber Dealers Association for final determination.

Second, And it is further agreed that the By-Laws of said Association and the method of procedure and practice of said Arbitration Committee shall govern in the determination of said matter.

Third, And it is further agreed that the determination of said

Committee shall be final and that both parties shall abide by the same.

In Witness Whereof, The parties hereto have hereunto set their hands and seals this   day of   , 19 .

[*Signatures*]

[*If for use in New York State, this form should be acknowledged as on page   .*]

The National-American Wholesale Lumber Association, Inc.

BY-LAWS COVERING ARBITRATION

Article XVII

Section 1. In case of a dispute between members of this Association or between a member of this Association and a member of another recognized lumber or other trade association arising out of the purchase or sale of lumber or other forest products,[2] either party may demand and shall be entitled to an arbitration of such difference upon request, in writing, to the Association and upon signing an arbitration agreement; provided, however, that disputes coming under the following three classifications shall be excepted:

(*a*) Disputes arising out of transactions originating prior to the date of application for membership of the member involved; but this Section shall not be construed to exclude disputes affecting members accepted under the provisions of Article III, Section 2, of these By-Laws.

(*b*) Disputes concerning lumber grades or tally shall not be arbitrated, but shall in the first instance be decided by some accredited inspector of some recognized inspection bureau or association, and his certificate shall be final in any arbitration proceedings between the parties as determining the grade of lumber in dispute at the time such inspection was made. But this section shall not be construed to exclude disputes where either of the

---

[2] The Board of Directors of the Association has interpreted this term "or other forest products," to mean "other products of the log."

parties concerned has unreasonably delayed official inspection, or refused to permit it upon the request of either party, or where the agreement between the parties makes no provision for inspection.

(c) Disputes which have previously been arbitrated.

Sec. 2. Any member of this Association failing or refusing to arbitrate on request of the Association under the foregoing section, or failing to abide by the result of an arbitration, shall be subject to expulsion as hereinbefore provided.

Sec. 3. A non-member failing or refusing to arbitrate on request of the Association or failing to abide by the result of an arbitration may be denied the privileges of further arbitrations at the discretion of the Executive Committee or Board of Directors.

Arbitration Procedure

APPROVED AND ADOPTED BY THE BOARD OF DIRECTORS, EFFECTIVE MAY 1, 1926

1. *Requests for Arbitration.*

(a) All requests for arbitration, whether from members or non-members, and all correspondence relating to arbitration shall, unless otherwise directed, be addressed to the headquarters of the Association at New York City, provided that correspondence on disputes between members located in British Columbia, Washington, Oregon, or California, shall be addressed to the Seattle office of the Association, from which point the arbitration may be handled. Requests for arbitration between two non-members shall be subject to acceptance by a majority vote of the Arbitration Committee.

(b) The party requesting arbitration shall sign an arbitration agreement and also shall submit a brief synopsis of the dispute, whereupon the Association will promptly take necessary steps to obtain the consent and agreement of the other party to arbitrate. Forms of arbitration agreement may be had upon application to the Association.

APPENDICES

(c) If the party complained of is a member he shall be requested to submit the case to arbitration, in accordance with the By-Laws. If the party is a non-member, he shall be invited to arbitrate. Should either party, whether a member or non-member, fail or refuse to arbitrate, the matter will then be referred to the Board of Directors or Executive Committee.

(d) No claim shall be arbitrated where the actual amount in dispute is less than $50, unless upon application of either disputant, the Executive Committee or Board of Directors directs that same be arbitrated because of importance or principle involved.

2. *Form of Submittal.*

(a) The detailed statement of claim must be filed by each party within 15 days after receipt by the association of the arbitration agreement properly executed by both parties; the statement must be submitted in duplicate; and the answer thereto, together with all correspondence or other evidence, must be filed by each party within thirty days after receipt of the statement of the adverse party. In the event of failure of either party to file his statement or answer within the times provided in this paragraph, the arbitration committee may proceed with the arbitration and make the award on the record before it. The Arbitration Committee may, if good cause be shown, extend the time for filing of the statement, answer or evidence by either party. Notice of the time within which detailed statement and within which the answer and evidence must be filed shall be served by the association on each party.

(b) The Association shall thereupon send to each disputant a copy of the other's detailed statement of claim and each party may then submit to the Association his answer or argument.

(c) All correspondence submitted by either party must be chronologically and neatly arranged, and exhibits marked in numerical order.

3. *Files Submitted to Counsel.*

The disputants shall have the right to request that the files be sent to the Counsel of the Association for a legal opinion, and such opinion shall be rendered to the arbitrators for their general guidance. An opinion must be rendered where both disputants request it, but should either of them request that no legal opinion be submitted, the arbitrators shall determine whether a legal opinion is required. The arbitrators at all times may call upon the Association Counsel for an opinion, but if the arbitrators conclude to dispense with a legal opinion both disputants shall be so informed, and upon the further request of either disputant the matter shall be referred to the Executive Committee or Board of Directors who shall finally determine whether a legal opinion shall be submitted. In rendering decisions, arbitrators shall state whether or not a legal opinion was submitted.

4. *Arbitration Committees.*

(*a*) Disputes between members shall be referred to a committee consisting of three members, to be appointed by the Association from a list of at least six members submitted by the Association to the disputants for approval.

(*b*) Disputes between members of this Association and non-members shall be referred to a committee of three; two shall be appointed by the Association from a list of at least six to be submitted to the disputants for approval, which list shall include at least three members, plus a similar number of members or non-members who may be suggested by the non-member's association; the two arbitrators thus appointed shall select a third to act with them before proceeding with the consideration of the dispute. The failure or delay of either party to object within 15 days to the list of suggested arbitrators shall be construed to convey approval of such arbitrators.

(*c*) Disputes between members of this Association and members of other recognized lumber or other trade associations shall, with the agreement of the non-member, be referred to a committee appointed as now provided in paragraph (*b*), provided that in a dispute between a member and such non-member, the Association of which the latter is a member shall have the privilege of naming one arbitrator, the National-American Wholesale Lumber Association to name the second arbitrator and the two thus appointed to select a third to act with them before proceeding with the consideration of the dispute.

5. *Selection of Committees.*

No case shall be sent for consideration or decision to a point where either party thereto resides, or has such connections as might suggest undue influence or personal prejudice, unless such action shall have been agreed to by both interested parties; provided, that disputes between parties located in the same city or district may be referred to arbitrators located in such city or district.

6. *Referring Cases to Committees.*

Arbitrations shall be referred to committees by means of a joint "Letter of Appointment," addressed and sent to each appointee, which shall briefly state the nature of the dispute and transmit copy of the regular "Instructions to Arbitration Committees." Each member of the committee shall be requested to notify the Association promptly should there be any reason why he cannot or should not serve. The committee shall be charged to carefully follow all instructions given, also, legal opinion of Counsel, if any, and to render its decision with as little delay as possible.

7. *Examination of Decision Rendered.*

Upon return of the files from the Committee to the Association the decision shall be carefully examined and in case the decision has not been prepared in accordance with the instructions, it shall be returned to the same or a similar committee for further attention.

8. *Return of Files with Decision.*

When the decision has been rendered in proper form the Association shall promptly send a signed copy of the decision to each party to the dispute, together with return of his file, receipt of which shall be promptly acknowledged. The parties shall also notify the Association in writing when the case has been settled in accordance with the decision rendered.

9. *Expenses and Charges Assessed as Costs.*

Members of Committees shall serve without any charge for their services. The Association shall pay any traveling or other necessary expense incurred by the Committee or any of its members and shall be reimbursed therefor in accordance with the finding of the committee. The latter shall definitely assess all such expenses as costs, against either or both parties to the case, as it may deem wise .

10. *Decision.*

The decision of a majority of the arbitrators, in all matters before it, shall be accepted by both disputants as final and binding.

11. *Instruction to Committees.*

A set of "Instructions to Arbitration Committees" has been regularly adopted by the Standing Committee on Arbitration and is hereby made a part of these rules and regulations.

12. *Reporting Decisions.*

The Association may publish to its members and the public at large any arbitration decision, or a synopsis thereof, omitting the names of the arbitrators and disputants.

13. *Arbitration Charges.*

For the purpose of partly compensating the Association for the additional expense incurred in the handling of arbitrations, the Association shall be entitled to a nominal charge of 5 per cent of the amount of money awarded under the arbitration decisions or collected through informal adjustment by the Association; the arbitrators shall in their decisions state whether one or both of the disputants shall pay this fee and shall name the amount on which the fee is to be based; a minimum charge of $5 shall be made on collections or awards up to $50, and a minimum charge of $10 shall be made on awards or collections from $50 to $200, provided that in no case shall the fee exceed $100.

APPENDIX XIV

THE RUBBER ASSOCIATION OF AMERICA, INCORPORATED; RULES
AND REGULATIONS GOVERNING ARBITRATIONS

I. *Controversies which may be submitted to arbitration.*—
Any controversy which might be the subject of an action in a
Court, between persons legally competent to manage their affairs,
may be submitted to arbitration except one relating to an estate
in real property in fee or for life; but a controversy as to the partition of real property, or as to boundaries, may be arbitrated.

The death of a party to a submission, or the appointment of
a committee of his person or property, operates as a revocation
of the submission if it occurs before the award is delivered, but
not if it occurs afterwards.

II. *Method of submitting controversies.*—If the parties to a
controversy agree to submit the matter to arbitration they shall
execute a submission in the form hereinafter provided and file
a copy thereof with the Secretary of the Committee on Arbitration and, at the time of such filing, each party to the submission
shall deposit with the Secretary the sum of Fifty Dollars; or

Any party, or parties, to a controversy with others may execute and file with the said Secretary, a submission in the form
hereinafter provided (each party depositing the sum of Fifty Dollars therewith) and request an arbitration with the other party
or parties named in the submission; whereupon the Secretary
shall notify such other party or parties that such arbitration has
been requested and call upon it or them to execute said submission. If executed by such other party or parties, it shall be
filed with the Secretary, and each such other party shall, when

filing the same, deposit the sum of Fifty Dollars. If the agreement is not executed and filed and the said deposits made by such other party, or parties, within three days after such notice from the Secretary, the deposit or deposits made by the party, or parties, requesting the arbitration shall be returned to them together with the submission which has been filed.

All submissions shall be in accordance with "Form A" hereto attached and shall contain a statement of the matter in controversy in concise but sufficiently comprehensive form to express the nature of the controversy and the points submitted for decision. They shall be duly executed and acknowledged by all parties to the submission before a notary or other official authorized to take acknowledgments of deeds, and, if signed by an agent or by one or more partners, shall be accompanied by duly authenticated power of attorney from the principal of the agent or from copartners not signing the submission.

III. *Hearings before the arbitrators.*—Within three days after the filing of the completely executed submission with the Secretary and the depositing of the moneys above provided for, the Committee on Arbitration shall, in writing, in accordance with "Form B," appoint an arbitrator or arbitrators, and shall at the same time give to the parties to such submission notice in writing of such appointment. The parties may, within two days after the receipt of the said notice, forward to the Committee written objections to the arbitrator or arbitrators appointed. Within two days after the receipt of the objection to the appointment, the Committee on Arbitration shall finally designate the arbitrator or arbitrators and give to the parties written notice of such designation. The above mentioned periods shall be reckoned exclusive of Sundays and holidays.

IV. *Hearings before the arbitrators.*—The arbitrator or arbitrators shall, within three days (exclusive of Sundays and holidays), after their final designation, notify the parties of the time and place of the first hearing, and shall thereafter designate the times and places for all continuances of the hearings, and shall at all times control the manner in which the questions in issue shall be presented.

The arbitrator or arbitrators shall, before hearing any testimony, be sworn in accordance with "Form C" unless the oath is waived by the written consent of the parties to the submission, or their attorneys.

The parties shall be entitled to be heard in person or by counsel, and may produce witnesses for examination; and the arbitrator or arbitrators may, by subpœna, require any person to attend before him or them as a witness, and to bring with him books or papers. A complete record shall be kept of all the proceedings.

All arbitrations in the City of New York shall be held in the rooms of the Rubber Association of America, Inc., which will furnish all reasonable facilities for conducting the arbitration, without charge over and above the fees hereinafter fixed.

The proceedings shall not be public unless so requested by the parties to the arbitration. But members of the Committee on Arbitration may be present at any of the hearings, and the records shall at all times be open to the members of The Rubber Association of America, Inc., and shall also be open to others upon the written order of the Committee on Arbitration.

If there are more than two arbitrators in any case, the decision of the majority shall be the decision in the arbitration, and the majority may adjourn hearings, require the production of witnesses and otherwise do all acts which a sole arbitrator or all of the arbitrators might do in the matter of the arbitration; except that all the arbitrators must meet together and hear all of the allegations and proofs of the parties.

All awards shall be made in writing and shall be executed and acknowledged before a notary public or other official authorized to take acknowledgments of deeds. An original of the award shall be furnished to each of the parties, and a copy shall be filed in the records of the Committee on Arbitration.

V. *Fees and expenses of arbitration.*—Each arbitrator shall be entitled to a fee of $10.00 for each case, and to reimbursement for all railroad and hotel expenses when hearings are held outside of the place of residence or place of business of the arbitrator, or when trips away from the place of hearing are required in conducting the arbitration proceedings. Additional fees may be awarded by the Committee on Arbitration in exceptionally protracted or involved arbitrations, not to exceed, in the case of any one arbitrator, Ten Dollars for each day spent in the business of the arbitration unless, at or before the commencement of the hearing, a different rate of compensation is fixed by written consent of the parties.

The Rubber Association of America, Inc., shall be entitled to receive the cost of stenographic notes and transcription thereof and all other of its expenses incurred strictly in connection with the arbitration, together with $10.00, in addition, for each arbitration.

Each party shall pay all expenses in connection with calling its own witnesses (except the reporting and transcribing of the testimony), but all of the other fees and expenses shall be paid by one or more of the parties, or shared between all of them, as the arbitrator or arbitrators shall decide to be just under the circumstances.

Any unexpended balance of the deposits made at the time of filing the submission shall, upon the completion of the foregoing arbitration, be returned.

VI. *Appeals.*—Any one or more of the parties may appeal to the Committee on Arbitration from the decision of the arbitrator, or arbitrators, by giving notice to such Committee, in accordance with "Form D," within five days (exclusive of Sundays and holidays) after receipt of notice of the award in the arbitration, and by paying $100.00. If more than one party appeals, the said Committee shall make such refunds that the Committee shall not receive more than $100.00 for each arbitration and that each appealing party shall pay an equal share of said $100.00.

Immediately upon the expiration of said period of five days, the Secretary of said Committee shall notify each party to the arbitration as to the appeals taken and shall, at the same time, fix a date and place for the hearing on the appeal, which hearing shall be upon the record made before the arbitrator, or arbitrators, supplemented by briefs and oral argument if any party so desires.

A majority of the members of the Committee on Arbitration shall constitute a quorum to hear any and all appeals, and each member who is to hear an appeal shall, before such hearing, be sworn in accordance with "Form C," unless the oath is waived by the written consent of the parties to the submission or their attorneys. All of the members constituting such quorum shall meet together and hear all of the allegations of the parties, and the majority decision of the members hearing the appeal shall be accepted as final by all parties.

The award on appeal shall be made in writing and shall be executed and acknowledged by all of those making it, one original to be furnished to each of the parties and a copy to be filed in the records of the Committee.

VII. *The intent in the arbitrations.*—The arbitrator, or arbitrators, and the Committee on Arbitration, in conducting arbitrations and appeals shall make their rulings, orders and decisions with the end in view of applying reason and enforcing equity and fair dealing in matters of trade and commerce, irrespective of technicalities, and with the least possible delays and expenditures consistent with a comprehensive investigation of each controversy presented.

In case of any question arising as to the interpretation of these Rules and Regulations, the decision of a majority of the members of the Committee on Arbitration shall be accepted by the parties as final and conclusive.

VIII. *Duties of secretary.*—The duties of the Secretary of the Committee on Arbitration (or, in his absence, the Assistant Secretary of the Rubber Association of America, Inc.), shall be as follows:

He shall receive and file all submissions, all copies of awards, give notice of all hearings and appeals, keep a docket of all cases, and such other books and memoranda as the Committee shall from time to time direct.

He shall render all necessary assistance to the Arbitrators, attend to their clerical work; receive and disburse all fees and costs and keep careful and accurate account thereof, under the supervision of the Committee on Arbitration.

IX. *Amendments.*—The Committee reserves full power to amend, add to or omit any of these rules from time to time, as may be found expedient.

THE SAME; FORM OF SUBMISSION

(Form A, above referred to.)

THE COMMITTEE ON ARBITRATION OF THE RUBBER ASSOCIATION OF AMERICA, INC.

and } Submission.

A controversy, dispute or matter of difference between the undersigned having arisen and relating to a subject matter the nature of which, briefly stated, is as follows: [Insert particulars here.]

We do hereby voluntarily submit the same and all matters concerning the same to such arbitrator or arbitrators as may be selected by a majority of the Committee on Arbitration of The Rubber Association of America, Inc., for hearing and decision pursuant to the By-Laws of The Rubber Association of America, Inc., and the Rules and Regulations adopted by the Committee on Arbitration of The Rubber Association of America, Inc., and pursuant to Article 84 of the Civil Practice Act of the State of New York, and we agree to stand to, abide by and perform the decision, award, order, orders and judgment that may therein and thereupon be made under, pursuant and by virtue of, this submission and of any appeal that may be taken by either party to the Committee on Arbitration of The Rubber Association of America, Inc., under the rules thereof. Should no appeal be made within five days of the date of receipt of notice of the finding of the arbitrators, or should an appeal, if taken, be withdrawn, or not be prosecuted in accordance with the Rules of the Committee on Arbitration governing such appeals, then such finding is considered as final; otherwise it shall be final only after the decision on said appeal. We do further agree that a judgment of the Supreme Court of the State of New York may be entered in any County in the State of New York upon any final finding herein.

We do also in all respects waive any right to withdraw from or revoke this submission after the arbitrator or arbitrators accept their appointment hereunder, hereby expressly and specifically waiving the provisions of Section 2383 of the Code of Civil Procedure.

Dated, New York.

THE SAME; ACKNOWLEDGMENT FOR AGENT

State of } ss:
County of

On this   day of   , 19 , before me personally came   , the attorney of   , known to me to be the person who, as such attorney, executed the foregoing instrument, and he being by me duly sworn, did depose and say that he, by a duly executed power of attorney hereto annexed, was empowered to execute and deliver said instrument for and on behalf of said   , and he acknowledged that he executed the same as the free act and deed of the said   therein described and for the purposes therein mentioned, by virtue of said power of attorney.

Subscribed and sworn to before me this   day of   19 .

THE SAME; APPOINTMENT OF ARBITRATOR OR ARBITRATORS
(Form B, above referred to.)

In pursuance of the foregoing submission, the undersigned, constituting a majority of the Committee on Arbitration named therein, hereby select and appoint   as arbitrator (or arbitrators).

Dated   [*Signatures.*]

In case objections have been filed to the original appointment and a second and final appointment is made, in accordance with Article III of the "Rules and Regulations Governing Arbitration of The Rubber Association of America, Inc.," there shall, in such final appointment, be here added the word "finally."

THE SAME; OATH OF ARBITRATOR

(Form C, above referred to.)

State of } ss:
County of }

The undersigned being duly sworn says that he is an arbitrator appointed under the foregoing submission; that he will faithfully and fairly hear and examine the matters in controversy and make a just award according to the best of his understanding.

Sworn to before me this
day of   , 19
Notary Public.

THE SAME; NOTICE OF APPEAL

(Form D, above referred to.)

To the Committee on Arbitration of the Rubber Association of America, Inc.

  and   } Notice of Appeal.

A controversy, dispute or matter of difference between the undersigned having arisen and having been arbitrated under the rules of the Committee on Arbitration of The Rubber Association of America, Inc., and we desiring to avail ourselves of the privilege of appeal as provided in said rules do hereby voluntarily request the same and all matters concerning the same to be referred to the Committee on Arbitration of The Rubber Association of America, Inc. or a quorum thereof, as Arbitrators selected by us for hearing and decision on appeal pursuant to the By-Laws of The Rubber Association of America, Inc., and the Rules and Regulations adopted by the Committee on Arbitration of The Rubber Association of America, Inc., and pursuant to Article 84 of the Civil Practice Act of the State of New York,

In accordance with said Rules and Regulations, we deposit, with this Notice of Appeal, One Hundred Dollars.

Dated, New York.

APPENDIX XV

AGREEMENTS TO SUBMIT FUTURE DISPUTES TO ARBITRATION

CLAUSE SUGGESTED BY CHAMBER OF COMMERCE OF THE STATE OF NEW YORK

Any dispute arising under, out of, or in connection with, or in relation to this contract, shall be submitted to arbitration under the rules, for the time being, of the Committee on Arbitration of the Chamber of Commerce of the State of New York.

ARBITRATION CLAUSE; ANOTHER FORM

Any differences arising between the parties to this contract do not invalidate same, but shall be settled by arbitration at New York, unless otherwise specified herein, and decision by such arbitration shall be final and binding on both parties.

THE SAME; ANOTHER FORM

All disputes and differences arising out of this contract shall be settled and finally determined in the City of New York, by arbitration in the following manner: Each party to this agreement shall appoint an arbitrator. If the two arbitrators so appointed cannot agree within a month after their appointment, they will select a third arbitrator. The decision in writing of the three arbitrators, or any two of them, shall be final and binding upon the parties therein, who shall conform to and abide by said decision. If either party fails to appoint his arbitrator within 14 days after notice in writing requiring him to do so, the arbitrator appointed by the other party shall act for both; his decision in writing shall be final and binding upon both parties, as if he had been appointed by consent, and both parties thereto shall conform to and comply therewith.

THE SAME; ANOTHER FORM

In case of any dispute between the parties hereto as to their rights hereunder against each other the same shall be settled by arbitration, as follows: Either party may, by written notice to the other, appoint an arbitrator. Thereupon, within ten days after the giving of such notice, the other shall by written notice to the former appoint another arbitrator, and in default of such second appointment the arbitrator first appointed shall be sole arbitrator. When any two arbitrators have been appointed as aforesaid, they shall, if possible, agree upon a third arbitrator and shall appoint him by notice in writing, signed by both of them in triplicate, one of which triplicate notices shall be given to each party hereto; but if ten days shall elapse after the appointment of the second arbitrator without notice of appointment of the third arbitrator being given as aforesaid, then either party hereto (or both) may in writing request the person who is at the time the Chairman or Acting Chairman of the Arbitration Committee of the Chamber of Commerce of the State of New York to appoint the third arbitrator, and upon appointment of the third arbitrator (whichever way appointed as aforesaid) the three arbitrators shall meet and shall give opportunity to each party hereto to present his case and witnesses, if any, in the presence of the other, and shall then make their award; and the award of the majority of the arbitrators shall be binding upon the parties hereto and judgment may be entered thereon in any court having jurisdiction. Such award shall include the fixing of the expense of the arbitration and assessment of same against either or both parties.

Agreement Adopted by the Public Service Commission for the First District of the State of New York with the Interborough Rapid Transit Company of New York

Article XXX. *Arbitration.*—If the Commission or the Lessee shall desire to submit to arbitration any matter of difference arising under any provision of this contract in respect of which it is therein provided an arbitration may be had, then such matter of difference may be submitted to arbitration. Such arbitration shall be conducted as follows: Either the City, acting by the Commission, or the Lessee, may give written notice to the other that it requires the matter arising hereunder to be submitted to arbitration, and shall at the same time name a disinterested person as an arbitrator, and accompany the notice by a written acceptance by the arbitrator of the nomination. Within thirty (30) days after the receipt of such notice, the party receiving the same shall name a disinterested person as an arbitrator, and give written notice of such nomination to the other party, the notice to be accompanied by a written acceptance by the arbitrator of the nomination. If the party to whom notice of arbitration is given shall not so nominate an arbitrator, who shall so accept, then the arbitrator named by the party giving the first notice shall be the sole arbitrator. The Commission and the Lessee shall upon the nomination of the second arbitrator select a third arbitrator; but if they fail to agree upon such third arbitrator within thirty (30) days after the date of the nomination of the second arbitrator nominated, the third arbitrator shall be nominated by the Chief Judge of the Court of Appeals of the State of New York; or if within fifteen (15) days after being requested by either the Commission or the Lessee to make such nomination, the said Chief Judge shall decline or fail to make a nomination, then an arbitrator shall be nominated, upon the request of the Commission or the Lessee and within a period of fifteen (15) days by an Associate Judge of said Court of Appeals in order of seniority; or if within such periods the said Judges shall decline or fail to make a nomination, then the third arbitrator shall be nominated by the President or Acting President for the time being of the Chamber of Commerce of the State of New York. The arbitrators shall hear the parties and their counsel or any statements or evidence which the parties or either of them desire to submit. The failure to give notice provided for in Article XXIX shall not preclude the party failing to give such notice from setting up counterclaims growing out of or incident to the matter as to which the other party shall have given such notice. Either party may, upon two (2) days' notice

(Saturdays, Sundays and Holidays excepted) to the other, bring on the subject in dispute for hearing before the arbitrators. Within thirty (30) days after such hearing commences, unless such time shall be extended for good cause by written order of the arbitrators or a majority of them, the arbitrators shall make their determination in writing in duplicate, one to be delivered to the Commission and the other to the Lessee. In case any vacancy shall at any time occur by reason of the death, resignation or inability to serve of any arbitrator, his successor shall be nominated in the same manner and within the same times (during which times the other periods of time prescribed for or in the course of the arbitration shall be suspended) as above provided for in case of the original nomination of such arbitrator and in case the successor arbitrator shall not be nominated within such times the remaining arbitrator or arbitrators shall be the sole arbitrator or arbitrators. Any determination by a majority of the arbitrators shall be final and conclusive. Every such arbitrator shall be deemed to be employed both by the City and the Lessee. The fees and expenses of the arbitrators (including necessary expenses for stenographic and clerical services) and the expenses of the parties shall be assessed as the arbitrators consider equitable and as they direct in their award, but such assessments so made shall not be charged to cost of construction, cost of equipment or to operating expenses. Every such arbitrator shall, before proceeding to consider the matter, be sworn as nearly as may be in the same manner as referees in actions at law are required to be sworn. Provided, however, that if in any case, or for any reason an arbitration cannot validly be had as aforesaid, then the City or the Lessee, if in no way responsible for the failure of the arbitration, may bring such action, suit or proceeding as either of them may be advised for the purpose of determining any of the matters for which an arbitration is herein provided.

APPENDIX XVI

FORMS OF SUBMISSION

GENERAL FORM OF AGREEMENT OF SUBMISSION

WHEREAS, controversies exist, and for a long time have existed, between us, A. B., of   , and Y. Z., of   , in relation to divers subjects:

Now, THEREFORE, we, the undersigned A. B. and Y. Z., do hereby mutually covenant and agree, to and with each other, to submit all and all manner of actions, cause and causes of actions, suits, controversies, claims and demands whatsoever, now pending, existing, or held by and between us, § to M. N., of   as arbitrator, who shall [*or,* to M. N., O. P., and Q. R., all of   , as arbitrators, who, or any two of whom, shall] arbitrate, award, order, judge, and determine of and concerning the same, with power to award the payment of the costs [and of the expenses] incurred in such arbitration. And we do mutually covenant and agree to and with each other that the award to be made by the said arbitrator [*or* arbitrators, or any two of them] shall, in all things, by us and each of us, and by the [*here add the word* "heirs" *if award may affect any interest in real property*], executors, administrators, and assigns of us and each of us, be well and faithfully kept, observed, and performed. Provided, however, that such award be made in writing, under the hand of the said arbitrator [*or,* hands of the said arbitrators, or any two of them], ready to be delivered to us, or either of us, on or before the   day of   ,   .

WITNESS our hands and seals, this   day of   ,   .
In presence of   A. B. [SEAL.]
[*Witness's signature.*]   Y. Z. [SEAL.]

NOTE.—Submission for use in the State of New York must be duly acknowledged.

THE SAME; WITH AGREEMENT FOR AN UMPIRE

[*As in last form, to the §; continuing thus:*] to M. N., and Q. R., all of   , as arbitrators, who shall arbitrate, award, order, judge, and determine of and concerning the same. [*Here insert, if desired,* with power to award the payment of the costs (and of the expenses) incurred in such arbitration.] And we do mutually covenant and agree to and with each other, that the award to be made by the said arbitrators shall in all things by us and each of us, and by the executors, administrators, and assigns of us, and each of us, be well and faithfully kept, observed, and performed. Provided, however, that such award be made in writing, under the hands of the said arbitrators, ready to be delivered to us, or either of us, on or before the   day of   , 19 . And provided that, in case the said arbitrators do not so make their award on or before said day, the questions above mentioned shall be, and are hereby, submitted to the decision of such third person as shall be then, or shall theretofore have been, appointed [in writing] by said arbitrators to act in such case as umpire; and the award so made and ready to be delivered by said umpire, on or before the   day of   , 19 , shall be valid and binding upon each of us, and the [*here add the word* "heirs" *if the award may affect any interest in real property*] executors, administrators, and assigns of each of us, in like manner as if it had been made by the arbitrators above named in person.

WITNESS our hands and seals, this   day of   , .
In presence of   A. B. [SEAL.]
   [*Witness's signature.*]   Y. Z. [SEAL.]

AGREEMENT FOR ARBITRATION OF PARTNERSHIP AFFAIRS

WHEREAS, a partnership was formed on the   day of   ,   , between the undersigned A. B., C. D., and E. F., which by its terms has not yet expired, but which the partners desire to terminate; and,

WHEREAS, they have been unable to agree upon the terms of dissolution, and various differences have arisen among them;

Now, THEREFORE, in consideration of the premises, and for a settlement of all questions between the parties connected with said partnership, the undersigned agree to submit their differences to arbitration and award of G. H., I. J., and K. L., whose decision duly made in writing and delivered to the parties on or before the   day of   , 19 , the undersigned severally and mutually agree to abide by and perform. The matters specially submitted to said arbitrators and upon which they are to make their award, are:

First: Upon what terms shall the said C. D. and E. F. purchase the stock and interest of said A. B., in all the partnership property of the said firm, including merchandise, furniture and fixtures, machinery at the factory, and real estate, the purchasers assuming all the partnership liabilities, and what security upon such purchase shall be given to the said A. B.

Second: Upon what terms shall the said A. B. purchase all the stock and interest of said C. D. and E. F., in the same partnership property, he assuming all the partnership liabilities, and what security upon such purchase shall be given by him to the said C. D. and E. F.

The arbitrators shall also determine which of the parties shall have the option of purchasing according to the terms awarded, that is, whether the option shall be given to the said A. B. to purchase the interest of the said C. D. and E. F. in said property, or to the said C. D. and the said E. F., to purchase the interest of the said A. B. in the same upon the terms awarded by them; and in case the party to whom such option is awarded does not, within thirty days after the execution and delivery of the award, elect to purchase according to its terms, then the other party to these presents shall, and hereby agrees to purchase according to the terms awarded, as the terms of the purchase by him or them.

In determining the matters so submitted, the arbitrators are to have submitted to them the articles of partnership executed between the partners, the partnership books, and any inventory, balance sheets and other statements appertaining to the partnership business, and also such books and papers of the former firm of A. B. & Co., as may be required in the premises, and may act upon their own judgment as to the values, or may take testimony, and after hearing the statement of the parties and their counsel, they shall make their determination and award upon a full consideration of all the claims, questions, and differences of and between the parties.

IN TESTIMONY WHEREOF, etc. [*Signatures and seals.*]

APPENDIX XVII

PRACTICE AND PROCEDURE BEFORE ARBITRATORS

NOTICE TO THE ARBITRATORS OF THEIR APPOINTMENT

Written notice is not important, but this form is the most convenient way of proceeding in most cases.

GENTLEMEN: You are hereby notified that you have been chosen arbitrators on the part and behalf of each of the undersigned, to arbitrate, award, adjudge, and determine as to certain matters of difference specified in the submission of the undersigned, which will be produced before you [*or*, to determine a controversy existing between us concerning, *here stating the matter as in the agreement or bond*], and to make your award on or before the   day of   ; and you are requested to meet the undersigned at the house of J. K., in the town of   , aforesaid, on the   day of   , 19 , at   o'clock in the   noon of that day, for the purpose of fixing upon a time and place for hearing the proofs and allegations of the said parties.

[*Date.*]   Yours, etc.

                                        A. B.

To M. N., O. P., and Q. R.   Y. Z.

NOTICE OF HEARING, TO THE ADVERSE PARTY

STATE OF   ,
County of   ,

In the Matter of the Arbitration

between A. B. and Y. Z.

SIR: Please take notice, that a hearing in the matter of the arbitration concerning certain differences between A. B. and Y. Z.,

will be had before the arbitrators, at the office of M. N., No. , street, in the city of , at o'clock in the noon, on the day of , 19 .
[Date.]
[Address.] [Signature.]

OATH OF ARBITRATOR

State of }
County of } ss.:

I, , the undersigned arbitrator, appointed by and , do swear that I will faithfully and fairly herein examine the matters in controversy between the before-named parties and will make a just award therein according to the best of my understanding.

Subscribed and sworn to before me this day of , 19 .

[Signature.]

OATH OF WITNESS

You do swear that the evidence you shall give to the arbitrators here present, in a certain issue joined [or, certain matters of difference] between A. B. and Y. Z., shall be the truth, the whole truth, and nothing but the truth; so help you God.

THE SAME; IF WITNESS AFFIRMS

You do solemnly and sincerely declare and affirm that in this proceeding between and , you will tell the truth, the whole truth, and nothing but the truth, so help you God.

AGREEMENT TO EXTEND THE TIME FOR MAKING THE AWARD

It is hereby mutually agreed between the parties to the within [or, annexed] submission, that the time for making ready the award be and hereby is extended to the day of , 19 .

Dated this day of , . [Signatures.]

APPOINTMENT OF UMPIRE, AFTER DISAGREEMENT OF ARBITRATORS

TO ALL TO WHOM THESE PRESENTS SHALL COME, We, N. N. and Q. R., of   , send greeting:

WHEREAS, by an agreement [or, bond], bearing date of the   day of   , 19 , differences were referred by A. B. and Y. Z. to our consideration, to hear, determine, and award upon the same,* and we are not able to determine such differences; we have, therefore selected and made choice of, and by these presents do appoint, S. T., of   , for umpire, to arbitrate, award, order, judge, and determine the said differences between the said A. B. and Y. Z., pursuant to said agreement [or, bond.]

WITNESS our hands, this   day of   , 19 .
[*Signatures.*]

THE SAME, BEFORE THE HEARING

[*As in preceding form to the*,* continuing thus:*] we, therefore, have selected and made choice of, and by these presents do appoint, S. T., of   , for umpire, to arbitrate, award, order, judge and determine the said differences between the said A. B. and Y. Z., pursuant to said agreement [or, bonds], in case we do not agree upon and make an award on or before the   day of   ,   .

WITNESS our hands, this   day of   , 19 .
[*Signatures.*]

APPENDIX XVIII

AWARDS

AWARD BY ABRITRATORS

[*Title*]

WHEREAS, matters in controversy between A. B. and Y. Z., of   , were by them submitted to the undersigned, M. N., as arbitrator [*or*, M. N., O. P., and Q. R., as arbitrators], as by their submission in writing [*or*, by the condition of their respective bonds of submission, executed by the said parties, respectively, each to the other], and bearing date the   day of   ,   , more fully appears. Now, THEREFORE, we, the arbitrators mentioned in the said submission [*or*, bonds], having [been first duly sworn according to law, and having] heard the proofs and allegations of the parties [*or*, of A. B., the said Y. Z. not appearing after due notice to him], and having examined the matters in controversy by them submitted, do make this award in writing [*or*, in writing and under seal]—that is to say † [*here state the things awarded to be done—see following forms*].

IN WITNESS WHEREOF, I [*or*, we] have subscribed these presents, this   day of   , one thousand nine hundred and   .

[*Signatures, and seals also, if required by the submission.*]
In the presence of
[*Witness's signature.*]   [*Acknowledgment, if required.*]

AWARD BY ARBITRATORS; SHORT FORM

In the Matter of the Arbitration of
    A. B. and Y. Z.

We, C. E. and F. G., having been duly appointed arbitrators in the matter in controversy existing between said A. B. and

Y. Z., as by the provisions of their submission in writing [*or,* the condition of their mutual bonds], executed by the said parties, respectively, and sealed with their respective seals, dated the   day of   ,   , will more fully appear, and after having taken the oath prescribed by statute, and having heard the proofs and allegations of the said parties, and due deliberation having been had, do hereby award, determine, and order [*or,* do make this award in writing]; that is to say—[*here insert decision of arbitrators.*]

IN WITNESS WHEREOF, we have subscribed these presents, this   day of   , 19   .

[*Signatures of arbitrators.*]

[*Acknowledgment.*]

AWARD SUGGESTED BY CHAMBER OF COMMERCE OF STATE OF NEW YORK

Supreme Court of the State of New York
County of New York

....
.... } In Arbitration

The undersigned [*names of Arbitrators*] having been appointed Arbitrators as to certain matters in difference between the above-named   and   , by a Submission executed by the said parties bearing date of   , as by reference thereto will fully appear, and having heard the proofs and allegations of the said parties and duly deliberated thereupon, do hereby award and determine and order that

In witness whereof we have hereunto set our hands and seals this   day of
In the presence of
    [*Witness.*]   [*Signatures.*]

STATE OF NEW YORK, }
County of New York   } *ss.:*

On this   day of   , before me personally came   ,   , to me known and known to me to be the individuals described in and who executed the foregoing instrument and they duly acknowledged to me that they executed the same.

AWARD BY UMPIRE

WHEREAS, matters in controversy between A. B. and Y. Z. were by them submitted to M. N. and Q. R., as arbitrators, as by their submission in writing [*or,* by the condition of their respective bonds of submission executed by the parties to each other], bearing date the   day of   ,   , more fully appears, whereby it was provided that in case said arbitrators should not make their award on or before the   day of   ,   , the said questions should be and were submitted to the decision of such third person as should be then, or should theretofore, have been appointed [in writing, *or,* in writing and under seal] by said arbitrators to act in such case as umpire, the award by such umpire to be made and ready to be delivered on or before the   day of   ,   ; and,

WHEREAS, the said M. N. and Q. R. met upon the said arbitration, and did not make their award between the said parties by the time limited in and by said submission [*or,* by the condition of the said bonds], and, in pursuance of the said submission [*or,* bonds], have chosen me as umpire [by appointment in writing, hereto annexed], to settle and determine the matters in difference between the said parties.

Now THEREFORE, I, the said umpire, having been first duly sworn according to law, and having heard the proofs and allegations of the parties [*or,* of A. B., the said Y. Z. not appearing after due notice to him], and having examined the matters in controversy by them submittted therein, do, therefore, make this award in writing [*or,* in writing and under seal]—that is to say, [*here state the things awarded to be done—see following forms*].

IN WITNESS WHEREOF, I have subscribed these presents, this   day of   ,   19   .
[*Signature, and seal also, if required by the submission.*]

In the presence of
   [*Witness's signature.*]

APPENDICES

Special Provisions to be Inserted to Cover Particular Cases

AWARD FOR PAYMENT OF MONEY IN FULL

The said Y. Z. shall pay or cause to be paid, to the said A. B., the sum of   dollars, at   , within   days from the date hereof, in full payment, discharge, and satisfaction of and for all moneys, debts, and demands and claims whatever [referred to in the submission] due or owing from him, the said Y. Z., to the said A. B., at any time before the date of said submission.

AWARD FOR DAMAGES FOR BREACH OF WARRANTY

That the said A. B. did sell to the said Y. Z. a certain horse on the   day of   last, warranting him to be sound in every respect, for the price of one hundred and fifty dollars. The said horse is, and was at the time of such sale, unsound, and worth only the sum of forty dollars; and the said A. B. should pay to the said Y. Z. one hundred and ten dollars for the difference in price, and thirty dollars for the expenses of keeping said horse, besides the costs of this arbitration.

AWARD FOR DELIVERY OF GOODS

That the said Y. Z. shall freely deliver up to the said A. B., on request by him to be made, one trundle-bed, and three pair of sheets thereto belonging, one mahogany table, one dozen chairs, and one silver tea set, all of which were the goods of the late M. N., deceased.

AWARD FOR DELIVERY OF WRITINGS

That the said A. B. shall freely deliver up to the said Y. Z., on or before the   day of   next ensuing the date hereof, at his dwelling-house in   aforesaid, all leases, deeds, and writings whatsoever concerning the estate of the said Y. Z., now in the hands and possession of the said A. B., or of any other person in trust for him, especially the leases of the dwelling-house [*etc., describing the particular papers*].

AWARD FOR DELIVERY OF WRITINGS TO BE CANCELED

That the said A. B. shall deliver up unto the said Y. Z. a certain indenture of mortgage made by   , to   , and dated on the   day of   ,   , canceled, or to be canceled.

AWARD FOR GIVING A BOND FOR PAYMENT OF MONEY

That the said A. B., within   days after notice of this award, shall well and sufficiently make, seal, and deliver to the said Y. Z. a bond or obligation in the penal sum of   dollars, conditioned for the payment of   dollars to the said Y. Z., his executors, administrators, and assigns, on or before the   day of   ,   , with interest at   per cent per annum, payable semi-annually from this date.

AWARD FOR ASSIGNMENT OF A MORTGAGE

That the said Y. Z. shall make, execute, and deliver to the said A. B., on or before the   day of   instant, a good and sufficient assignment of a certain bond and mortgage, executed by one I. J. to said Y. Z., etc.; and the said A. B. shall pay, or cause to be paid, to the said Y. Z., the sum of   dollars, immediately upon the execution and delivery of the said assignment.

AWARD FOR SPECIFIC PERFORMANCE OF AGREEMENT TO ASSIGN A LEASE

That the said A. B., or his heirs, shall and do, on or before the   day of   next ensuing the date hereof, make and execute to said Y. Z. a good and sufficient conveyance of his interest as lessee for years of a certain farm in the possession of the said A. B., situate at   , according to the true intent and meaning of certain articles of agreement, bearing date on or about the   day of   , and made between the said

A. B. of the one part, and the said Y. Z., of the other part, or as near the same as the present circumstances will admit.

AWARD FOR SPECIFIC PERFORMANCE OF CONTRACT TO CONVEY LAND

That A. B. shall, on or before the   day of   next, by such deed or deeds as the said named Y. Z., his heirs or assigns, or his or their counsel, shall advise, well and sufficiently grant, convey, and assure unto the said Y. Z., his heirs and assigns, forever, a certain piece of ground, situated in   , and known and described as follows [*describing it*]. And that upon the execution of the said conveyance, the said Y. Z. shall pay, or cause to be paid, unto the said A. B. the sum of   dollars, and shall also give security by bond and a mortgage of the premises (if required) for the payment of the sum of   dollars, in manner following—to wit, etc.

PROVISION FOR THE DISCONTINUANCE OF ALL SUITS

And we do further award, that all actions and suits commenced, brought, or depending between the said A. B. and Y. Z., for any matter, cause, or thing whatsoever, arising or happening at the time of, or before their entering into the said submission [*or,* bonds of arbitration], shall, from henceforth, cease and determine, and be no further prosecuted or proceeded in by them, or either of them, or by their, or either of their means, consent, or procurement.

PROVISION FOR THE DISCONTINUANCE OF SUIT, WITH COSTS

And we do further award, that the said Y. Z. shall forthwith cease to prosecute, and shall discontinue a certain suit commenced by him, against the said A. B., in the   court of   county, now pending and undetermined in said court; and the said A. B. shall pay, or cause to be paid, to the said Y. Z., on or before the   day of   , the sum of   dollars, in full satisfaction of the costs, charges, and expenses incurred by the said Y. Z., in and about the prosecution of his suit as aforesaid.

PROVISION FOR GENERAL RELEASES

And we do further award that the said A. B. and Y. Z. shall, within   days next ensuing the date hereof, execute unto each other, under seal, mutual and general releases of all actions, cause and causes of actions, suits, controversies, claims, and demands whatsoever, for or by reason of any matter, cause, or thing, from the beginning of the world down to the date of the said submission [*or,* said bonds].

PROVISION FOR COSTS OF THE ARBITRATION

And we do further award, that the sum of   dollars, being the expenses and charges incident to this arbitration, shall be paid by the said A. B. [*or,* by them, the said A. B. and Y. Z., in equal shares].

INDEX

Administration purposes, tribunals for, 71, 76, 151-153.

Admiralty disputes, 107-110.

Alaska, powers over arbitration, 82, 83; U. S. courts in, 83.

Amalgamated Clothing Workers, 11.

Amendments to exchange and trade rules, how effected, 5, 45; of uniform contracts, 35.

American Arbitration Association, organization, purposes, research and publication division, 149, 150.

American Bar Association, services for arbitration, 108, 109.

American Bar Association Journal, articles on legal conciliation, 158.

American Federation of Labor, organization of, 11; history of, 126; fight against Bolshevism, 126, 127.

American Spice Trade Association, contracts, of, 39.

American Wholesale Lumber Dealers' Association, 255.

Amicable relations preserved through arbitration, 98.

Anthracite coal mining scale agreement, 139; as extended Feb. 17, 1926, 246, 247; for anthracite and bituminous scale agreements in full, 246, note.

Appointment, notice to arbitrators of, 281. See Forms.

Apprenticeship, common law indenture of, 17-19; rights under, 17-19; seven years required, 38. See Guilds.

Arabs, early merchants, 23; laws, customs of, 23; introduced arithmetic into Europe, 23. See also Merchants.

Arbitration, under rules of court, 145, 196-198, 207-210; see Chicago, New York; official administrative by non-judicial functionaries, 151-153; fence-viewers, 151, 152; wreck masters, opening roads, tax assessments, 152; in England, 152, 153; see Conciliation; compulsory and voluntary, fields for, distinguished, 159-161; compulsory, relates to future disputes, 160, 161; see Commercial Courts. of future disputes, arguments for and against, 167-171; Judge Harlan S. Stone for, 168; U. S., N. Y., N. J. and Mass. arbitration laws cover future disputes, 168; merchants know their own needs, 169; who have worked for broad statute, 169, 170; U. S., N. Y. and N. J. broad statutes passed unanimously, 169, 170; conflict of laws, 170, 171; merchants understand commercial, arbitration 171.

before permanent tribunal or by appointed arbitrators, 176; will to arbitrate increasing, 76; cultivation of will to conciliate or arbitrate, 176, 177; clause for, in Motion Picture Exhibition Agreement, 189-191; see Forms;

plan for offering facilities for, 248-254; suggestions for conduct of, 252-254.
agreements to submit disputes to, forms of, 273-276; practice and procedure before arbitrators, 281-283; forms of awards, 284-290.
tribunal, recognized, official, experienced, fellow-member experts, 4, 5, 21, 22; see Expert; regards larger interests and proposes amendments, 5; proper standard for judging, 7, 8; in Clothworkers' Guild, 19-21; arbitration clauses lessen disputes, 103; see Forms; in place of mandamus, 148, 149; narrow form of explained, 108; broad form of explained, 108; experience of N. Y. Chamber of Commerce with, 87-113; see Chamber of Commerce of State of New York; administrative by non-judicial functionaries, 71, 76, 151-152; see also Arbitrator, Commercial Arbitration, Common Law Arbitration, Industrial Arbitration, Statutory Arbitration, Jewish Court of Arbitration.
Arbitration Foundation, Inc., 111, 112, 149, 150.
Arbitrator, oath of, Municipal Court of Chicago, 197, 198; should not be chosen at time, 176; see Arbitration.
Argentine Republic, arbitration with, 143, 144.
Arithmetic, introduced by Arabs, 23.
Armour & Co., employee representation plan, 138.
Association of British Chambers of Commerce, 112, 145.
Athens, maritime disputes at, 32, 33.

Atmosphere, ethics are an, 37, 41, 42, 44; of confidence under Bethlehem Steel plan, 132, 133.
Attorney-in-fact, arbitrator was, at common law and his authority revocable, 62, 63.
Austria, commercial courts in, 33.
Award, enforcement of, like court judgment, 75; not enforceable without statute or by another action, 63, 89; see Forms.

Bakers, English guild of, 17.
Belgium, commercial courts in, 33.
Bernheimer, Charles L., appointed judge, 93; original investigations on arbitration, 94, 95; chairman of special committee on arbitration of New York Chamber of Commerce, 95; report of special committee, 95, 96; chairman of committee on arbitration since 1911, 95; time devoted by, 110, 111; insurance on life of, 111; president of Arbitration Foundation, Inc., 111; suggestions for conduct of arbitrations, 252-254. See also Chamber of Commerce of State of New York.
Bethlehem Steel Corporation, report on, 132-138.
Bituminous coal mining scale agreement, 139, 240, note.
Boards of Trade, conduct of, 5-7; conditions in, 48. See Commercial Arbitration.
Bolshevism, labor's fight against, 126, 127.
Bond, to arbitrate, 65.
Brazil, arbitration with, 143, 144.
Business, change in methods of doing, 9-15; objects of organized, 187, 188. See Organization.
Business ethics, spread of by New

INDEX

York Chamber of Commerce, 112, 113, 116; Judge Gary shows growth of, 113-116; former corporation practice as to, 114, 115; growth of, in craft guilds, 22; among medieval merchants, 29; improvement of, 34, 35, 113-116. See Organization.
Business Organization. See Organization.
By-laws, rules and regulations of exchanges, etc., design of, 3-5.

Calcutta, Black Hole of, 122.
Calder, John, report of, upon Bethlehem Steel Corporation, 132-136.
California, court conciliation in, 157.
Campbell, Lord, opinion in Scott vs. Avery, 65, 66.
Capital, organization of, 10, 11.
Chamber of Commerce of the State of New York, history of arbitration in, 88-116; original objects, first meeting, monthly appointment of arbitration committees, 87; charters, 87, 88; action during Revolutionary War, 88-90; letter from British Superintendent General, 89, 90; committees on arbitration and appeals, 90; agitation for commercial court, 90, 91; Court of Arbitration for the Port of New York, 91-93; services and death of Judge Fancher, 92, 93; appointment of successor, 93; lapse of arbitration after Judge Fancher's death, 94, 95; special committee for reëstablishing arbitration, 95, 96; report and new plan, 95, 96; official list of arbitrators, 96, 101, 102, 252-254; how arbitrators appointed, 96; résumé from annual reports of committee on arbitration, 96-106; educational work of committee, 96-103; effect of existence of chamber's system, 98; conciliation and adjustment, 98-105; see Conciliation; big brother work, 99, 100, 110; George Washington's will, 100; informal arbitration, 100, 101; transactions with foreigners, 101, 103, 105; intervention in court, 102, 107; cancellations, 102, 103; international arbitration treaties, 103, 110; value of arbitration clauses, 103; speed of action, 103; scope of committee's labors in arbitration, conciliation, mediation and fact finding, 103-105; list of articles and countries involved in arbitrations, 104, 105; mediation and fact determining explained, 106; action during World War, 106; technical nature of disputes, 106; changes in law and rules governing intrastate, interstate and international disputes, 81-86, 106-110; laws governing intrastate, interstate, admiralty and international disputes explained, 107; relations with bar associations, 107-109; narrow form of statute in Illinois and Oregon, 108; broad forms in New York, New Jersey, Massachusetts, 108, 109; U. S. Arbitration Act, passage of, 109-110; urging uniform contracts, 110; insurance upon life of Charles L. Bernheimer, 110, 111; The Arbitration Foundation, 111, 112, 149, 150; leadership of merchants, 112; spread of eth-

ical and friendly spirit, 112, 113, 116; form of award, 285, 286.
Chamber of Commerce of U. S., work for arbitration among members, other chambers, in international chamber of commerce, and with South American Republics, 143-145; success in international activities, 144, 145.
Chambers of commerce, activities of, 145; arbitration under rules of, 159, 160; voluntary arbitration in, 160, 161; suggestions to, for offering arbitration facilities, 248-254.
Chicago, municipal court of, rule governing arbitrations, 196; submission, 196, 197; oath of arbitrator, 197, 198.
Chicago Association of Credit Men, action to encourage commercial arbitration, 69-77; report of Samuel Rosenbaum, 69-77.
Church, growth of, 10, 11. See Organization.
Civil Practice Act, article, 84, of New York, 201-207.
Cleveland, court conciliation in, 157.
Clothworkers' Guild, ordinances of, 19-21, 181-186.
Clubs, growth of, 10, 11. See Organization.
Coal Mining, bituminous and anthracite scale agreements, 139, 246, 247.
Collective bargaining and industrial arbitration, 128-140. See Industrial Arbitration.
Collective conscience of a business community, 99; experience of association members, in drawing uniform contracts, 72.
Collectivism, results of, 6, 7.
Colorado Fuel and Iron Co., employee representation plan, 138.
Columbia, arbitration with, 143, 144.
Commercial Arbitration, strict or pure, defined and habitat shown, 3-8; used by self-governing organization with power to enforce mandates, members engaged in homogeneous dealings under self-imposed rules or uniform contracts, 3, 4; general object to simplify transactions, improve business organizations, 4, 187, 188, 269; nature and expertness of tribunal, 4, 5; see Expert; larger interests recognized, 5; how amendments made, 5, 35, 45, 269; underlying ethical and guild spirit, 5; gradual growth of better ethics, 5-7; how ethical spirit grows and minimizes disputes, 6, 7; relates exclusively to future disputes, 7; gyroscopic action, 7; only proper standard, 7, 8, 77, 166; connection with present tendency to organize and suborganize along ethical lines, 9-15; how it minimizes disputes, 41-52; business organization induces amicable settlement, conciliation, arbitration, official interpretation of rules, 41-52; relative degrees of litigation, 42; New York Stock Exchange, transactions of, and arbitration and litigation in, 42-45; New York Clearing House Association, transactions of, and arbitration and litigation in, 45-47; New York Produce Exchange, objects of, transactions, arbitration and litigation in, 47, 48; nature of, in exchanges and trade associations doing homogeneous business, 48, 49; Motion Picture Producers and Distributors of America, Inc,

INDEX

arbitrations under rules of, in 1923, 1924, 1925, 49-52; anecdote of Gen. U. S. Grant, 52; should be extended, 166; conclusions as to, 165, 166. *See also* Arbitration.

Commercial Clubs, suggestions to, for offering arbitration facilities, 248-254.

Commercial Courts, 33, 55, 56; in Europe, England and U. S., 162; successors of consular courts, 162, 163; in England, 163; U. S. District Courts as, 164; nature and functions of small claims courts, 164.

Common law, nature, origin and scope of, 55-61; English slow to enter business, 55, 56; related chiefly to feudal rights and not to trade, 56; struggle between Normans and Saxons over race assimilation, 56, 57; crudeness of law of contracts under, 57-59; English kings, 57; little use of writing in England, 57, 58; writing used by European merchants, 58; real not personal property, important under, 59; common law not fruitful soil for commercial arbitration, 60, 61; English justice slow and unsatisfactory, 60; must be changed by statute, 63, 64, 66, 67, 81, 82, 85, 86.

indenture of apprenticeship, 17-19. *See* Common Law Arbitration.

Common Law Arbitration, frequently a compromise, 60; frailties and failures of, 62-68; nature of, 62; right of either party to withdraw before actual award, 62; arbitrators were attorneys in fact, 62, 63; whose authority may be withdrawn, 62, 63; bonds to arbitrate, 65; not before experts or permanent tribunal or for future disputes, 62-64; common law rule of, must be changed by statute, 63, 64, 66, 67, 81, 82, 85, 86; agreement for, of future disputes was against public policy and non-enforceable, 62, 64-66; reasons for this rule, 64, 65; reversal of rule in Scott vs. Avery, 65, 66, 81, 85, 94, 95, 107; U. S. took over and followed old English rule, 66, 67; no commercial or gyroscopic advantages in, 68; *see* Statutory Arbitration; changes in England of law regarding, 69-77; report of Samuel Rosenbaum for Chicago Association of Credit Men, 69-77; action in Liverpool, 69, 70; English Arbitration Act of 1889, 70, 77, 81, 82; rarity of commercial trials in English courts, 71-76; use of uniform trade contracts, 71-77; F. O. B. contract, 74, 75; how arbitrators selected, 71-76; status of arbitration in England, 71-77; conclusions as to, 166-168. *See also* Arbitration, Forms.

Community, duty of master and servant to, 130.

Compromise, under common law arbitration, 60-63.

Conciliation, in exchanges, etc., 4, 46; in English court procedure, 76; by committee on arbitration of N. Y. Chamber of Commerce, 99, 102-106; in industrial arbitration, 129-139; in Bethlehem Steel plan, 132-134; extended facilities for, 145; in Jewish Court of Arbitration, 147-149; in New York Chamber of Commerce and other bodies,

154, 155; legal conciliation defined, 156; in Norway, Denmark, North Dakota, Minneapolis, Cleveland, Milwaukee and New York City, 157; courts of, authorized in some early state contributions, 157; forms of, 157, 158; New York Legal Aid Society, 158; conclusions as to, 175; rules on, in New York Municipal Court, 209, 210.

Contracts, nature of, 49, 112, 113; sacredness of, 5; history of, in England, 57-59; adoption of uniform, 97; uniform, value and function of, 35; keeping of, 41, 42; in English trade associations, 72.

Corn Laws, 124.

Costs of arbitration, award for, 290.

Court of commerce cases, 163.

Courts, arbitration as relieving, 77, 175, 176; how arbitration regarded by early English, 59, 60; of non-experts, 30; intervention of New York Chamber of Commerce in, 110; rules of, for conduct of arbitration, 85; arbitration under rules of, 145, 196-198, 207-209; not required for amending exchange rules, 5.

consular, 26-29; of law merchant, 28, 29; forms of, 27; commercial, derived from consular courts, 27, 28; celerity of trials in, 28; court of the dusty feet, 28.

Cowdin, Elliott C., argument of, 31-33.

Craft Guilds. See Guilds.

Crusades, effect of, on commerce, 23. See Merchants.

Definition of conciliation, 148, 156; of expert witnesses, 30, 31; of mediation, 106; of merchant, 23.

Delivery of goods and writings, awards for, 287, 288.

Denmark, commercial courts in, 33; court conciliation in, 156, 157.

Discontinuance, award for, of suits, 289, 290.

Ecuador, arbitration with, 143, 144.

Education on arbitration, record of New York Chamber of Commerce, 96-102; American Arbitration Association, 149, 150.

Electrical Construction Industry, arbitration in, 135, 136.

Elliott, Andrew, 88-90.

Employee representation plan, 128-139; of various companies, 132-138.

England, powers of Parliament, 81, 82; guilds of, see Guilds; opposition to extraterritoriality in, 27, 28; slow to accept law merchant, 56; common law related chiefly to feudal estates, 56; Arbitration Act of 1889, 70, 77, 81, 82; court of commerce, 163; housing, factory, industrial, political conditions before and during Industrial Revolution, 119-125; membership of House of Commons, 123, 124. See Common Law, Common Law Arbitration.

English Industrial Revolution. See Industrial Revolution.

Equity, questions involving, before craft guild tribunals, 21, 22.

Ethics, an atmosphere, 37; growth of, in exchanges, 38, 39; and ethical spirit grow gradually, 5, 177; growth of, during past 25 years, 113-116; no thought of,

under common law arbitration, 60; as basis of collective bargaining, 130, 131, 139, 174.
Europe, international merchants of medieval. *See* Merchants.
Exchanges, chief objects of, 5-7, 13, 36-38; 41, 42; technicality of dealings on, etc., 13; control by stronger members, 38, 39; conditions in, 48; power over members, 71; arbitration by, 97. *See* Commercial Arbitration.
Existing disputes, common law applies only to, 67. *See* Future disputes.
Expert and speedy decisions required by organized business, 30-33; decisions by, imperative, 30-40; evidence not required before expert arbitrators, 30; evidence, nature of, in courts of law, 30, 31; definition of expert witnesses, 30, 31; witness when not needed upon arbitration committees of exchanges, etc., 30-33; value of explained by Elliott C. Cowdin, 31-33; tribunals needed, 171, 172, 31-33; administrative arbitration, 151-153; no tribunal at common law, 63, 64; but in industrial arbitration, 131-139; and in Jewish Court of Arbitration, 145-149.
Extension of time to make award, 282.
Extraterritoriality of consular courts, 27, 28; England opposed to, 27, 28.

Factory conditions during English Industrial Revolution, 123.
Fairs, international, 23-28; for wholesale dealings, 23-25; transactions at, 23-29; at Stourbridge, 24, 25; Vanity Fair, 25; peace of God, freedom from local law, consular courts and their speedy action, 26-29.
Fair Law, 26, 28, 55.
Fancher, Enoch L., 92-94.
Fence-viewers, functions of, 151, 152.
Ferris, Frank A., 95.
Feudal System, meaning of, 119; in connection with labor, 119-125.
Florence, commerce of, 23.
Foreign transactions, arbitration of, 101; dealings with foreigners, 101, 103.
Forms of arbitration clauses: in sale note of London Corn Trade Association, 73; in London Oil and Tallow Trades Association, linseed oil in barrels, 73; in Refiners Beet Contract of Sugar Association of London, 73; in Institution of Gas Engineers, Society of British Gas Industries, 73, 74; in F. O. B. contract of Timber Trade Federation of the United Kingdom, 74, 75; in contract of Motion Picture Producers and Distributors of America, Inc., 189-191; in agreements, 273-276; in New York Public Service Commission with Interborough Rapid Transit Co. of New York, 274-276.
of submissions in Municipal Court of Chicago, 196, 197; in Municipal Court of New York City, 208; in Massachusetts, 219; of National Wholesale Lumber Dealers' Association, 258, 259; of Rubber Association of America, Inc., 270, 271; general form, 277; with agreement for an umpire, 278; of partnership affairs, 278-280.
practice and procedure before

arbitrators; notice to arbitrators of appointment, 281; notice of hearing, 281, 282; oath of arbitrator, 282; oath of witness, 282; affirmation of witness, 282; extending time to make award, 282; appointment of umpire before hearing, or after disagreement of arbitrators, 283.

awards, by arbitrators, 284, 285; form suggested by New York Chamber of Commerce, 285, 286; by umpire, 287; special provisions to cover each particular case; for payment of money in full, 287; for damages for breach of warranty, 287; for delivery of goods, 287; for delivery of writings, 287; for delivery of writings to be canceled, 288; for giving bond for payment of money, 288; for assignment of mortgage, 288; for specific performance of agreement to assign lease, 288, 289; same, of contract to convey land, 289; for discontinuance of all suits, 289; for discontinuance of suit with costs, 289, 290; for general releases, 290; for costs of arbitration, 290; in Municipal Court of New York City, 208, 209.

miscellaneous; oath of arbitrator, Municipal Court of Chicago, 197, 198; oath of arbitrator, Rubber Association of America, Inc., 272; judgment, Municipal Court of New York City, 209; notice to appear in New York Municipal Court in conciliation proceedings, 210; acknowledgment for agent, 271; of submission, 286; appointment of arbitrator or arbitrators, 271;

appeal, notice of, Rubber Association of America, Inc., 272.
of common law indenture of apprenticeship, 17-19.
France, commercial courts in, 33.
French Revolution, 124, 125.
Future disputes, agreement to arbitrate against public policy under common law, 62, 64-67; industrial arbitration of, 129-139; arbitration of, 160; under craft guilds, 21. See Arbitration.

Gary, Elbert, article by, 113-116; fight for better ethics, 116.
Geneva tribunal of arbitration, 91.
Genoa, commerce of, 23.
Georgia has not adopted Uniform Negotiation Instruments Law, 85.
Germany, commercial courts in, 33.
Gompers, Samuel, fight against Bolshevism, 127.
Grace, Eugene G., 134.
Grant, Gen. U. S., anecdote of, 52.
Grocers' Board of Trade, arbitration by, 91.
Grocers, Worshipful Co. of, 22.
Guilds, spirit of, 6, 7; developed arbitration, 9; municipal guilds and guilds merchant, arbitration under, and nature of, 16; were religious fraternities, 16; English craft guilds, origin of, 16, 17; were homogeneous, religious, fraternal and mystical, 16, 17; religious names, 17; hallmoots, 17; apprentices and journeymen, 17-19; early indenture of apprenticeship, 17-19; nature of guild ordinances, 19; Clothworkers' arbitration ordinance, 20, 21; related to future disputes and common welfare, 21;

INDEX

involved important legal and equitable questions, 21, 22; produced code of ethics, 22; ordinance of Grocers' Guild, 22; arbitration under, not of common law type, 61; traditions of, 36; ordinances of Clothworkers', 181-186.

Gyroscope, function of commercial arbitration like that of a, 7, 68.

Habitat, natural, of strict commercial arbitration, 3-8.

Hallmoots of English guilds, 17.

Hart Schaffner & Marx plan, 134, 135, 137, 138; text of labor agreement, 229-245; preamble, 229, 230; objects of company, union and workers, 229, 230; administration, board of arbitration, trade board, 230-234; chairman of trade board, 232; deputies, 232, 233; shop representatives, 234, 235; procedure, 235-237; adjustment by deputies, docket and records, direct complaints, decisions, appeals, hearings, enforcement, 234-237; wages, hours, overtime, price-rate committee, changing operations, 237-240; preferential shop and preferences, 240, 241; working conditions, 241, 242; general provisions, 243; loyalty to agreement, 244, 245; wages, 245.

Hawaii, powers over arbitration, 82, 83; U. S. courts in, 83.

Hentz, Henry, 95.

Homogeneous, products, etc., arbitration by organizations whose members trade with each other in, 3-5, 13, 16, 45, 48, 67, 75, 159; Jewish court, 147.

Honor, business, 98-101. See Ethics.

Housing conditions during English Industrial Revolution, 121, 122.

Hughes, Charles E., 110.

Illinois, arbitration law of, 108, 192-195; municipal court of Chicago. See Chicago.

Indiana, court conciliation in, 157.

Individualism, evils of, 6, 7.

Industrial Arbitration, English Industrial Revolution of 1760, 119-126.

former feudal relations between master and servant, 119, 120; no industrialism, 119, 120; services in war valued, 119, 120; personal loyalty and manhood value, 120, 129, 130; rule of liability of paid servant, 120; when labor became a commodity, 121; increase of pauperism, 121-124; bad agricultural and city conditions, 121-123; housing and factory conditions, 121-123; unceasing foreign war, debt and taxation increase, political conditions, Corn Laws in England, 123, 124; relation of costs and wages, 123, 124; effect of French Revolution, 124, 125.

formation of and loyalty to trade unions, 125, 126; arbitration banned by trade unions, 126; development of unions in America, 126; American Federation of Labor, 126; action of, against Bolshevism, 126, 127; Samuel Gompers' position, 127; Bolshevist denunciation of Samuel Gompers, 127.

collective bargaining distinguished from, 128; resembles commercial type, 128, 131, 136, 137,

139, 140; provisions for, in collective bargains, 128-130; loyalty of labor, to community and state, 130; ethics as basis of, 131, 132; by Bethlehem Steel Corp., report on, by John Calder, 132-136, 138; by Hart, Schaffner & Marx, 134, 135, 137, 138, 229-245; by Electrical Construction Industry, 135, 136; N. Y. and N. J. Arbitration laws cover labor disputes, 137; employee representation agreements, 138; rapprochement of capital and labor, 138, 139; anthracite and bituminous coal mining agreements, 139; conclusions as to, 172-175.

Industrial Revolution, English, 119-126, 129, 130; scars of, 139, 140. See also Industrial Arbitration.

Industrial Workers of the World, 11.

Institution of Gas Engineers, arbitration clause of, 73, 74.

Insurance on life of Charles L. Bernheimer, 111.

International Chamber of Commerce, conciliation and arbitration by, 144.

International disputes, 106-110.

International Merchants of Medieval Europe. See Merchants.

Interpretation, official, of rules, 4, 46, 47.

Interstate Cotton Seed Crushers Association, objects of, 188.

Interstate disputes, jurisdiction of, 81-86, 106-110, 223.

Intrastate, disputes, 81-86, 106-110

Italy, commercial courts in, 33.

Jewish Court of Arbitration, organization, objects, procedure, arbitrators, 145-149; trials, 147; statistics of, 147; conciliation in, 147, 148; illustrations, 148, 149.

Kiwanis Clubs, growth of, 10, 11; suggestions to, for offering arbitration facilities, 248-254.

Labor, organization of, 10, 11; original English status of, 119, 120; paid rent by military service, 119, 120; served through successive generations, 120; manhood, value of, 120; then a commodity to be bought in cheapest market, 121; condition during English Industrial Revolution, 121-123; conditions in, 119-126; lockouts and strikes, 125, 126; debt and taxation in England, 123; wages in England, 121, 123, 124; various forms of agreements with, 128-130; attitude of American workman to his shop, 135. See also Industrial Arbitration.

Law, questions of, in arbitration proceedings referred to court, 76; freedom of merchants from local, 26-28; law's delays, 30-33. See also Courts, Legislation, Law Merchant.

Law Merchant, origin of, 15; outgrowth of consular courts, 27-29; basis of our commercial law, 28, 29; objects and field of, 55; adopted in England, 57.

Legislation, provisions applicable to transactions throughout world, 76; required to change common law, 63, 64, 66, 67, 81, 82, 85, 86; to change court rules, 85; not required for amending exchange rules, 5. See Law.

INDEX

Lex Mercatoria. *See* Law Merchant.
Litigation, avoidance of, not primary object of commercial arbitration, 7; will to litigate decreasing, 76; decrease of, 42-52; prevention of, 45.
Liverpool, cellars in, 122.
Liverpool Corn Trade Association, 70.
Liverpool Cotton Association, 70.
Liverpool General Brokers Association, 70.
Lloyds, 76, 77.
London, housing in, 122.
London Chamber of Commerce, report of, 72.
London Corn Trade Association, arbitration clause in sale note of, 73.
London Oil & Tallow Trades Association, arbitration clause of, 73.
Lumber, by-laws and procedure of national lumber dealers associations, 255-264; arbitration clause of Timber Trade Federation of United Kingdom, 74, 75.

Magna Charta, as to foreign merchants, 26.
Malynes, 101.
Manchester, cellars in, 122.
Manchester, England, Chamber of Commerce, 103.
Mandamus, arbitration in place of, 148, 149.
Manhood Value of Labor, 129-139; feudal relations, 130; community and state, duty of master and servant to, 130; now recognized, 174.
Market value of labor, 119-126.
Markets, local, transactions at, 25.
Massachusetts arbitration law, 109, 219-222.

Mediation, systems of, 99; by committee on arbitration of N. Y. Chamber of Commerce, 103-106.
Medicine, practice of, 38.
Medieval Europe, International Merchants of. *See* Merchants.
Merchants, international, of medieval Europe, developed arbitration, 9; Arabs first, their forms, customs, laws adopted, 23; Saracens introduced arithmetic into Europe, 23; post-Crusades trade, 23; merchant defined, 23; did business through international fairs, 23, 24; nature of transactions at such fairs, 24-26; Stourbridge Fair, plan and conduct, 24, 25; Vanity Fair described, 25; local markets, 25; peace of God or of Church at, 26; freedom from local laws, 26-29; merchants' consular courts, 27-29; celerity of fair and consular courts with no appeal, 26-29; extraterritoriality at fairs, 26, 27; provisions of Spanish law and Magna Charta, 26, 27; four classes of consular courts, 27, 28; promptness of decisions, 28, 29, 32, 33; arbitration, local and itinerant, 28; evolution of law merchant or lex mercatoria, and European commercial courts, 28, 29; value of judge, expert in trade customs, 29; high commercial honor of, 29; speed, need of, in deciding commercial disputes, 30-33. *See* Arbitration, Expert.
Merchants' Association of New York, referendum by, 103.
Michigan, court conciliation in, 157.
Milwaukee, court conciliation in, 157.

Minimizing of disputes under business organization, 41-52; reasons for this, 41, 42; transactions of and arbitration in New York Stock Exchange, 42-45; in New York Clearing House Association, 45-47; in New York Produce Exchange, 47, 48; in other exchanges and trade associations, 48, 49; in Motion Picture Producers and Distributors of America, Inc., 49-52.

Minneapolis, court conciliation in, 157.

Motion Picture Producers and Distributors of America, Inc., arbitration clause of, 189-191; arbitration under, 49-52.

Municipal Guilds, English, 16. See Guilds.

National-American Wholesale Lumber Association, Inc., by-laws and procedure for arbitration, 259-264.

National Wholesale Lumber Dealers' Association, by-laws and forms for arbitration, 255-259.

Negotiable Instruments Law, 85.

Newcastle-on-Tyne, court trials at, 28.

New Jersey, arbitration law, 108, 109; passed unanimously, 170; includes labor disputes, 137; text of, 211-215.

New Jersey State Chamber of Commerce, proposed uniform arbitration rules of, 248-251.

New York City, court conciliation in, 157; municipal court of, rules for arbitration, 207-209; rules for conciliation, 209, 210; Jewish Court of Arbitration in, 145-149.

New York State, arbitration law, 108, 109; includes labor disputes, 137; contract to be construed under laws of, 191; text of arbitration law, 199-201; passed unanimously, 170; civil practice act concerning arbitration, 201-207; decision by court of appeals of, 102; Civil Practice Act of, 201-207.

New York Chamber of Commerce, report on prevention of unnecessary litigation and standardized contracts, 14. See •Chamber of Commerce of State of New York.

New York Clearing House Association, 4; not incorporated, 11; operations of, 45-47; influence of, 112.

New York Cotton Exchange, 95.

New York Legal Aid Society, conciliation by, 158.

New York Produce Exchange, objects and operations of, 47, 48, 187; arbitration by, 91, 95, 112.

New York Public Library, holds original minutes of arbitration committees, 88.

New York State Bar Association, report on prevention of unnecessary litigation and standardized contracts, 14.

New York Stock Exchange, not incorporated, 11; operations of, 42-45, 112; objects of, 187; arbitration by, 91; arbitration with non-members, 159.

Non-expert, courts, 46, 64; judges, 49, 50. See also Expert.

Norman struggle with Saxon races, 56, 57. See also England.

North Dakota, court conciliation in, 157.

Norway, court conciliation in, 157.

INDEX

Notices to and before arbitrators, 281, 282.
Nutmegs, Yankee wooden, 35.

Oaths. *See* Forms.
Objects, homogeneous, 47; of arbitration, 269. *See also* Commercial Arbitration, Exchanges.
Official list of arbitrators. *See* Chamber of Commerce of the State of New York; in New Jersey, 249; formation and use of, 252-254; in English trade associations, 75.
Ohio, court conciliation in, 157.
Ordinances of Clothworkers' Guild, 19-21, 181-186.
Organization, present tendency for, along altruistic and ethical lines, 9-15; business, follows ancient rules, such as those of medieval merchants and craft guilds, 10, 11; *see also* Guilds, Merchants; nature of, 10-15; increasing tendency to, 10; growth of churches, clubs and fraternal organizations, 10, 11; altruistic objects, 11, 12; of labor and American Federation of Labor, 11; pamphlet as to commercial and industrial organizations, 11, 12; chambers of commerce and similar bodies in the U. S., 12; arbitration in connection with such organizations, 12, 13; arbitration only one method, but essential, 12, 13; nature of business of wholesale exchanges, etc., 13, 14; value of standardized contracts, 14; origin of law merchant, 15; how unethical practices compel, 34; service and business honor characteristics of, 34, 35; increasing sacredness of contracts, 35, 36; uniform contracts, 35, 36; *see* Contracts; ethical objects of, 36-40; growth of club or guild spirit, 36-40; nature of business ethics, 37; *see* Ethics; improvement in trade methods by experts, 37, 38; English apprenticeship law, 38; regulation of medicine, 38; gradual growth of professions and regulated business, 38, 39; objects of, 42.
Oregon, arbitration law, 109, 216-218.
Orr, Alexander E., 95.

Panama, arbitration with, 143, 144.
Paraguay, arbitration with, 143, 144.
Partnership, clause for arbitration of affairs of, 278-280.
Peace of God or the Church, 26.
Pennsylvania System, employee representation plan, 138.
Philippines, powers over arbitration, 82, 83.
Pisa, commerce of, 23.
Plague, London, 122.
Porto Rico, powers over arbitration, 82, 83; U. S. courts in, 83.
Procedure simplified by arbitration, 171, 172.
Professions, beginnings and growth of various, 38.
Property, distinction between real and personal under common law, 59.

Railway Brotherhoods, 11, 136.
Release, award for general, 290.
Revocation of common law agreement to arbitrate, 63, 64; 252, 253; rule changed in England, 75. *See* Statutory Arbitration.

INDEX

Revolutionary War, arbitration by New York Chamber of Commerce during, 88-90.
Richman, Louis, services in Jewish Court of Arbitration, 148, 149.
Roosevelt, Theodore, action of, in regard to corporations, 115.
Rosenbaum, Samuel, report on commercial arbitration in England, 69-77. See also Common Law Arbitration.
Rotary Clubs, growth of, 10, 11.
Rubber Association of America, Inc., objects of, 187; rules and regulations governing arbitration, 265-272.
Rules, of court, arbitration and conciliation under. See Courts.
Russia, commercial courts in, 33.

Salford, cellars in, 122.
Saxon struggle with Norman conquerors, 56, 57. See also England.
Scandinavian Sawmillers' Association, 75.
Scott vs. Avery, decision in and effect of, 65, 66, 81, 85, 94, 95, 107; law in American colonies and states, 66, 67.
Service increasing in business, 34, 35.
Small Claims Courts, 164, 175.
Society of British Gas Engineers, arbitration clause of, 73, 74.
Spain, law of, as to merchants, 26; commercial courts in, 33.
Specific performance, award for, 288, 289.
Standard, proper, for judging arbitration, 7, 8, 77, 166.
Standard Oil Co. of New Jersey, employee representation plan, 138.
State, duty of master and servant to, 130.

Statutes. See Legislation.
Statutory Arbitration, governmental administrative arbitration, 76; law questions referred to courts, 76; will to arbitrate growing, 76; English, applicable in all parts of empire, 76, 77; differing rules for obtaining in England and U. S., under federal and state laws, 81-86; rules covering international, interstate, maritime, federal, state, dependency and territorial powers, 82-86; overlapping jurisdictions in U. S., 82-86; list and powers of U. S. courts, 83-85; of state courts, 84; lack of uniformity in statutes and court rules, 85; statutes required to amend common law, 63, 64, 66, 67, 81, 82, 85, 86; conclusions as to, 167-171; should be in broad form of statute, 167-171; work of New York Chamber of Commerce and other bodies for broad statute, 169, 170; disadvantages of, 172; when revocation not allowed, 192, 199, 211, 220, 223, 265.
Stone, Harlan S., 168.
Stourbridge, fair at, 24, 25; court of the dusty feet, 28.
Sugar Association of London, 73.
Survey Graphic, articles on legal conciliation, 158.

Talcott, James, 95.
Timber Trade Federation of the United Kingdom, arbitration clause of, 74, 75.
Time saved by arbitration, 30-32. See Commercial Arbitration.
Trade Associations, conduct of, 5-7; power over members, 71, 72; conditions same as in exchanges,

INDEX

48, 49; arbitration by, 97; suggestions to, for offering arbitration facilities, 248-254. *See also* Contracts.

Trade Unions, causes for formation of, 125; struggles by, 125, 126; in U. S., 126. *See* Labor.

Treaties, commercial. *See* U. S.

Tribunal. *See* Arbitration, Expert.

Umpire. *See* Arbitration, Forms.

Unethical acts, effects of in unorganized business, 34-36, 41; set forth by Judge Gary, 114-116. *See also* Ethics.

Uniform Contracts, nature of, 49; collective experience of members in drawing, 72. *See* Arbitration, Contracts.

U. S., American colonies took over common law as of July 4, 1776, 66.

U. S., overlapping jurisdictions of federal, state and local courts and laws, 82-86; powers of federal government and courts, 82-86.

U. S. Arbitration Act, drawing and passage of, 109, 110; excludes most labor disputes, 137; text of, 223-228; passed unanimously, 168-170.

U. S. Arbitration Treaties, 110.

U. S. Chamber of Commerce. *See* Chamber of Commerce of U. S.

U. S. Dept. of Commerce, list of commercial and industrial organizations of the U. S., 11, 12; duties of, 37, 103.

Umpire, appointment of, after commencement of arbitration, 283; before hearing, 283; award by, 286.

Uruguay, arbitration with, 142, 144.

Vanity Fair, description of, 25.

Venezuela, arbitration with, 143, 144.

Venice, commerce of, 23.

Warranty, award for damages for breach of, 287.

Washington, George, will of, 100.

Weavers, English guild of, 17.

Welfare, common, considered in organized bodies, 5, 21.

Wisconsin, court conciliation in, 157.

Witness, oath and affirmation of, 282.

Wreckmasters, functions of, 151, 152.

Writing, in early England and Europe, 57, 58; European merchants accustomed to written contracts, 58.

Writings, award for delivery of, 287, 288.

Yankee Wooden Nutmegs, 35.

Yorktown, siege of, 89, 90

Zinovieff, Gregory, fight against American Federation of Labor, 127.

(1)